THE SIEGE OF TYRE

THE
SIEGE
OF
TYRE

ALEXANDER THE GREAT
AND THE GATEWAY TO EMPIRE

DAVID A. GUENTHER

WESTHOLME
Yardley

Facing title page: Alexander the Great from a first century AD Roman mosaic of the
Battle of Issus. (*Museo Nazionale, Naples*)

©2024 David A.Guenther

Maps by Paul Rossmann © Westholme Publishing

Westholme Publishing, LLC
904 Edgewood Road
Yardley, Pennsylvania 19067
Visit our Web site at www.westholmepublishing.com

ISBN: 978-1-59416-428-6

Also available as an eBook.

Printed in the United States of America.

To my wife, Dawn:
Το ῥοδοδάκτυλος Ἠώς
—Homer, *The Odyssey*

CONTENTS

Illustrations

MAPS

HALFTONES

An unnumbered gallery follows page 88

A Note on Sources, Names, and Dates

Over the last twenty-three centuries, few people in the Western world have been written about more than King Alexander III of ancient Macedonia—Alexander the Great. Yet despite this longstanding celebrity, there exist today no first-hand accounts of the events of his life. Virtually everything we know about Alexander comes to us from preserved writings of Greek and Roman historians, all of whom lived and wrote hundreds of years after Alexander's death. The story that is retold in this book is based on the writings of five of these historians, known to us as Arrian, Curtius, Diodorus, Justin, and Plutarch, with the first three providing most of the information pertaining to the siege of Tyre. While these writers had access to accounts written by Alexander's contemporaries, in some cases written by men who had accompanied the Macedonian army on its epic march across the Persian Empire, those sources are lost to us.

In writing this book I have relied on four translations of Arrian's *Anabasis of Alexander*. Three of these translations—by P. A. Brunt, Martin Hammond, and Pamela Mensch—are cited in the notes as:

Arrian, *Anabasis of Alexander*, trans. P. A. Brunt (Cambridge, MA: Harvard University Press, 1976).

Martin Hammond, trans., *Arrian: Alexander the Great, the Anabasis and the Indica* (Oxford: Oxford University Press, 2013).

James Romm, ed., *The Landmark Arrian: The Campaigns of Alexander*, trans. Pamela Mensch (New York: Anchor, 2012).

The text of Arrian quoted in Appendix B is from:

E. J. Chinnock, trans., *The Anabasis of Alexander, or, The History of the Wars and Conquests of Alexander the Great, Literally Translated with a Commentary, from the Greek of Arrian the Nicomedian* (London: Hodder and Stoughton, 1884).

According to the editors of *The Oxford Handbook of Warfare in the Classical World*, "The spelling and presentation of Greek names and technical terms is a thorny issue over which scholars continue to wrangle, much to the confusion of nonspecialists."[1] For the names of people and places mentioned in this book, I have used those that I thought would be most familiar to modern English speakers, for example, "Alexander" rather than the Greek Alexandros (or Ἀλέξανδρος), "Asia Minor," and "Greece." In many cases the names with which we are most familiar are the ones that came down to us from those used by the ancient Greeks or Romans. For example, the Greeks referred to the people of Tyre (and other coastal cities of the eastern Mediterranean) as *Phoinikes* (plural of *Phoinix*), "Phoenicians," whereas the people living in Tyre would not have used that term to describe themselves.[2] We call them Phoenicians (and we call Iranians Persians) because that's what the Greeks called them. The Phoenicians living in Tyre called their city Sur, from the Semitic word for rock. The Greeks called it Tyros (Τύρος), and the Romans Tyrus.[3] Throughout the book I refer to Alexander's homeland as Macedonia rather than Macedon, although some scholars prefer the latter term.

The spelling of ancient names for people and locations follows *The Landmark Arrian: The Campaigns of Alexander*.[4] For example, the Greek god is Herakles rather than Heracles, and the Macedonian general is Krateros rather than Craterus. All quotes use American English spelling, even if the original used British spelling. For example, armor and harbor rather than armour and harbour.

The word "uncertain" appears often in this book because serious scholars disagree about many of the basic facts relating to Alexander and his campaign. For example: How long was the *sarissa*, the feared weapon of the Macedonian phalanx? Where exactly was the Panaros River, site of the battle of Issus? Were the walls of Tyre really 150 feet high? How were the oars and rowers of a quinquereme arranged? In cases like these, I present all of the scholarly views and let the reader decide, although I have attempted to identify which views seem to reflect a consensus.

All dates given are BC unless otherwise noted. I follow the standard format for citing classical prose sources: book number, chapter number, and, if applicable, section within a chapter. For example, "Arrian *Anabasis of Alexander*, 1.18.5" refers to book 1, chapter 18, section 5.

Introduction

This book tells the story of how Alexander the Great ended the naval power of the Persian Empire. In 334, at the start of Alexander's campaign, the Persian fleet was the most powerful naval force in the world. The Greek historian Arrian writes that the Persians had four hundred warships, all first-class ships with experienced crews from the maritime provinces of the empire—Phoenicia, Cyprus, Egypt, and the coastal cities of Asia Minor—their decks loaded with marines and well-paid veteran Greek mercenary infantry.[1] Alexander knew he couldn't leave this powerful force at his back to threaten Greece and Macedonia while he marched into Asia. Yet to oppose them, Alexander had a mere 160 ships: his own Macedonians plus a cobbled together force of Greek allies of questionable loyalty. He knew he could never defeat the Persians in a naval battle.

So he didn't try. Instead, he adopted the strategy of defeating the Persian navy from the land. His plan was to capture the coastal cities that were the home bases of the ships in the Persian fleet—the places where the ships were resupplied and repaired, where the crews were recruited, and where the families of the sailors and marines had their homes.

Robin Lane Fox writes that this strategy "needed two years' faith and patience to succeed" and that it was "shot through with short-term danger. Nevertheless finance and numbers made it the one sound option. Alexander, at least, had the foresight and daring to pursue it to its hazardous end."[2]

The end was indeed hazardous. It came two years later, at the Phoenician city of Tyre.

THE SIEGE OF TYRE

PROLOGUE
The Prophecy

The modern city of Tyre occupies a narrow peninsula on the eastern shore of the Mediterranean Sea, clinging like a barnacle to the Lebanese coast. But twenty-three centuries ago, at the time the events described in this book occurred, Tyre was an island, small and rocky, separated from shore by half a mile of sometimes-stormy sea.

For centuries the kings of Tyre maintained good relations with their Canaanite neighbors, including, to the south, the biblical kingdoms of Israel and Judah. In Jerusalem, King Solomon may have relied on skilled craftsmen and engineers from Tyre for the construction of his temple, using cedar beams and other building materials supplied by Tyre; he may have incorporated design elements from Tyre's temples as well.[1] In the Kingdom of Israel, King Ahab's wife Jezebel, whose "prophets of Baal" famously clash with the prophet Elijah in I Kings 18, was a royal princess of Tyre, and her god Baal was a Phoenician deity.[2]

In the year 587, a Babylonian army destroyed Jerusalem and sent the inhabitants into exile. Tyre reportedly responded to this Judean disaster with glee, seeing it as the removal of a trading rival and an opportunity to expand its influence in the region. In Babylon, the news of Tyre's joyful response to Jerusalem's destruction incensed one of the exiled Jews, a man we know as the prophet Ezekiel. Ezekiel's anger (and perhaps a voice from God) compelled him to make the following prophecy:

> The word of the Lord came to me: Son of man, because Tyre said concerning Jerusalem, "Aha, the gate of the peoples is broken, it has swung open to me; I shall be replenished, now that she is laid waste," therefore thus says

the Lord God: Behold, I am against you, O Tyre, and will bring up many
nations against you, as the sea brings up its waves. They shall destroy the
walls of Tyre, and break down her towers; and I will scrape her soil from
her, and make her a bare rock. (Ezek. 26:2-4 RSV)

Ezekiel goes on to explain who will be the agent of Tyre's destruction:

I will bring upon Tyre from the north Nebuchadnezzar king of Babylon,
king of kings, with horses and chariots, and with horsemen and a host of
many soldiers. He will slay with the sword your daughters on the mainland;
he will set up a siege wall against you, and throw up a mound against you,
and raise a roof of shields against you. He will direct the shock of his battering rams against your walls, and with his axes he will break down your
towers. . . . [Y]our stones and timber and soil they will cast into the midst
of the waters. (Ezek. 26:7-12 RSV)

Ezekiel's prophecy continues on in this vein for quite a while, through
chapters 27 and 28, and includes this line:

Behold, I will bring strangers upon you, the most terrible of the nations;
and they shall draw their swords against the beauty of your wisdom and
defile your splendor. (Ezek. 28:7 RSV)

We know with hindsight that Ezekiel was only partially correct in his
prophecy. Although Nebuchadnezzar did besiege Tyre for thirteen years
(585 to 572), the island city was never captured.[3] The Babylonians never
broke down Tyre's towers and walls, never cast Tyre's stones and timber and
soil into the midst of the waters.[4] Nebuchadnezzar wasn't the "most terrible
of the nations" that God had in mind. But God is nothing if not patient.
After 250 years, other "strangers" did come to Tyre, and they weren't Babylonians.

They came from Macedonia, the wild land to the north of Greece. They
were fierce and bold and reckless, an army the likes of which the world had
never seen, carving their way across Asia, straight through the might of the
Persian Empire. They were led by a twenty-three-year-old military genius
who thought he was a god. To his men, perhaps he was.

His name was Alexander.

And he was coming for Tyre.

PART I

The Long March

"Arrian, Diodorus, Quintus Curtius, Plutarch, and Justin, despite their diversity, all furnish a Greek memory of the event, and the silence of Phoenician sources deprives us of any comparison. Furthermore, these accounts are largely posterior to the event. They fall more under the genre of heroic history, of myths associated with the sometimes revered, sometimes criticized figure of Alexander the Conqueror, founder of an empire that was as ephemeral as it was memorable."

—Corinne Bonnet, "The Hellenistic Period and Hellenization in Phoenicia," in *The Oxford Handbook of the Phoenician and Punic Mediterranean*

ONE

THE
SYRIAN GATES

I t was early morning in the fall of 333 (late October or early November—
the exact date is uncertain),[1] and the veteran soldiers of Alexander's
Macedonian army awoke to find they were in serious trouble. It wasn't that
their location was bad. They were camped near the seaside town of Myriandros, on the Gulf of Issus, nearly three hundred miles north of Tyre. The
gulf was formed where the southern coast of Asia Minor, part of the
province of Cilicia, makes a sharp right turn to become the coast of northern Syria, part of the large province with the odd name Beyond-the-River
(Akkadian: Eber-Nari), which covered all of the lands of the Persian Empire
west of the Euphrates River.[2] A short distance to the east of their camp the
men could see foothills of the Amanus mountain range, running north-
south along the coast, isolating the narrow strip of shoreline on which the
army was camped from the inland expanse of the Syrian plain beyond.

The men had just endured a punishing two-day forced march, trying to
reach a strategic pass through those mountains—called the Syrian Gates—
before the Persian army of King Darius III could block it. Although Alexander

had no maps, he would have known from Xenophon's *Anabasis* that his army could travel from Mallos, in Cilicia, where he first received news of the location of Darius's army, to Myriandros, at the Syrian Gates, in two days of hard marching.[3] Xenophon recorded his march through this same area in 401 as consisting of twenty-five *parasangs*. There is no general agreement among historians as to whether a Persian *parasang* is a unit of time or of distance. Robin Lane Fox argues twenty-five *parasangs* would be equivalent to twenty-five hours of hard marching. However, Donald W. Engels argues that it would be impossible for the army to march from Mallos to Myriandros in two days; he suggests the two-day march began at the town of Issus, about halfway between Mallos and Myriandros. P. A. Brunt writes that in counting the two days of the march, it is probable that the counting begins at a place between Mallos and Myriandros.[4]

A heavy rainstorm during the night had halted the army's progress at Myriandros, near the western entrance to the Syrian Gates,[5] and now, before they could resume their march, shocking news arrived in a grisly fashion. One version of the story is told by the Roman historian Quintus Curtius Rufus in his *History of Alexander*. According to Curtius, on the previous day a small party of sick and injured Macedonians had been left at a makeshift field hospital in the town of Issus. There the men had been captured by Persians, who had brutally cut off their hands and cauterized the bleeding stumps with red-hot irons—Curtius uses the Latin word *adustis* (singed or burnt). On the orders of the Persian king, the mutilated men were shown the vast size of the Persians' encampment and then released, the expectation being that they would spread fear throughout Alexander's army.[6] A few of these men survived their mutilation and walked all night in the rain to reach the Macedonian camp and warn their comrades of the danger.

Alexander's veteran soldiers, although hardened to the brutality of warfare, were stunned and angered by what had been done to these men, but they were also confused. The Persian king and his army were supposed to be on the other side of the mountains, on the Syrian plain, where Alexander was hurrying to confront them. So what Persians had committed this atrocity? Where had they come from? And worst of all, what were they doing *behind* the Macedonian army? Alexander had been so certain that the Persians were still camped east of the mountains, where they had last been detected, that he hadn't kept track of their subsequent movements. When he heard that Darius and his army were behind him, at first he refused to believe the news.[7] He ordered some of his men to take a ship and sail north along the

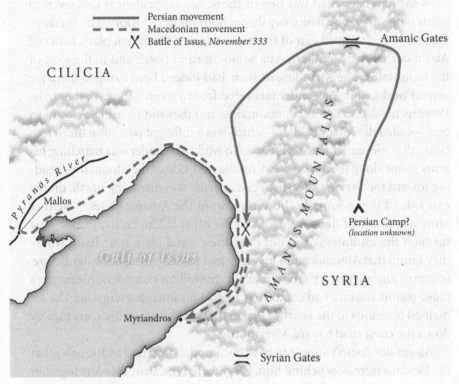

MAP 1. Movements before the Battle of Issus.

coast, back the way the army had marched the day before, and find out exactly who these Persians were and, more importantly, *where* they were.

The report came back quickly: a vast Persian army occupied the coastal plain just to their north, less than a day's march to their rear, blocking the narrow passage that ran between the sea on the west and the mountains on the east. The Persians were behind them, cutting them off from their line of retreat, cutting them off from the Greek cities on the Aegean coast of Asia Minor, and cutting them off from Macedonia, and home.

According to J. F. C. Fuller, "There can be little doubt that [Alexander] had blundered badly—over-eagerness had led him into a trap."[8] Not only was the army cut off, but the men were worn out from the two days of hard marching, some of it in the rain. There were signs that the local inhabitants were keeping the Persian scouts well informed about Alexander's movements; none of them thought the Macedonians had much of a chance.[9]

What had happened was one of those odd coincidences that seem to occur with surprising frequency throughout military history. The Persians, who had been camped east of the mountains on the Syrian plain, believed Alexander to be in southern Asia Minor, farther north and to the west of the mountains. The Macedonian army had indeed been camped there for several weeks while Alexander recovered from a fever.[10] To reach them, the Persians needed to cross the mountains, and they did so using a northern pass—called the Amanic Gates—which was a different pass from the Syrian Gates that Alexander planned to use. So while Alexander was marching his army south along the Syrian coast, on the west side of the mountains, heading toward the Syrian Gates, the Persian army was marching north, on the east side of the mountains, heading toward the Amanic Gates.[11] Neither army was aware of the movements of the other.[12] The Persians came west through the mountains and out onto the coastal plain near Issus, where they found that Alexander and his army had passed through the day before. In one of ancient history's most inexplicable military blunders, Alexander's failed reconnaissance had completely missed his intended target, and he remained oblivious to the nearby Persian threat as he urged his army rapidly down the coast road toward Myriandros.[13]

Alexander doesn't appear to have been unduly worried by the news that the Persians were now behind him. He gathered the army's leaders together and tried to shore up their confidence by reminding them of past successes in the face of tough odds. As generals have done throughout history, he assured them that the gods were on their side and that their strategy was sound, giving them a speech that inspired and encouraged them and their men.[14] Then he ordered the army to rest and eat, after which he turned them around and headed back north, along the narrow coastal road beside the mountains, toward where the Persians were waiting.

Reading Alexander's speech today, a modern reader gets the impression that rather than feeling trapped by the Persians, he now had them exactly where he wanted them: close to hand and easy to find. He didn't care that they were behind him—he just wanted to get at them and kill them. Exactly where that happened didn't really matter.

TWO

"MEN WHO DINE ON SHARPENED SWORDS"

The story of how Alexander and his army ended up on the border of Syria, cut off from home, and seemingly trapped by the Persians, begins a year and a half earlier, in spring 334, when the army was ferried across the Hellespont (modern Dardanelles) from Europe to Asia Minor by the Greek and Macedonian ships of Alexander's fleet. In making the crossing, the Macedonians used cargo ships and 160 triremes. The triremes were fast, oared warships, but they were long and narrow and had limited space for the soldiers and horses of Alexander's army. Some of the triremes would have been modified and reconfigured into transports by removing rowing benches, sacrificing speed for space. Other triremes would likely have towed the slower cargo ships. Alexander himself, accompanied by sixty warships, sailed to the site of Homeric Troy, where he landed and made sacrifices. Some of these sixty ships were triremes, while some may have been larger warships of Alexander's personal squadron.[1]

The army and navy that Alexander led to Asia Minor were technically part of an allied Greek force operating under terms of an alliance between

Macedonia and most of the city-states of mainland Greece. The alliance had been formed four years earlier, in 338, by Alexander's father, Philip II of Macedonia, following Philip's victory over a Greek army at the Battle of Chaeronea. At a critical point in that battle, eighteen-year-old Alexander achieved his first military success by personally leading a charge that shattered the famed Sacred Band of Thebes, thus ensuring the victory.[2] Philip's victory on the battlefield effectively ended Greek resistance to Macedonian hegemony and resulted in the formation of the Council of Corinth, at which Philip was proclaimed leader of the forces of the Greek alliance.[3]

Philip's goal in uniting the Greeks was to bring about a combined Macedonian-Greek army and navy that he would lead in a campaign against the Persian Empire, at that time the largest empire the world had ever known. Under its current king, Darius III, the Persian Empire stretched, north to south, from the Black Sea to the southern border of Egypt, and west to east, from the shores of the Aegean Sea to beyond the Hindu Kush Mountains of Afghanistan. Philip's stated reason for the campaign was to avenge wrongs committed against the Greeks during the invasion by the Persian king Xerxes in 480, when Greek temples were said to be desecrated and the city of Athens was burned.[4] Philip's real motivation is unclear, although it may have simply been his belief that Persia at that time was militarily weak and ripe for conquest. Greek victories on land and at sea during decades of conflict with Persia may have given Philip confidence that despite the Persian Empire's vast size, its armies could easily be overcome by Greek valor, arms, and tactics.[5]

Philip had made careful preparations for the campaign against Persia, including sending an advance force to Asia Minor to seize and hold a bridgehead. The Persians pushed them back but left the Macedonians clinging to a thin stretch of Asian coastline, primed for a future invasion.[6] Unfortunately for Philip, he was assassinated in 336 before the campaign could begin, and so the responsibility fell to his son and heir, Alexander, who was acclaimed leader of the Greek allied force.[7] Two Greek city-states were notably absent from the allied army. One, Sparta, refused to take part in any military action in which a Spartan general was not in command. Alexander let them go, believing a war against Sparta was not worth the trouble.[8] The Spartans would continue to be a thorn in Alexander's side, creating a distraction during the early part of the campaign through their continued overtures to Persia. The other Greek city-state not taking part was Thebes, which, at the news of Philip's death, had rebelled against the forced alliance, and as a consequence the city had been sacked and destroyed by Alexander as both a punishment to the Thebans and a warning to the other Greeks.[9] With that accomplished, the allied army set off to war.

Alexander's army was what would today be termed a combined arms force, comprising several different types of units, each having a specific function.[10] Combining these different units created a force that was more flexible and powerful than any one would be individually. There were heavily armed cavalry squadrons for massed shock attack, and lightly armed squadrons for reconnaissance and skirmishing; there were armored infantry battalions in slow-moving massed formations, and light infantry skirmishers able to move quickly over rough, uneven terrain; there were archers and slingers and javelin men to attack from a distance, and engineers and siege equipment for breaking into fortified cities. It was all Philip's creation. Victor Davis Hanson writes of the Macedonian army, "They were quick and travelled lightly,"[11] which fit perfectly with Alexander's style of leadership.

They were also brutal. Hanson writes that the Macedonians "were known as thugs by the *polis* Greeks: in Demosthenes' words they were little more than beasts 'who always had their hands on weapons.'"[12] The Greek playwright Mnesimachos wrote a comedy poking fun at Philip and his hard-bitten soldiers, portraying them as men for whom fighting is as natural as eating: "Do you realize that your fight is against men who dine on sharpened swords, and gulp down flaming torches as a delicacy?" is part of one line from the play.[13]

The core of Alexander's army was the Macedonian heavy infantry, the phalanx, sometimes referred to as the Foot Companions. The phalanx typically formed up in dense rectangular units that were sixteen ranks deep, but these could be combined into deeper rectangles of thirty-two or sixty-four ranks when necessary. Unlike the typical citizen-soldiers mustered by the Greek city-states, these were highly trained full-time professionals, and they could march and move in formation like a modern drill team. Their armor was similar to that of classical Greek hoplites: shields (Greek: *aspis*), bronze helmets (*korus*), and cuirasses (*thōrax*) of bronze, leather, or linen to protect the upper body, although it may be the case that only the first few ranks of the phalanx wore cuirasses.[14] Minor M. Markle argues that there is no evidence Macedonian infantry wore cuirasses at all, and Nick Sekunda writes "most modern authorities do not believe that the infantry were so heavily equipped."[15]

The primary weapon of the phalanx was a long pike. There is some question as to whether the men had greaves (Greek: *knēmis*) for leg protection and carried swords (*xiphos*). Fuller writes that they wore "leggings" and carried a "short sword." Lane Fox writes that the front rank "probably sported greaves against enemy missiles" and that the men wore short daggers on their hips that were "very much a last resort." Sekunda writes "we can probably assume that all the infantry were issued with swords." Simon Anglim et al. write "muscled greaves were also common," and "it is likely that knives or short swords would have been carried."[16]

Philip had introduced two innovations that drastically increased the fighting power of the Macedonian phalanx. First, the traditional spear carried by Greek heavy infantry was discarded in favor of a much longer pike, called a sarissa (Greek: *sarisa* or *sarissa*), approximately eighteen feet long with a foot-long iron blade and a metal butt spike for balance.[17] There is some uncertainty about the length of the Macedonian sarissa used by Alexander's men. Here are some estimates by modern scholars:

"13 to 14 feet in length" (Fuller)

"its longest variety was eighteen feet long" (Lane Fox)

"these tough spears . . . were riveted together to a length of sixteen feet" (Lane Fox)

"according to Polybius . . . the sarissa was 6-7m (19.4-23ft) long" (Anglim et al.)

"the longest *sarissai* measured 12 cubits (18 feet)" (Sekunda)

"nearly 18 feet and more" (Hanson)

"varied in length only between about four and a half and five and a half meters" (Markle)

"it is not possible to give a precise measurement as estimates vary" (John Warry)[18]

Philip's second innovation was to reduce the size and weight of the traditional Greek round infantry shield so his men could carry it on their back or left shoulder, slung by a strap around the neck, thus freeing both hands to wield the sarissa.[19] Regardless of length, the sarissa was undoubtedly heavy and difficult to control, requiring two hands to wield effectively. But in the hands of Alexander's highly drilled phalanx, the weapon presented any enemy with a bristling forest of sharpened iron blades protruding from the first five ranks, presenting a "hedgehog-like front" and looking "like the quills of a metal porcupine."[20]

A second infantry component in the Macedonian army was a unit called the Shield Bearers (Greek: *hypaspists*). The exact nature and armament of the Shield Bearers has long been the subject of scholarly debate.[21] Here are some arguments made by modern scholars:

"[they had] better armor and shorter pikes . . . [and they] were usually the first infantry forces to follow behind the cavalry" (Hanson)

"how the [Shield Bearers] were armed and equipped is not known" (Fuller)

"it is logical to assume that they were more lightly equipped than the Foot Companions" (Sekunda)

"ancient sources do not describe [the Shield Bearers] in any detail, and many historians presume that they simply formed an elite unit within the phalanx, while others see them as commando-type light infantry" (Anglim et al.)

"the part of the Macedonian infantry under Alexander the Great normally armed with the hoplite panoply were the [Shield Bearers]" (Markle)[22]

The Shield Bearers, because of their name, likely carried a large hoplite shield that required the use of their left hand and arm and thus ruled out wielding a sarissa. However, the fact that the Shield Bearers were often selected for fast pursuits suggests they could leave behind their heavy armor and fight as light infantry when necessary. Lane Fox considers the Shield Bearers to be the "most lethal" troops in Alexander's army, and calls them "the finest foot force in antiquity."[23]

The army also contained allied Greek soldiers. The League of Corinth provided seven thousand heavily armed hoplites from the various member city-states and also five thousand mercenaries—both hoplites and light infantry. James Romm argues that the allied Greek soldiers were "classed as allies but essentially hostages." He writes that their contribution to the army was minimal, since they fought with spears rather than the sarissa, and that they were included in the expedition to ensure that their home cities in Greece remained loyal to Alexander.[24] Philip also raised troops from the peoples living on the borders of Macedonia: Thracians, Paeonians, and Illyrians.[25]

Several different types of light infantry units formed an important part of Alexander's army. To provide missile weapons Philip had hired archers from Crete and slingers from Rhodes.[26] According to Fuller the Cretans were reputed to be "the most skilled bowmen of their day."[27] But the best light infantrymen were the javelin-armed skirmishers from a tribe called the Agrianians (or Agrianes) whose homeland was in the southwest corner of

present-day Bulgaria. They were referred to as peltasts because of the type
of shield they carried, and Lane Fox calls them "the Gurkhas of the Macedonian army." These tough soldiers were often chosen to make night attacks
or to climb rough terrain.[28] Fuller calls them "superb javelin-men." Because
the Agrianian king had been a friend of Alexander's, this unit is thought to
be one that Alexander added to Philip's original army.[29]

The main cavalry force of the Macedonian army was the Companion
Cavalry, a unit that Lane Fox calls "the finest cavalry in history."[30] Based on
images from ancient coins and paintings, scholars think the cavalry horses
of ancient Greece were smaller and heavier than modern breeds, and they
had no horseshoes.[31] There were no stirrups or saddles, so the troopers had
to work hard to stay on their horses during combat.

The main weapon of the Companion Cavalry was a lance (Greek: *xyston*)
of tough cornel wood. Cornel wood comes from the cornelian cherry tree
(*Cornus mas*), which is commonly found on wooded mountain slopes in
Macedonia, and its range extends into the Balkans. Because of its elasticity
and hardness, it was prized as the best material for spears, javelins, and
bows.[32] The cavalry lance was shorter than a sarissa, and despite the tough-
ness of the cornel wood, it often broke during combat.[33] Because of this,
the lance had spearheads fixed to both ends so a trooper whose lance shattered could simply reverse the weapon and continue fighting with the stub
end.[34] A sword was used as a secondary weapon since the lance was likely
to be lost once it had been thrust into the body of an enemy.[35]

The armor of the Companion Cavalry was a cuirass of linen, leather, or
metal, a fringed leather skirt to protect the rider's groin, and shoes that were
open at the front like sandals. There were no greaves or horse armor. Helmets were of the Boeotian type, which Lane Fox describes as resembling "a
fluted sou'wester of metal" that was sometimes worn with a metal neck
guard. The troopers also had fringed leather shoulder guards.[36]

It seems clear that Greek and Macedonian cavalry did not carry shields,
perhaps because the cavalry lance required two hands to wield effectively.[37]
In describing Sasanian heavy cavalry of a later era, Michael J. Decker writes
"there is no easy way to cope with a shield alongside the use of the long and
heavy two-handed lance."[38] If this lack of a shield seems odd, particularly
in view of the fact that Roman auxiliary cavalry are often portrayed with
shields, consider that eighteenth and nineteenth century AD European cavalry—Napoleon's cuirassiers and lancers or Wellington's dragoons for example—had no shields and had as their primary weapons sabers and lances,
not at all dissimilar to those of Alexander's Macedonian cavalry.

A second important component of the Macedonian cavalry was a unit called the Mounted Scouts, consisting of men recruited from the recently acquired Thracian borderlands, although their officers may have been Macedonians. As their name implies, the primary role of the unit was reconnaissance, and consistent with that role, the scouts were lightly armored and may have worn only helmets. Because they are sometimes referred to as *sarissophoroi*, or being armed with a sarissa, some scholars argue that Alexander had equipped the scouts with the infantry sarissa rather than with the cavalry lance.[39] Armed in this manner, the unit could take part in pitched battles, the troopers wielding their long sarissas with both hands and controlling their horses using only their knees.[40] If sarissas came in different lengths, it may be the case that the cavalry sarissa used by the scouts was shorter than the infantry weapon used by the phalanx. In addition to the sarissa or cavalry lance, both the scouts and Companion Cavalry likely also used javelins when they were on scouting or reconnaissance duty.[41] Fuller writes that the scouts "usually operated like Cossacks." Although the role of the light cavalry in battle was to cover the army's flanks, the scouts were sometimes found at the head of a charge against the enemy.[42]

The army also contained two thousand heavy cavalrymen from Thessaly who were armed and armored like the Companion Cavalry and whose performance in battle was nearly their equal. There were also 1,200 light cavalry from Thrace, Paeonia, and Odyrsia, and a contingent of Greek mercenary cavalry.[43] All of these would have been available to Alexander when he began his invasion of Asia Minor.

Philip had trained the Macedonian army to march fast over long distances. While soldiers in contemporary Greek and Persian armies used servants to carry their personal gear, Philip's men carried their own armor, weapons, and food, with servants used only to carry camp supplies. There were no long baggage trains or hordes of camp followers with Philip's army.[44] Cavalry troopers were allowed one servant each, and the infantry one servant for each ten men. The men carried military gear only, and on a march, sometimes up to thirty miles a day, each soldier carried thirty days' provisions as well as their arms and armor.[45] The soldiers were well trained and motivated and could move quickly when necessary. They were incredibly tough, hardened by the thirty-mile-a-day marches with full provisions, and able to keep to a minimum the number of carts, wagons, slaves, and servants that accompanied them. This ability to move fast over long distances without being tied to supply lines was a key feature of Alexander's future success.[46]

One additional unit accompanied the army: a small group of military engineers. This unit was likely started by Philip to devise and improve siege equipment—catapults, rams, and towers—used to capture fortified cities. The Greeks referred to such equipment as a "machine" (Greek: *mēchanēma*).[47] If Philip was not the creator of this unit, he added to it and incorporated it as an integral part of his army.[48] Siege warfare under Philip and Alexander gradually became more sophisticated, and the military engineers developed technologies that would be used extensively in the wars waged by Alexander's successors.[49] It has also been suggested that these engineers developed a "naval siege unit," either under Philip or Alexander, that specialized in techniques for assaulting walled cities and harbors from the sea by mounting siege machines on specially designed ships.[50] If such a naval siege unit did exist within the Macedonian army, it would find its greatest challenge at Tyre.

With the allied army that crossed the Hellespont into Asia Minor, Philip had created a fearsome weapon with which to strike at the Persian Empire. But Philip was dead, and his young son was now king. Whether Alexander could wield that weapon as his father had, and defeat a proud and ancient empire, was the unanswered question in the minds of Alexander's soldiers.

The answer would not be long in coming.

THREE

INVASION

The army that accompanied Alexander to Asia Minor was not large by modern standards, especially when measured against the size of the empire it was meant to conquer. Arrian gives the numbers as thirty thousand infantry, including light infantry and archers, and five thousand cavalry. Lane Fox gives the following breakdown, taken from Diodorus Siculus (Diodorus): thirty-two thousand infantry, which included nine thousand Macedonian Foot Companions, three thousand Macedonian Shield Bearers, one thousand foreign skirmishers, seven thousand allied Greeks, and seven thousand light troops from Thrace and Illyria; six thousand cavalry, which included eighteen hundred Macedonian Companion Cavalry, eighteen hundred heavily equipped Thessalian cavalry, and a few allied Greek and lightly armored Thracian and Paeonian cavalry units. An advance force, already in Asia Minor holding a small bridgehead, contained the Macedonian Mounted Scouts. Together with the Macedonian and allied Greek infantry in the advance force, Alexander's army totaled forty-three thousand.[1]

After crossing the Hellespont and making landfall in northwest Asia Minor in spring 334, Alexander had time to consider how best to proceed, as there was no immediate Persian attack. While Philip's plan had been to liberate the Greek cities along the Aegean coast, Alexander's initial instinct, given his temperament, may have been to look for a fight. He sent out cavalry to reconnoiter the area and find the enemy: one squadron of Companion Cavalry and four squadrons of Mounted Scouts.[2]

Two Persian provincial governors (satraps) and their local leaders met in council to decide how best to oppose the invasion. Arrian reports that the forces at their disposal consisted of about twenty thousand cavalry and about the same number of Greek mercenary infantry. Diodorus reports that the Persians had more than ten thousand cavalry and one hundred thousand infantry, which seems far too high for the infantry, even if it includes local levies in addition to the Greek mercenaries. Fuller guesses the actual strength of the mercenaries to be around five thousand.[3] Whatever their numbers, it is likely the Greek mercenary infantry in Persian service was outnumbered by Alexander's infantry.

One of the satraps' military advisers, Memnon of Rhodes, argued that the safest plan was a scorched-earth policy—withdrawing their forces, burning their crops and cities, and drawing the Macedonians farther into the interior of Asia Minor, where they could be isolated and destroyed. This plan, while sensible, was rejected by the council. The satraps and other Persian officials were wealthy landowners with large holdings in the surrounding countryside; the crops and houses they would be burning would in many cases be their own. One of the satraps said he would not allow any of the houses in his province to be burned.[4]

Alexander's army met the Persian force at the Granicus River (now called the Biga River), which runs north to empty into the Sea of Marmara in northwest Asia Minor. The Macedonians, approaching from the west, found the Persian army drawn up and waiting on the east bank. The river was shallow and approximately twenty-five yards across, and the banks must have been low enough for cavalry to cross. The Persians had their cavalry lining the riverbank in front of their mercenary infantry. According to E. Badian, "the river itself was no obstacle, but the banks would be manageable only where the gravel slopes offered an easy means of access and exit. The Persian cavalry would in effect have to watch the gravel slopes on their side."[5]

As the units of the Macedonian army reached the river, they spread out from their marching columns and formed up along the bank in a line of battle, infantry in the center and cavalry on the flanks. It was late in the afternoon, and the Macedonians were tired, having marched all day. For a while both armies stood, watching and waiting.

Two conflicting accounts of the ensuing battle have survived, one by Arrian and one by Diodorus. The story recorded by Arrian portrays Alexander as impetuous and bold, almost to the point of recklessness. Arrian writes that after a short pause, Alexander ordered cavalry from the right wing to attack, led by the Mounted Scouts, sending them obliquely across the river to stretch and thin out the Persian line. While the Persians were beating off this initial attack, Alexander led the Companion Cavalry in a charge up the gravel slopes of the opposite bank and into the mass of waiting Persian horsemen. The rest of the army plunged into the river and attacked the Persians on the opposite bank. According to Plutarch, Alexander "seemed to be acting like a frenzied and foolish commander rather than a wise one."[6]

Diodorus tells a contrasting story that portrays Alexander as cautious, not daring to cross the river in the face of Persian opposition. In this version, the Persians were waiting for Alexander to cross, knowing his army would become disordered in the crossing and be vulnerable to a counterattack. Alexander in turn was unwilling to risk an attack, and the day ended with both armies camped on opposite sides of the river, the Macedonians on the west bank and the Persians on a hill east of the river. The following morning, Alexander made a surprise dawn attack and crossed the river before the Persians were awake and could assemble their army. By the time the Persians formed up for battle, the Macedonians were ready and waiting on the east side of the river.[7]

In his 1973 book *Alexander the Great*, Lane Fox argues that Diodorus's account is likely correct, writing that the Macedonians made a dawn river crossing that caught the Persians by surprise, because the Persian camp was probably located far from the river, and the Persian army's practice was never to fight before first light.[8] He goes on to argue that Arrian's account was a dishonest way of highlighting Alexander's boldness, and he based this conclusion on the fact that Arrian's source was Alexander's official historian, whereas Diodorus's source was a historian who had nothing to gain from praising Alexander.[9]

Writing in a subsequent book, Lane Fox seems to reconsider his view that Arrian's account was wrong. He writes that Arrian's version was based on accounts made by Alexander's officers but that there also existed an alternate version of the battle, written by an ancient historian who was not present at the event. In this alternate version, Alexander waited until dawn to make a surprise river crossing. Lane Fox argues that any alternate version of the battle should only add to, not supersede, the officers' account that is reflected in Arrian. In the case of the crossing of the Granicus, Lane Fox sees no reason for Alexander's officers to write biased accounts, and he therefore concludes that the bold river crossing described by Arrian should be the accepted version.[10]

An even stronger argument that Arrian's version was correct is made by Badian, who writes that the traditional view among scholars is that Arrian is right and Diodorus is wrong. He says this point needs to be emphasized because "Diodorus' error is—inevitably—from time to time revived and defended by modern *paradoxographoi*." Badian goes on to argue that the account in Diodorus can't be taken seriously as a description of a real battle since it failed to explain what prevented the Persians from setting up their camp in a spot from which they could guard the riverbank. (Whether Diodorus is a reliable historian vis-a-vis Arrian will become important in later chapters in trying to understand what occurred during the siege of Tyre.) According to Badian, Diodorus would have us believe that not only did the Persians neglect to even watch the river they were trying to defend but that somehow Alexander knew the river would be unguarded at dawn and was thus able to take advantage of the Persians' incompetence to get his whole army across unmolested.[11]

Peter Green, in an extensive appendix to his book, argues that the two inconsistent accounts of the battle given by Arrian and Diodorus are both partially true to the extent that they are describing two engagements in what Green views as a two-day battle. According to Green, Alexander's initial impetuous attack with the Companion Cavalry—as described by Arrian—was met on the opposite riverbank by the Persians' disciplined mercenary infantry. The attack was beaten off by the mercenaries, forcing Alexander to retreat and regroup. "Alexander's first brush with the Persians had ended in humiliating failure," Green writes. Realizing that another cross-river assault was futile, Alexander instead led his army on a secret night crossing farther downstream, out of sight of the Persians. The following morning the Macedonians were able to take the Persians by surprise, leading to the cavalry encounter that Diodorus describes.[12]

Regardless of how and when the Macedonian army crossed the river, the soldiers soon found themselves engaged in ferocious hand-to-hand fighting. In Arrian's account, Alexander led the Companion Cavalry in a charge aimed straight at the leaders in the center of the Persian cavalry line. The conflict quickly dissolved into a series of personal battles as frantic riders hacked and stabbed at one another in a confused and bloody melee.[13] In

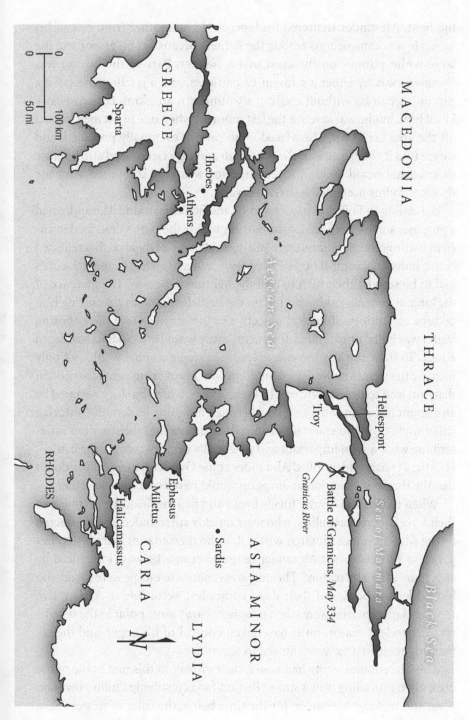

MAP 2. Greece and Asia Minor.

the fight, Alexander shattered his lance and got another from one of his men. He was conspicuous among the fighters because of his armor and the large white plumes on the crest of his helmet. Part of the helmet was chopped away by either a scimitar or battle-ax, and a javelin penetrated a gap in his cuirass without causing a wound. An attacking Persian nearly killed him, but he was saved at the last moment when one of his men hacked off the attacker's arm. The Macedonian cavalry eventually prevailed, and we are told it was because of their strength and experience, and also because their cornel wood lances proved superior weapons compared with the shorter javelins used by the Persian cavalry.[14]

According to Fuller, Arrian's focus on the fighting around Alexander had a purpose, and modern readers cannot appreciate the tactics described in ancient battle accounts without recognizing that many of these clashes reflected heroic individual combat between opposing leaders. Leaders of ancient armies had to be seen by their men to lead the fighting in person. The presence of the king or general, risking his life on the battlefield, meant that killing him became an important tactical objective of the enemy. Once the opposing leader was killed or wounded, the enemy army would often panic, leading to a rout. To fight and slay the enemy leader in single combat would not only increase the victorious leader's reputation with his men but could more often than not lead to decisive victory. In Fuller's view, when the story narrated by an ancient historian contains a duel between opposing leaders, the historian isn't simply trying to entertain or introduce drama into the story but is describing what was an important and potentially decisive event in the battle.[15] Had the Persian leaders killed Alexander at the Granicus, there is little doubt that the threat of Macedonian invasion would have ended then and there.

When the Persian cavalry finally broke and fled the field, they abandoned their Greek mercenary allies, who were quickly surrounded and massacred by the Macedonians. Plutarch writes that the mercenaries had tried to negotiate a surrender, but Alexander refused because he was "influenced by anger more than by reason." The only mercenaries to escape were those who hid under the bodies of their dead comrades. According to Arrian, two thousand mercenaries were taken prisoner,[16] so at some point in the slaughter, Alexander's reason must have taken control of his anger, and the remaining mercenaries were allowed to surrender.

The Macedonian army had won a clear victory in this first battle of the campaign, prevailing over a strong Persian force, justifying Philip's invasion plan, and making Alexander, for the time being, the ruler of western Asia Minor. What now?

As it turned out, the strategy Alexander would adopt and the route he would take over the next eighteen months—leading to the confrontation with Darius near the Syrian Gates—were driven by one overriding concern: the Persian navy. It was Persian command of the sea that worried Alexander now. The battle at the Granicus had proved to him and his men that they could defeat the Persians on land. What about the Persian fleet?

FOUR

THE INFLUENCE
OF SEA POWER

After the victory at the Granicus, Alexander headed south, making for Sardis, capital of the wealthy province of Lydia. The Persians offered no resistance, and capturing the treasury at Sardis made Alexander, in the words of Lane Fox, "richer than Croesus," a reference to an earlier Lydian king whose defeat by the Persians two hundred years before had led to the incorporation of Lydia into the Persian Empire. Llewellyn-Jones writes that "Croesus was unspeakably rich, vulgarly wealthy, and, like a latter-day Russian oligarch, had absolutely no qualms about putting his affluence on conspicuous, ostentatious display."[1] Now Alexander had the money he needed to pay his soldiers and, equally important, his sailors.

From Sardis, Alexander turned southwest toward the Aegean coast, following Philip's plan to liberate the Greek cities from their Persian overlords—which essentially meant forcing them to change their allegiance from a Persian king to a Macedonian one. At first, things went well as city after city came over to him. News of the outcome of the Granicus battle caused the mercenaries who garrisoned Ephesus to abandon that city, taking two triremes with them.[2] But things changed at the port of Miletus, where Alexander found that the Persian commander—a man who had previously offered to surrender the city—reversed his decision and was determined to resist the Macedonians. According to Arrian, this was because news had reached Miletus that the Persian fleet was nearby and on the way to defend the city.[3]

Alexander's luck held, and his own fleet reached Miletus before the Persians. The Macedonian ships sheltered on the small island of Lade, across a narrow strait to the west of Miletus, and Alexander protected them with a force of allied troops and mercenaries. When the Persian fleet arrived three days later, it landed on the Mycale peninsula north of Miletus, separated from the city by a wide bay. Outside the city's walls, Alexander's engineers prepared the siege machines, and as soon as they were ready began the assault. At the same time, the Macedonian ships rowed out from Lade and quickly forced their way into the harbor before the Persians could react. The Macedonians filled the harbor entrance with a row of triremes, their prows facing out in such a way that they completely blocked the narrow opening.[4] Without access to the harbor, the ships of the Persian fleet were unable to offer assistance to the besieged city, while Alexander's men and machines assaulted it from the land.

Ancient authors disagree about the size of the Persian fleet. In Arrian's account there are four hundred ships, while Diodorus writes that there are three hundred.[5] Whatever the number, it was clear that the Persians had considerably more ships than the 160 available to Alexander. Without prior knowledge of the Persian fleet's location, its arrival at Miletus would have caught Alexander by surprise. He suddenly found himself faced with superior Persian sea power, a strategic problem that would affect the route of the Macedonian army and take two years to solve. Lane Fox writes that "for the first time in Asia Alexander was outnumbered."[6]

It isn't clear why the Persians arrived too late to intercept the Macedonian fleet at Miletus. Earlier they had missed a chance to stop Alexander during the initial crossing of the Hellespont. Modern scholars have offered various theories to explain these delays. Romm writes that they had "been held up for other obligations and by the poor sailing conditions of the spring weather." Others have attributed their late arrival to luck, but Edward M. Anson argues that it is hardly "credible that Alexander would have staked his entire expedition on the chance that the Persian fleet would be late." Anson considers the various reasons proposed for the failure of the Persians to stop Alexander's crossing to Asia Minor and concludes that the most likely reason is because the Macedonians controlled both the European and Asian coastlines at the crossing point. In Anson's view, the Persian fleet was available in the Aegean much earlier but unable to act effectively against Alexander's smaller fleet in the narrow confines of the Hellespont.[7] This doesn't explain why they were late at Miletus.

Regardless of the reason for their tardiness, the Persian fleet was there now, and Alexander had to deal with it. What to do? He abandoned his usual recklessness and emphatically rejected the notion of fighting the Persians at sea. He explained to his generals that it would be irrational to fight the larger Persian fleet with his own smaller one. He also pointed out that the Persian crews, from Cyprus and Phoenicia, were well trained and experienced, whereas his own crews were relatively inexperienced. Alexander wasn't willing to waste the bravery of his men in an endeavor as risky as a battle at sea. If the Macedonians did lose a sea battle, they would forfeit the advantage they had gained from the victory at the Granicus, and a defeat would likely cause some of the city-states of Greece to rebel against the Macedonian alliance.[8]

Alexander then interpreted for his men an omen they had all seen, when an eagle had landed on the shore behind one of their beached ships. He told his men that the eagle was on the side of the Macedonians but that because the eagle was standing on dry land rather than on one of the ships, the omen meant that Alexander would defeat the Persian fleet from the land.[9] This strategy of defeating ships from land makes some sense when the nature of ancient warships is taken into account. These ships, particularly triremes, had very little space on board to store water and food, and there were no cooking facilities and no sleeping quarters for the crew. This meant the ships had to return to shore at least once a day to allow the crew to cook meals, get fresh water, and sleep. Lane Fox refers to these ships as "glorified racing-eights."[10] The *Oxford English Dictionary* defines an "eight" as "a boat for eight oarsmen," and the term is sometimes used by modern scholars as a metaphor for the long, narrow, oared warships of the ancient Mediterranean.

Although the term "racing-eight" may be a useful way to illustrate an ancient warship's limited carrying capacity and crew space, Cynthia M. Harrison argues that historians originally applied the term to ancient warships based on the mistaken belief that the ships were very lightly built. She points out that "no one seemed to doubt the validity of attributing to a trireme, a 170-oared vessel with hand-worked timbers, the physical properties of an eight-oared racing shell made of molded plywood."[11]

The Persian fleet had been using a base on the Mycale peninsula, across the bay to the north of Miletus. Each day the Persians would row south from Mycale and cross the bay, hoping to lure the allied Macedonian fleet out of the harbor to fight in the bay, where the Persians could utilize their greater numbers to advantage. However, there wasn't a source of water available at Mycale, and so each night the Persians had to row to the mouth of the Maeander River, a few miles away. Noting this, Alexander sent his cavalry and three battalions of infantry to secure the beaches at the mouth of the Maeander where the Persians were trying to land, preventing them from disembarking. After inconclusive skirmishing between ships from the two fleets, and unable to obtain water and other provisions nearby, the Persians eventually gave up. They abandoned their base at Mycale, sailing away to the island of Samos to reprovision, leaving Miletus in Alexander's hands.[12]

Although Alexander had been successful at Miletus, it was clear to him that as long as the Persians had access to the numerous Aegean islands from which they could resupply their ships at will, his strategy of defeating their fleet from land was doomed to fail. At this point he took an extraordinary and somewhat controversial step: he disbanded his own fleet and sent the ships and their crews home.[13]

Arrian gives several reasons for Alexander's decision to disband the allied fleet. First, he writes that Alexander was short of money to pay the sailors. Second, Alexander didn't believe his fleet was strong enough to face the Persians, and he did not want to risk its destruction. Finally, since Alexander now controlled Asia Minor, he no longer needed a navy. He could simply capture all the cities along the coast and thus deprive the Persians of the bases they needed to repair and resupply their ships and recruit new crews. This reasoning was consistent with Alexander's interpretation of the omen involving the eagle, which suggested to him that he could defeat the Persian ships from the land.[14]

Clearly, if he was "richer than Croesus," Alexander was not short of money. However, Lane Fox points out that the ships of his allied fleet required thirty-two thousand crewmen (160 ships x 200 crewmen per ship), and the cost of paying these men ran to 160 talents per month, a gigantic sum. Although Alexander possessed the wealth captured at Sardis, and he would receive the tribute payments that the newly liberated cities had been sending to Darius, he may still have been concerned about running out of cash with which to pay his soldiers and sailors. And while the allied Greek city-states were obligated to provide ships for Alexander's fleet, they may not have been responsible for paying the wages of the crews that manned them.[15]

Waldemar Heckel writes that the arguments given for Alexander's decision to disband his fleet are not convincing. There were many Aegean islands with cities and ports capable of supporting the Persian fleet, and
Alexander couldn't possibly secure them all. Besides, the home ports for
most of the Persian ships were on the island of Cyprus, or the coast of
Phoenicia, hundreds of miles away from Miletus, with the army of Darius
likely barring the way. Arguments that Alexander's fleet was too expensive
were also not convincing, since with each city that surrendered to him,
Alexander's source of revenue increased. According to Heckel, Alexander's
main concern was to avoid a disastrous naval defeat and the defection of
his Greek allies. But Heckel argues that disbanding the fleet had important
negative consequences that should have been anticipated. First, the assault
on the city of Halicarnassus, which like Miletus refused to surrender, was
made more difficult without a fleet. Second, the Persians were able to re-
capture Miletus as soon as the Macedonians moved on. And third, the absence of the Macedonian fleet left the Persians free to roam the Aegean and
attack coastal cities that were loyal to Alexander.[16]

Lane Fox defends Alexander's decision to disband the fleet, writing that
once he realized that the Cypriot and Phoenician ships in Persian service
would remain loyal to Darius, it made sense to send his own ships home
because his smaller, less-experienced fleet would never be able to defeat the
Persians at sea. Had he kept his fleet intact, he would still have needed to
capture the port cities of Phoenicia and Cyprus that were the home bases
of the Persians' allied ships. However, Lane Fox also points out the negative
consequences of Alexander's action: the Persians would be able to strike
anywhere around the Aegean (the same argument made later by Heckel),
and they would also be able to foment rebellion among the allied Greek
city-states.[17]

According to Romm, another reason for Alexander to disband his navy
was fear that the Greek crews manning the allied ships would desert. Those
crews could sail for home much easier than could the hired mercenaries or
allied troops in Macedonian service. Romm states that "many historians
judge this to be the primary reason for Alexander's surprising decision to
send his ships home." Diodorus gives still another reason for dismissing the
fleet, although this one is perhaps less plausible than the others. Diodorus
argues that Alexander was concerned about the willingness of his men, particularly the allied troops and the mercenaries, to face the army of Darius
in the battle that was certain to come, and that by sending his ships home
he would be forcing the men to fight by cutting off any hope they might

have of escape.[18] Diodorus is accusing Alexander of adopting the same tactic used twenty centuries later by the Spanish conquistador Hernán Cortés, who reportedly scuttled (or burned) his ships on the coast of Mexico, thereby eliminating any possibility that his men could retreat.[19] Alexander's men would conquer, or they would die. There was no going back.[20]

There were at least three flaws in Alexander's strategy of disbanding his fleet. First, the Macedonians were unable to effectively garrison the entire coastline of Asia Minor, and as soon as the army moved on from one location, the Persians were free to land mercenaries and marines behind them and recapture coastal cities and ports. Second, the Aegean is full of islands, and they provided potential bases for the Persians to resupply and repair their ships, out of reach of the land-bound Macedonians. Third, if the Persians could take control of the Hellespont, they could not only stop Macedonian reinforcements, but they could also intercept Black Sea grain ships, thus cutting off essential food supplies to Athens and other Greek city-states allied with Alexander. All of these problems would start to manifest themselves the following spring when the Persians began their naval counteroffensive.

For now, however, Miletus was captured by a successful siege, aided by the powerful catapults deployed by Alexander's engineers. When he disbanded his fleet, Alexander kept behind a few ships that would be used to transport his siege machines, including twenty ships from Athens. The fact that Alexander kept these ships to transport the siege machines illustrates how important the machines were for his overall strategy and implies that there already existed within the army at this time a specialized engineering unit.[21] The siege machines—catapults, rams, and towers—were designed to be disassembled for easy transport, either by ship or, if inland, by carts or even mules, and the engineers would be responsible for this, as well as for reassembling the machines at future sieges. The machines were complex pieces of equipment (particularly the catapults) and would be difficult to re-create from scratch on-site at each besieged city.[22]

From Miletus the army continued south along the Aegean coast, liberating cities, Greek and non-Greek, and converting them into taxpaying members of Alexander's growing empire. The major fortified port of Halicarnassus resisted, necessitating another siege. Halicarnassus had long been a loyal part of the Persian Empire. During Xerxes's invasion of Greece in 480, the city had provided a naval contingent led by its queen, Artemisia. At the climax of the naval Battle of Salamis, Artemisia's ship rammed and sunk an allied Persian ship in a frantic effort to escape the defeat. Xerxes, watching from shore and thinking Artemisia had sunk a Greek ship, is reported by Herodotus to have said, "My men have become women, and my women men."[23] In escaping, Artemisia had tried to fool the pursuing Greeks into thinking hers was a Greek ship by having her archers shoot Persian sailors who had survived her ramming and were trying to swim for shore.[24]

One hundred fifty years after Salamis, Halicarnassus was still a reliable Persian ally. The city was garrisoned by a large force of hired mercenaries, and the harbor was guarded by triremes from the Persian fleet. The rowers and marines from the Persian ships were also available to help defend the city.[25] Capturing Halicarnassus would be harder than taking Miletus. The Macedonians assembled their siege machines and attacked the walls of the city, while the defenders fought back fiercely, at times sallying out and trying to set fire to the towers. The Macedonians beat back each counterattack and eventually broke through the walls and captured the outer city. The remaining defenders fell back, retreating to a fortified citadel where they continued to hold out.

After assessing the strength of the citadel's defenses and the determination with which the Persians and their mercenary allies were fighting, Alexander decided to break off the attack. The nature of the ground around the citadel made any assault difficult, and capturing the fortress was not considered to be worth either the time or loss of life that would be required. Instead, Alexander left behind three thousand of his own mercenary infantry and two hundred cavalry and moved on with the rest of the army.[26]

Although the citadel at Halicarnassus remained in Persian hands, and Miletus would soon be recaptured by the Persians, the fact that Alexander had within a few months stormed and captured two of the most strongly fortified harbors in Asia Minor was a remarkable achievement and certainly far exceeded anything his father had accomplished. Lane Fox writes that "as a besieger, [Alexander] stands without equal in the ancient world," and he argues that Alexander's success was due to a strategy of attacking several parts of a city at the same time with multiple weapons, which strategy invites "the lucky break."[27] Two years later, at Tyre, Alexander would find a lucky break hard to come by.

After leaving Halicarnassus, Alexander split his army, sending back to Macedonia on winter leave all the soldiers who had recently married, both to raise their morale and to ensure a stable birth rate back home. He sent a large contingent of cavalry back to Sardis along with any excess supply wagons. The rest of the army continued marching south through the province of Caria, then turned east to follow the coastline through the provinces of

Lycia and Pamphylia, sticking with the strategy of trying to defeat the Persian fleet from the land. According to Lane Fox, the Persian ships could only travel about thirty miles before they needed to come in to shore, and Alexander's goal was to cut off those ships from the series of landing places along the coast that they would need to travel from the Aegean back to their home ports in Phoenicia and Cyprus.[28]

Eventually, however, with winter coming on, Alexander abandoned the coast and turned north into the heart of Asia Minor, meeting up with the rest of the army at the Phrygian city of Gordion (often spelled Gordian), ancient capital of the legendary King Midas. The reunited army wintered in Gordion waiting for spring, when there would be grass for the cavalry horses and the recently married men who had been sent home would return along with other reinforcements.[29] It was here that Alexander famously cut the "Gordian knot." Unfortunately, Arrian writes, "I cannot say with confidence what Alexander actually did about this knot, but he and his suite certainly left . . . with the impression that the oracle about the undoing of the knot had been fulfilled."[30]

That spring of 333, while Alexander waited in Gordion for his reinforcements to arrive, the Persians began their naval counteroffensive in the Aegean. According to Lane Fox, the commander of the Persian fleet had several courses of action available to him. First, in the absence of a Macedonian fleet, the Persians were free to force those Aegean cities that had gone over to Alexander to switch their allegiance back to Persia. Second, the Persians could combine their forces with those Greek city-states that were hostile to Alexander, such as Sparta, and support a war against Macedonia, forcing Alexander to return home. Finally, the Persians could seal off the Hellespont to Greek shipping, preventing any reinforcements or supplies from reaching Alexander in Asia Minor.[31] However, because Alexander's reinforcements had already reached Asia Minor and were on their way to Gordion, and because the Macedonian army tended to gather supplies locally rather than from home, even the loss of the Hellespont, the Aegean cities, and the Macedonian homeland might not have been enough to cause Alexander to abandon his campaign. But it was doubtful his soldiers would follow him farther into Asia knowing their homes were being threatened.[32]

Persian naval activity in the Aegean was relentless, and it forced Alexander to reverse his decision of the prior year and reassemble his fleet.[33] He appointed men to lead the new Greek-Macedonian fleet and provided them with five hundred talents to cover the expenses of prosecuting the naval war in the Aegean. To Antipater, his regent in Macedonia, and the men who were charged with defending the cities of Greece, he sent six hundred talents, and he ordered his Greek allies to send ships to guard the Hellespont and the crossing to Asia Minor.[34] However, N. G. L. Hammond argues that "the Macedonian fleet, as opposed to the Greek fleet, had not been disbanded and was holding the Hellespont, and that Alexander sent large sums of money to two Macedonian officers there . . . who were to reassemble the Greek fleet."[35]

With the arrival of spring weather and with his army now reinforced, Alexander turned southeast, heading once again for the coast of Asia Minor. He resumed his tactic of sticking close to the coastline to deny landing places to the Persian fleet.[36] It was rugged country, but their rapid march prevented Persians from fortifying a strategic pass, the Cilician Gates, which led through the Taurus Mountains from central Asia Minor to the coast.

At this point Alexander got a lucky break that reduced Persian naval activity in the Aegean. Darius had been gathering an army at Babylon with the intention of marching to confront Alexander, either in Asia Minor or Syria. The Persian army tended to be strong in cavalry but weak in disciplined infantry, relying instead on hired Greek mercenaries for this purpose. To get as many mercenaries as he could, Darius ordered the commander of the Persian fleet to take the Greek mercenaries already under his command and transport them by sea from the Aegean to the coast of Phoenicia from which point they would be able to march overland and join the Persian army at Babylon. Sometime in summer 333, these mercenaries were landed at the Phoenician port of Tripolis and marched inland to join Darius. The fact that these ships were able to sail from the Aegean to Tripolis in Phoenicia suggests that Alexander's strategy of securing the coastline of Asia Minor against use by the Persian fleet was not successful. The ships that carried the mercenaries—nearly two hundred vessels, according to Lane Fox—would remain at Tripolis until the mercenaries returned. A. B. Bosworth writes that as a result of this transfer of ships and mercenaries, "the war in the Aegean flagged irretrievably, and the Macedonian admirals were able to reach parity with the enemy by the beginning of 332."[37]

While campaigning along the southern coast of Asia Minor, waiting for news of Darius and hoping that his re-formed Aegean fleet would have more success against the Persian navy than his strategy of denying them shore bases, Alexander became seriously ill, which required the army to halt for some time at Tarsus while he recovered. While we don't know the exact nature of Alexander's illness or how long it took him to recover, Lane Fox suggests it was a serious one and his recovery delayed the army's movement from early July until mid-September. All that time, while Alexander lay in his sick bed and the army was stalled, Darius had been assembling his own army at Babylon and was counting his men before forming them into their units. When the Persian army was at last ready, Darius led them west, heading for the plains of Syria and a place where he would have room to use his greater numbers, and in particular his cavalry, against Alexander's army.[38]

Near the end of summer, when Alexander was finally recovered and able to resume the march, the Macedonian army continued east along the coast, heading for the city of Mallos on the Pyramos River in the province of Cilicia. While Alexander was at Mallos a report reached him that Darius and his army had been spotted, camped on the Syrian plain at a place called Sochi, a two-day march from the Syrian Gates. Alexander assembled his generals and told them that Darius had been located. According to Arrian, his men were eager at long last to meet the Persian king and his army in battle, and they urged Alexander to move without delay.[39]

Wasting no time, he sent a force of cavalry ahead to secure the vital Syrian Gates leading from the coast through the mountains and into central Syria. He knew from Xenophon's account that with hard marching, the army could be at the Syrian Gates in two days. The next day the army headed out to find and destroy Darius and the Persians.[40]

Alexander followed the coast road, turning south around the Gulf of Issus and into northwest Syria, through the narrow gap between the mountains and the sea. From there the road turned east through the Syrian Gates. He hoped to catch Darius by surprise.

To do so he would have to hurry.

FIVE

THE KING'S BATH

At Myriandros, near the Syrian Gates, Alexander allowed his wet, tired men to eat and rest for a day, sending a small reconnaissance force of cavalry and archers back north on the coast road toward Issus, looking for the Persian army that was somewhere behind them. Then, as evening was coming on, the whole army turned around and began marching north, trying to reach and occupy another set of gates—these unnamed by Arrian—before the Persians could fortify the narrow gap between the mountains and the sea. Fuller calls this spot the "Jonah Pass," Lane Fox calls it the "Pillar of Jonah Pass," Bosworth calls it the "Pillar of Jonah," and W. W. Tarn calls it the "Jonah Pass." The name refers to a tower or pillar located on this spot where, according to biblical tradition, a great fish "vomited out Jonah upon the dry land."[1]

Upon reaching the pass around midnight, the men were relieved to find it unoccupied. The army camped there for the remainder of the night, making sure to set out a line of pickets: Alexander would not be surprised twice.[2]

The men must have been anxious, knowing the Persians were nearby and in all likelihood Alexander would attack the next day. They would not be facing a provincial army like the one they had beaten at the Granicus. Darius had spent a year assembling his men, gathering them from across the empire. Macedonian scouts reported an enormous number of enemy campfires, such that the whole coastal plain was ablaze with light.[3] The Macedonians may have been men who dined on sharpened swords, but they must have worried nonetheless.

Was Alexander worried? Curtius writes that he grew anxious as he waited for the battle. Up until then he had enjoyed the favor of the goddess Fortune, but he knew the goddess could be fickle, and he knew that the next day would reveal the outcome, good or bad, of his great adventure. Weighing his chances, Alexander thought the potential prize was worth the risk, and even though there was considerable doubt about the battle's outcome, "yet one thing at least was certain, that he would die nobly and with great glory."[4] Curtius does not record the thoughts of Alexander's soldiers.

At dawn the Macedonian army descended from the narrow pass and onto the wider plain beside the sea, its units spreading out from marching column into battle line as the terrain allowed. The battalions of the phalanx were brought forward and formed into their dense rectangles, their sarissas held vertically as they marched, giving the units the appearance of porcupines with iron-tipped quills waving in the air.[5] Curtius writes that the phalanx was formed in thirty-two ranks rather than their usual sixteen because the narrow terrain wouldn't allow them to extend any farther.[6] On the left side of the battle line the hoofs of the allied Greek cavalry horses splashed in the sea, while on the right the archers and Agrianian javelin men edged into the foothills.[7]

They soon found the Persians, deployed and waiting behind a small river that Arrian calls the Pinaros. Scholars are unable to agree on the location of this river. Lane Fox argues for the modern Payas, a small stream that runs down from the mountains to empty into the Mediterranean. Fuller argues for the Deli, a river farther north. Tarn also argues it was probably the Deli. Engels argues that the Deli is too far from the Pass of Jonah for the Macedonians to have reached it before dark, and therefore the Payas must be the location of the battle. Bosworth points out that the Pinaros was just one of many streams that came down out of the mountains to empty into the Mediterranean, and because over the centuries the courses of these streams have changed so much, the location of the battlefield can't be pinpointed with certainty.[8]

The number of men in each army is hard to determine. Tarn writes that Alexander had fewer men than at the Granicus, perhaps twenty thousand to twenty-four thousand infantry, and five thousand cavalry, and Fuller relies on Tarn's numbers. Lane Fox writes that the Macedonian forces were probably a little over twenty-five thousand. Estimates for the Persian army are also difficult, although Arrian's assertion that it numbered six hundred thousand is clearly too high.[9] Tarn writes, somewhat unhelpfully, that the Persian army at Issus may have been larger than Alexander's but that it may also have been smaller. Fuller writes that there were likely over ten thousand Greek mercenaries in Persian service.[10]

If the Persian force did outnumber the Macedonians, as is likely, the narrowness of the battlefield took away this advantage. Choosing to fight in a narrow defile was a strategic mistake for which the Persian king was about to pay dearly. In Darius's defense, he may have expected Alexander to continue his march eastward through the mountain pass of the Syrian Gates and onto the wide Syrian plain, where the Persian army could follow and come upon the Macedonians from behind. Curtius writes that local peasants told Darius that Alexander's army had reversed direction and was now marching back north to meet the Persians. Darius found this difficult to believe since he was convinced that Alexander was still marching through the Syrian Gates. Alexander's rapid turnabout caught the Persians by surprise.[11]

The Battle of Issus, as it came to be called, was hard fought, and was over fairly quickly. The Persians massed their cavalry on their right, on the seashore where the level ground provided an excellent field for a cavalry charge. Sensing that his left flank was vulnerable, Alexander quickly sent over the Thessalian cavalry, who met the Persian charge on the beach and fought desperately to hold off the enemy horsemen. In the center, the uneven ground of the riverbank caused the files of the phalanx to lose their cohesion as they advanced on the Persian line, creating gaps in the sarissa hedgehog that were exploited by the more heavily armored Greek mercenaries on the Persian side. Had the battle continued as an infantry struggle, this could have been decisive.

But in the end, none of that mattered—the battle was won by the Companion Cavalry on the Macedonian right. Formed into their distinctive wedge formation, with Alexander at the point, they slammed into the weak Persian left wing at an angle, carving a path toward the center of the Persian line. Alexander spotted Darius in his royal chariot, and he led his men directly toward the Persian king, hoping that by killing Darius himself he could win the victory single handed.[12] The Macedonian troopers, with their cornel wood lances, stabbed and thrust their way through the mass of Persians, who fought desperately to protect their king. Men were falling all around the Persian king's chariot.[13] Sometime during this confused fighting, Alexander received a minor sword wound to his thigh that did nothing to slow his attack.[14] Darius's bodyguards, realizing that their king was in danger of death or capture, forced the royal chariot to turn around. Darius rapidly escaped the battlefield, followed by most of his army; he was safe, but with his withdrawal the battle was effectively over.

The historians' accounts of the battle provide a dramatic image of the Persian king fighting from his royal chariot while his bodyguards were cut down around him, until he was finally forced to turn and run for his life, pursued by a fearsome Alexander on horseback. This image of the battle is supposedly the basis for the scene depicted in the famous Alexander mosaic from Pompeii, which Bosworth argues was based on a contemporary painting.[15]

Alexander and his men pursued the fleeing Persians as darkness approached, killing what fugitives they could and trying desperately to overtake Darius. After a while the Persian king abandoned his chariot and threw away his shield and weapons, including his bow, fleeing on horseback. In the end he was saved by the coming of night. When it became too dark to see, Alexander called off the pursuit, and he and his men returned to the Persian camp, taking with them as booty the chariot, shield, and bow of the Persian king.[16] Despite his best effort, Alexander couldn't catch Darius.

As is often the case with victorious armies, the Macedonians turned to looting. With the coming of night the remnants of the Persian army were able to escape, leaving their camp open and unguarded for the Macedonians to plunder.[17] And there was much to plunder. According to Llewellyn-Jones, "the peripatetic royal court was, to all intents and purposes, a movable city." In addition to the king's household, the entire royal court and all of the government officials traveled with the king. There were servants for the king and his household, and scribes to keep royal records. The wives and concubines of the royal harem were there, along with all the various musicians, artists, dancers, and singers required to entertain them. Herds of livestock and their keepers traveled with the king, as well as tame animals and those in cages for the amusement of the royal entourage. To interpret omens and read signs, the king required priests and astrologers to accompany him. Finally, the royal treasury accompanied the king on campaign.[18] Despite the vast wealth that the Macedonians found in the Persian camp, Darius had sent most of his treasury to Damascus for safekeeping before the battle.[19]

Llewellyn-Jones explains that the tent of a Persian king wasn't like other tents. "When the court went travelling, the royal tent became the center of empire. It was a colossal structure, made from colorfully woven textiles and leather panels which were supported from a framework of columns thirty feet high, gilded and studded with jewels." The tent was essentially a portable palace, and as such was large enough to hold royal banquets for dozens of guests. The interior was filled with expensive furniture and artwork, and was splendidly decorated with the sorts of fine fabrics that would normally be found in a king's palace.[20]

According to Diodorus, the camp "included much silver, no little gold." The camp also included expensive clothing, jewelry, weapons, and furniture belonging to the Persian nobles and their wives and families who had all accompanied the king on campaign. The amount of wealth in the Persian camp was so great that the victorious soldiers couldn't carry it all, despite being used to marching with heavy loads. Curtius writes that the Macedonians plundered so much loot that they became overloaded and the men soon began to discard items of lesser value along the roadsides whenever they found something more valuable to steal.[21]

In addition to much silver and no little gold, there were also many women in the Persian camp, and so there was rape. Curtius writes, "And now they had reached the women, from whom their ornaments were being torn with the greater violence the more precious they were; force and lust were not sparing even their persons." The camp was soon filled with the screams and cries of the women as the soldiers cruelly assaulted them, regardless of their rank, status, or age.[22]

Diodorus also describes these assaults on the women in the Persian camp: "The lot of these captured women was pathetic in the extreme." Many of them were from the nobility and had all their lives been guarded and pampered, living in harems and protected from men. Now they were running through the camp in terror, pursued by drunken soldiers who tore at their clothing and jewels. Some women threw themselves at the soldiers' feet and begged for mercy. Others ran barefoot over rough ground out into the darkness in a desperate attempt to escape. Still others gathered in groups and called out for help that never came. Women whom the goddess Fortune had favored all of their lives now experienced the fickle nature of that goddess—they were dragged by the hair, beaten with fists or spear butts, and their clothing was ripped off.[23]

Included among the captives was the family of Darius: his mother, his wife—who Arrian claims was also his sister—two teenaged daughters, and a young son.[24] It was common for Persian kings to marry their sisters or nieces for dynastic reasons. Llewellyn-Jones writes that "the concept of 'incest' was of no importance when building a dynasty."[25] These royal women were apparently not molested by the troops, perhaps because they were housed in Darius's royal pavilion, which was kept off-limits and reserved for Alexander. Inside the tents of the pavilion, the servants of Darius stood guard over the wealth contained there, keeping it safe for their new master. They were left untouched by Macedonian soldiers who had secured the pavilion and guarded it for Alexander's return.[26] Macedonian royal pages soon came and took over the tent of Darius, where both a dinner and a bath had been prepared for the Persian king. The tent was ablaze with the light of many lamps and torches, and its vast wealth provided the pages with a glimpse of the riches that awaited Alexander and his followers in the conquest of all Asia.[27]

Plutarch provides an exquisite vignette of Alexander after the battle, writing that when he returned from his pursuit of Darius, he found that "his men had picked out for him the tent of Darius, which was full to overflowing with gorgeous servitors and furniture, and many treasures. Straightway, then, Alexander put off his armor and went to the bath, saying: 'Let us go and wash off the sweat of the battle in the bath of Darius.'"

"'No, indeed,' said one of his companions, 'but rather in that of Alexander; for the property of the conquered must belong to the conqueror, and be called his.'"

It was Alexander's bath now.

"And when he saw the basins and pitchers and tubs and caskets, all of gold, and curiously wrought, while the apartment was marvelously fragrant with spices and unguents, and when he passed from this into a tent which was worthy of admiration for its size and height, and for the adornment of the couch and tables and banquet prepared for him, he turned his eyes upon his companions and said: 'This, as it would seem, is to be a king.'"[28]

PART II

Phoenicia

The Phoenicians are a clever branch of the human race and exceptional in regard to the obligations of war and peace, and they made Phoenicia famous. They devised the alphabet, literary pursuits, and other arts too; they figured out how to win access to the sea by ship, how to conduct battle with a navy, and how to rule over other peoples; and they developed the power of sovereignty and the art of battle.

—Pomponius Mela, *Description of the World*

SIX

BABYLON . . . OR
PHOENICIA?

A lexander's victory at Issus not only defeated the Persian army, it scat-
tered the survivors in all directions, in the words of Lane Fox, "like
sparks from a stamped-out fire." Taking advantage of this chaos, Alexander
quickly sent a small force to Damascus to take control of the Persian treasury, which had been sent to that city before the battle. The Macedonians
met no resistance there from the royal caretakers, and according to Curtius
they captured 2,600 talents of "coined money," 500 pounds of "wrought silver," 30,000 men and "7,000 pack-animals carrying burdens on their backs."[1]
Alexander was once again richer than Croesus.

Alexander now faced a crucial decision based on geography: in which
direction should he take his army? Darius would in all likelihood flee east
to Babylon, or even farther, to Susa, nearer the Persian heartland. There he
could gather the remnants of his defeated army and augment them with
fresh levies from the eastern provinces. The Persian Empire was vast and
its manpower almost limitless. Given enough time, Darius could easily raise
another army larger than the one at Issus. To prevent this, Alexander could

hurry after the Persian king, crossing Syria and advancing deep into
Mesopotamia, harrying Darius and disrupting his attempt to re-form his
army.

Appealing as that prospect must have been for someone as bold and impetuous as Alexander, it failed to deal with the problem of the Persian navy,
which was still intact in the Aegean. Ironically, one of the effects of the land
victory at Issus was to reduce somewhat the number of ships available to
the Persians. The Greek mercenaries who had landed on the coast at Tripolis
the previous spring and marched to Babylon to join Darius now fled from
the disaster at Issus and made their way back to Tripolis. They found that
the ships that had brought them from the Aegean the previous summer
were still there, drawn up on the shore. They launched as many of these
ships as they had rowers to man them and burned the rest to prevent them
from falling into the hands of the Macedonians. From Tripolis they sailed
to Cyprus, and then on to Egypt, where they hoped to find safety.[2] By taking
some of the ships to Egypt and destroying the rest, the mercenaries converted what was a temporary loss of ships for the Persians into a permanent
one.

The victory at Issus also had a more indirect effect on naval activity in
the Aegean. The loss of the treasury at Damascus meant Darius had no way
of getting cash to his admirals to pay their sailors. The only parts of the Persian Empire that paid tribute using minted coins were the provinces of Asia
Minor, and these were now in the hands of the Macedonians. Eventually
the Persian admirals would run out of money with which to pay the crews
of their warships.[3] With the Persian navy weakened, the Greek fleet that
Alexander had ordered reassembled the previous year now seemed to be
achieving results. Alexander's fleet intercepted and defeated a Persian force
that had been sent to the Hellespont, sinking or capturing all of the enemy
ships.[4]

Although the Persian fleet was weakened, it was still capable of not only
retaking Greek cities—either on the coast of Asia Minor or on Aegean islands—but also of carrying the war to Greece itself. Arrian relates the following anecdote: The Persian admirals sailed to Siphnos, an island in the
Aegean near the coast of the Peloponnese, with one hundred of their best
ships. There they were met by the king of Sparta, a man named Agis, who
had come with only a single trireme. Agis asked the Persians to provide him
with money and as many ships and men as they could spare to support him
in a war against Macedonia. In the end, Agis got thirty silver talents and ten
triremes from the Persians. Romm writes that "Arrian gives no context to

explain this sudden appearance of Agis, the Spartan king who was about to shake up the Macedonian order in Europe." In 338, when Philip had organized the League of Corinth, Sparta had refused to join, and since that time had resented first Philip's and then Alexander's control over Greece. While too weak to take on Macedonia on its own—even in Alexander's absence—with the backing of Persian money, ships, and soldiers a Spartan army would be able to overturn Macedonian hegemony and take on the role of leader of the Greeks.[5]

The victory at Issus came as a shock to the Persian admirals as well as to those back in Greece whose loyalty to Alexander was uncertain.[6] Romm argues that the thirty talents and ten triremes Agis received from the Persians was nowhere near what the Spartan king wanted or needed for a war against Macedonia. The Persian admirals were likely planning on giving the Spartans more aid, but after learning of the defeat at Issus they changed their minds and focused their attention instead on providing direct support to Darius in Asia.[7]

In the end, Alexander saw the problem posed by the Persian fleet as being so critical to the success of the invasion that dealing with it took precedence over going after Darius. The way Alexander would deal with the problem, however, was not by engaging the Persian fleet in a naval battle but by resurrecting his old approach of beating the fleet on land. Only this time he wouldn't just occupy deserted coastlines to deny the sailors a place to sleep and cook dinner; this time he would capture the home bases of the Phoenician ships making up the bulk of the Persian fleet. He knew where these sailors and their families lived, and he was going after their homes, their parents, and their children. Alexander's success in Asia, argues Lane Fox, "depended on his strategy in the sea-ports, and he knew it." As Tarn points out, "His immediate objective was Phoenicia and the ruin of the Persian fleet." Waldemar Heckel notes that scholars have called Alexander's failure to chase Darius a "strategic error" and have argued that Alexander should have pursued the Persian king to prevent him from forming a new army. In Heckel's view "this strategy fails to take into account the threat of the Persian fleet and the danger of extending the lines of communication and supply."[8]

Theodore A. Dodge explains the decision this way: "Many critics have enquired why Alexander, immediately after the battle of Issus, did not sharply follow Darius, and penetrate to Babylon and Susa, seek to control the Persiad Kingdom from its center, and prevent Darius from accumulating another army. . . . But the truth was that Alexander had vastly more grave fears for his rear and for Macedonia than dread of any force in his front."

Dodge goes on to explain that because the Persian fleet still controlled the Aegean and could theoretically show up anywhere along the Mediterranean coast, from Asia Minor to Egypt, it would be foolish for Alexander to march into the interior without subduing it. That Alexander's "schemes of conquest were broad and sensible, is by nothing so well shown as by his patient waiting and working here on the coast before he ventured beyond the Euphrates."[9] Given Alexander's temperament and his tendency to rush headlong into danger, the fact that the phrase "patient waiting" should describe his approach here speaks to how important it was to him to neutralize the Persian fleet.

Edmond F. Bloedow offers a contrary view, arguing that "a different strategy [by Alexander] would have been much more economical and also much more beneficial in the long run. Immediately (or very soon) after Issus, Alexander could/should himself have gone in pursuit of Darius— something which modern critics have been at pains to argue away. *Instead of dispatching* [the Macedonian General] *Parmenion to Damascus,* [Alexander] *should have sent him to take care of the coast of Phoenicia and anything else that was deemed appropriate in the area.*" (emphasis in original)[10]

The coastal cities of Phoenicia, home ports for many of the ships of the Persian fleet, lay along the eastern shore of the Mediterranean. From north to south the principal ports were Arados, Tripolis, Byblos, Sidon, and Tyre. Colonists from these Phoenician cities had founded many of the cities on the island of Cyprus, which also provided ships for the Persian fleet, and Cyprus had long chaffed under Persian rule. Twelve years earlier, sensing Persian weakness, Cyprus had joined some of the Phoenician cities and Egypt in rebelling. It turned out to be a mistake, and all had been crushed by the vengeful Persian king Artaxerxes III.[11] Cypriot anger toward Persia still simmered, and Alexander hoped that if he detached the Phoenician ships from the Persian fleet, the ships of Cyprus would come over to him as well. His plan was to move south down the coast, offering liberation from Persian control, convincing each of the cities in turn to join in his campaign. He was confident that all of them would, and in the end, all did—all but Tyre.

But that was in the future. Alexander and his army still had a long way to go to reach Phoenicia. The small offshore island of Arados, northernmost of the Phoenician cities, was 150 miles south of the Issus battlefield, with two mountain ranges to be crossed. His men, now laden with booty from the Persian camp, retraced their route south, back through the Jonah Pass. The richness of the loot instilled in the common Macedonian soldiers a strong desire for more of the gold, silver, women, and luxurious goods they

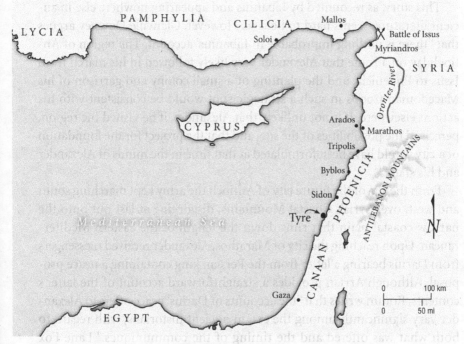

MAP 3. Phoenicia and the eastern Mediterranean.

had found in the tents of the Persian nobles. Plutarch writes that the Macedonians, having gotten a taste for the spoils to be had from success in a war in Asia, "were like dogs in their eagerness to pursue and track down the wealth of the Persians."[12] Turning southeast, they wound their way over the Amanus Mountains by way of the Syrian Gates and forded the Orontes River near the site where, in the year 300, Alexander's general Seleucus would found the city of Antioch.

Six hundred years later, the Greek writer Libanius, fiercely proud of the origins of his hometown of Antioch, wrote a fascinating—and fanciful—account of Alexander's visit to the site. Libanius writes that Alexander found a spring at the site of the future city and declared the water there to be so sweet it was like his mother's milk. He named the spring after his mother, Olympias, built a shrine on the spot, and said he would found a city there when his campaign had ended. In the meantime, he started the foundation for a temple dedicated to the god Zeus Bottiaios, named for the Bottiaei, a tribe that lived in the region of Thrace where Alexander had been raised.[13]

This story, as recounted by Libanius and appearing nowhere else in ancient literature, seems hard to believe. However, Glanville Downey argues that "there is nothing improbable in Libanius' account. The region of Antioch lay on a route that Alexander very likely followed in his march from Issus to Phoenicia, and the planting of a small colony and garrison of his Macedonian troops in such a strategic spot would be consistent with his actions elsewhere. It is not unlikely that Alexander, if he visited the region, perceived the possibilities of the site, and that the project for the foundation of a city would have been formulated at that time in the minds of Alexander and his staff."[14]

From the site of the future city of Antioch the army kept marching south and west, over Syria's Coastal Mountains, disgorging at last out onto the narrow coastal plain that runs down the length of the eastern Mediterranean. Upon reaching the city of Marathos, Alexander received messengers from Darius bearing a letter from the Persian king containing a peace proposal. Although Arrian provides a straightforward account of the letter's contents, Romm writes that "the accounts of Darius' peace offers to Alexander vary significantly among the extant ancient historians, with regard to both what was offered and the timing of the communiques." Lane Fox writes that "Darius' letters to Alexander are disputed and muddled in the histories."[15]

Arrian writes that the Persian messengers, in addition to bringing Alexander the letter, had been instructed by Darius to speak in person with him and to beg for the release of Darius's mother, wife, and children. In the letter, Darius argues that there had been an ancient friendship between Macedonia and Persia and that Alexander was an unprovoked aggressor. Darius claimed he was only defending his kingdom and that the outcome of the Battle of Issus had been decided "as some god had willed." Further, "as a king he begged a king to restore his captive mother, wife and children; and he was ready to make friendship and an alliance with Alexander." There is no mention by Arrian of any offer of payment to Alexander for the release of Darius's family.[16]

In comparing Arrian to the other historians—Curtius, Justin, and Plutarch—Romm writes that Curtius "agrees with Arrian that Darius wrote to Alexander shortly after Issus and proposed a treaty of alliance, but also relates an extravagant offer of ransom for the royal captives." Arrian will report this ransom offer in a second letter that occurs much later. Justin seems to agree with Curtius, and Plutarch seems to agree with Arrian "but places [the letter] at a different point in the war, about a year and a half later."

Romm concludes that "the historical accounts have in this instance become contaminated" and that "the truth about what Darius offered (if anything) and when is very hard to recover."[17]

While there may be disagreement among the historians about the content and timing of this first letter from Darius, Alexander's response is clear. In his letter back to Darius he provides a long list of grievances, both of Greece against Persia and personally of Alexander against Darius, whom he accuses, for example, of paying to have Philip assassinated. Romm writes that most of these charges "to the best of our knowledge, are specious."[18] In his letter, Alexander goes on to say that if Darius wants his family back, he should come to Alexander in person and ask for them, regarding Alexander as "lord of all Asia," and they will be returned. In the future, Darius should address Alexander as "king of Asia," and he should not consider himself as Alexander's equal. The letter concludes with this warning: "if you claim the kingship, stand your ground and fight for it and do not flee, as I shall pursue you wherever you are."[19]

Philip's goal of freeing the Greek cities of Asia Minor and waging a war of revenge against Persia was expanding. Alexander now saw the kingship of the whole Persian Empire waiting to be taken. It only required daring.

Despite Darius's offer, there would be no peace.

SEVEN

THE PURPLE LAND

As the Macedonian army approached the Phoenician coast, the first thing the men noticed may have been the smell. Throughout antiquity, Phoenicia was famous for the production of a type of fabric dye that ranged in color from pale rose to deep purple—a color so dark it was almost black. The dye was derived from the bodies of certain types of sea snails, called murex, that lived in great numbers along the Mediterranean coast. One byproduct of the large-scale dye production was dead, rotting snail carcasses that accumulated in enormous piles around the dye factories, creating an awful stench. According to Nina Jidejian, "large heaps of broken shells of *Murex brandaris* and *Murex trunculus* have been found at Tyre and also at Sidon, sites of ancient dye factories." The Greek geographer Strabo writes that the great number of dye works around Tyre in his day made the city "unpleasant to live in." Donald Harden suggests "it was best to have the 'factory' on the lee side of the town, as the odor was not pleasant."[1]

Because only a tiny amount of dye could be extracted from each snail, the dye was incredibly expensive, so much so that the color purple came to be associated with the very wealthy, resulting in the idea that the wearing of purple clothing was a sign of royalty. The value of purple cloth was compared with that of pearls.[2] According to the Greek writer Athenaeus, "Even kings did not have much fabric of this sort in that period, and they went to great lengths to obtain it; for purple dye cost its weight in silver."[3] It has been estimated that applying purple dye to raw wool would make the wool thirty times more valuable.[4] Ville Vuolanto writes that the Roman sumptuary law *lex Oppia* "provided that no woman should . . . wear luxuriously colored (versicolor) clothing. . . . Most scholars argue that by the versicolor clothing, Livy denotes purple, a luxury dye in the Roman world."[5]

The Bible records that King Solomon, wanting Phoenician purple cloth to adorn his new temple in Jerusalem, asked King Hiram of Tyre, "So now send me a man skilled to work in gold, silver, bronze, and iron, and in purple, crimson, and blue fabrics."[6] Purple cloth was also associated by the Greeks with the god Herakles, whom the Phoenicians knew as Melqart. A Greek myth tells the story of how purple dye from Tyre was first discovered by Melqart-Herakles while he was walking along the shore of the Mediterranean, accompanied by a nymph named Tyros. During the walk, Melqart's dog bit into a large sea snail, and as a result the dog's mouth was stained purple. Seeing this, Melqart took some cloth, stained it with the purple dye, and presented it to the nymph, who was delighted with the gift. This type of snail, and the dye it produced, became so important to Tyre that an image of a murex appears on Tyrian coins in the fourth century.[7]

Phoenicia is not a country, like Macedonia, or a Persian province, like Celicia, or a city-state, like Athens or Sparta. It is simply the name given by the Greeks (and later the Romans) to a group of seaport cities hugging the Mediterranean coastline of Syria. The Greek word for Phoenician (*Phoinikes*, plural of *Phoinix*) is first found in Homer and appears to be related to a color—dark red, purple, or brown.[8] Michael C. Astour argues that the word has a Semitic rather than a Greek origin and was borrowed by the Greeks from the Phoenicians themselves. However, he agrees that the word refers to the color purple.[9]

Although the cities of Phoenicia are ancient, dating back thousands of years, and the Phoenicians had a written language, few written records have survived. Most of what is written about them comes from a variety of other sources, such as stone monuments and clay tablets found in archaeological digs in cities of their various conquerors—Assyrians, Babylonians, Persians—as well as surviving accounts by Greek and Roman historians, who often saw Phoenicians as trading rivals or enemies. Because the modern

Lebanese sites of Phoenician cities are still densely populated, archaeology is limited in its ability to provide information about the past. Also, centuries of shifting sand and silt have changed the ancient coastline, sometimes, as at Tyre, quite dramatically. Some of the best archaeological evidence about ancient Phoenicia comes not from the eastern Mediterranean but from hundreds of miles away, at the sites of western colonies in North Africa (Carthage), Sicily, and Spain. Harden argues that "there is more archaeological and literary evidence about Carthage than about all the other Phoenician cities combined."[10]

Much of our knowledge of the Phoenicians comes from the Bible, since the kingdoms of Israel and Judah were close neighbors, and trade was carried on between the two regions. Phoenician cities are mentioned in historical accounts, such as the books of Kings and Chronicles, as well as in books by prophets, such as Ezekiel and Isaiah. King Solomon's relationship with the Tyrian king Hiram is mentioned in connection with the building of the temple in Jerusalem. For example, 1 Kings 8-12 (RSV) relates the following information about a contract whereby Hiram provides timber to Solomon in exchange for wheat and oil:

> And Hiram sent to Solomon, saying, "I have heard the message which you have sent to me; I am ready to do all you desire in the matter of cedar and cypress timber. My servants shall bring it down to the sea from Lebanon; and I will make it into rafts to go by sea to the place you direct, and I will have them broken up there, and you shall receive it; and you shall meet my wishes by providing food for my household." So Hiram supplied Solomon with all the timber of cedar and cypress that he desired, while Solomon gave Hiram twenty thousand cors of wheat as food for his household, and twenty thousand cors of beaten oil.[11] Solomon gave this to Hiram year by year. And the Lord gave Solomon wisdom, as he promised him; and there was peace between Hiram and Solomon; and the two of them made a treaty.

According to Mark Woolmer and Glenn E. Markoe, the Phoenicians were also famous for making glassware, and products made from glass were considered valuable in the ancient world. The primary ingredient for glassmaking was sand, which was mixed with "calcium carbonate and sodium and potassium alkalis (such as that obtained from plant ash). Once assembled, these components would be mixed together to form a paste which would then be heated to a temperature of around 1,050 degrees centigrade [1,890 degrees Fahrenheit] to ensure that the various elements fused together. The molten paste could then be poured into a mold and left to slowly set, or, alternatively, it could be carefully shaped whilst it was gradually cooling."[12]

Apparently the sand along portions of the Phoenician coast was exceptionally suited for making glass. The geographer Strabo writes: "Between [Acre] and Tyre is a sandy beach, which produces the sand used in making glass. Now the sand, it is said, is not fused here, but is carried to Sidon and there melted and cast. Some say that the Sidonians, among others, have the glass-sand that is adapted to fusing, though others say that any sand anywhere can be fused." The historian Pliny the Elder attributes the invention of glass to the Phoenicians and writes that there is a part of the Phoenician coast where "the beach stretches for not more than half a mile, and yet for many centuries the production of glass depended on this area alone."[13]

Cedar wood, purple cloth, metalwork, pottery, and glass were all valuable exports that the Phoenician seamen carried across the Mediterranean in their tiny ships. But according to Harden, the "highest and most enduring memorial" of the Phoenicians is the alphabet. "This is where they impinge most strongly on all subsequent civilizations of Old World origin. All Indo-European and Semitic tongues—indeed all subsequent alphabetic scripts—have employed the medium invented by the Phoenicians and rapidly adopted by many other nations round about them, including the Greeks." Including, after many centuries, the Latin alphabet with which this book is written. Madadh Richey writes, "Herodotus understood the Greeks to have acquired their alphabet from the Phoenicians. . . . Minus a few dissenting voices . . . scholars generally agree with this genealogy."[14]

Phoenician cities were relatively small in physical size compared with others in the near east. Sidon was probably the largest, at around 150 acres. Tyre probably covered no more than 40 acres. The typical Phoenician city comprised a lower district containing the business area and residential quarter, and an upper district containing temples, administrative buildings, and palaces. This upper district was often separately walled, although it does not appear to have been so at Tyre. Glen E. Markoe writes that "the commercial life of the Phoenician city was invariably organized around its port facilities, wharves and warehouses. The focus of activity was the broad market square or plaza, which was generally located in proximity to the main harbor and city entrance. Heavy industrial activity (metal-working, purple dye production) tended to be segregated in the periphery of the lower town—often near the harbor itself or at the rear of the settlement." He adds that "large-scale buildings were marked by handsomely dressed walls of marginally drafted ashlar masonry. As one would expect, internal access within such a closed urban environment was extremely tight, with routes of communication consisting of long narrow alleys or passageways. The resulting picture is that of a densely built-up urban amalgam."[15] Other buildings were made from brick or clay, and the upper stories of multilevel houses may have been made of wood.[16]

Although the cities of Phoenicia were part of the Persian Empire, this was not necessarily a bad thing for the inhabitants. Corinne Bonnet writes: "The organization of the vast [Persian] Empire had enabled Phoenician cities to thrive as it brought new dynamism to trade routes from the peripheries to the center, and vice versa. The potential of the provinces was developed, the road network was well maintained, and government networks of people and infrastructure were solidly established. . . . Each Phoenician kingdom managed its own development with its own dynasty and governing bodies, while being subject to annual tribute."[17]

The Phoenicians were a religious people who worshiped a pantheon of gods, the greatest of which was El, who was sometimes depicted as a bull. The wife of El was Asherat, and their son was Baal. Archaeological excavations at Ugarit (a Syrian coastal city north of Arados) revealed a temple to Baal that dates to the early second millennium. Much of our knowledge of the religions of Canaan comes from clay tablets discovered at Ugarit, which contain records written in an alphabetic cuneiform script that differs from Phoenician.[18]

The word "El" is simply the Semitic word for "god," and so the supreme god could be referred to by other names as well. The name of the chief god of Tyre, Melqart, contains the Phoenician word "milk," which means king or ruler, and "qart," which means city, and the god is sometimes referred to as Baal Melqart. The Greeks identified Melqart with Herakles, and he was an important god of the Carthaginians as well. The Carthaginians would send an annual delegation to Tyre to pay homage to Melqart and to pay tithes to Melqart's temple. Melqart's image appears on coins from as far away as Gades (modern Cadiz, Spain).[19] In chapter 9, Melqart-Herakles and the annual Carthaginian delegation will play a critical role in Alexander's decision to besiege Tyre.

Two Phoenician religious practices will likely seem troubling to a modern reader. The first is described by Harden as "religious prostitutes, both women and boys. Such a practice was common form in Phoenician sanctuaries, at least in the east. Herodotus records it in Cyprus, and the early fathers have much to say of it in Phoenicia. It also existed in the west, for representations of 'temple boys' occur more than once on Carthage stelae."[20] This type of sacred or temple prostitution is believed to have been practiced by other ancient cultures.

Markoe writes, "Sacred prostitution formed another long-established Phoenician institution, associated particularly with the cult of Astarte." He continues, "Astarte's procreative powers manifest themselves in her association with cults of ritual prostitution. Her celebrated sanctuary at Eryx was renowned for it; surviving inscriptions reveal the spread of its cult both to Sardinia and to North Africa. A text from the former records the names of two sacred prostitutes in the service of Erycine Astarte: a mother and daughter." Woolmer and Markoe write that some scholars "hypothesize that women (and sometimes men) were employed to have sexual intercourse with worshippers in an effort to induce the gods to copulate with one another (an act which it was thought would ensure the fertilization of the natural world)."[21]

Here is how Herodotus describes one form of the institution:

> The foulest Babylonian custom is that which compels every woman of the land once in her life to sit in the temple of Aphrodite and have intercourse with some stranger. . . . When a woman has once taken her place there she goes not away to her home before some stranger has cast money into her lap and had intercourse with her outside the temple. . . . After their intercourse she has made herself holy in the goddess's sight and goes away to her home; and thereafter there is no bribe however great that will get her. . . . There is a custom like to this in some parts of Cyprus.[22]

However, Stephanie Lynn Budin argues that "sacred prostitution never existed in the ancient near east or Mediterranean." Her book *The Myth of Sacred Prostitution in Antiquity* "reconsiders the various literary data that have given rise to the sacred prostitution myth and offers new interpretations of what these may have actually meant in their ancient contexts." She devotes an entire chapter to a line-by-line analysis of the Herodotus account of the Babylonian practice on Cyprus, concluding, "In the end, the sacred prostitution Herodotus describes . . . is not real. Rather than a historical reality, it is an almost poetic description of the current, conquered state of Babylon that pulls together a number of important themes running throughout the Histories."[23] Whether sacred prostitution was, in fact, practiced by the Phoenicians, and if so, to what extent, are questions currently being debated by scholars.

The second aspect of Phoenician religion that modern readers find troubling is the sacrificing of human infants and children. Paolo Xella writes, "Any discussion of Phoenician and Punic religion must include the issue of the tophet. Known conventionally through the biblical term . . . these are open-air child cremation sanctuaries."[24] Harden writes that excavations at the precinct of Tanit at Salammbo, Carthage, provide sufficient evidence "to show conclusively that the ancient stories of Phoenician and Canaanite infant sacrifice to 'Moloch' were only too true. . . . It is now clear that other peoples' detestation of the Phoenicians for such a practice was founded on fact." He goes on, "Two inscriptions from the Tanit precinct at Carthage expressly mention infant sacrifices. . . . It would be nice to think that as time went on the infant sacrifices became rarer and substitutions of small animals and birds were more common, and we may hope that that is what the contents of the Tanit urns will indicate when they have been fully studied."[25]

Markoe writes that the western Mediterranean Phoenician colonies were infamous for a "form of sacrificial rite involving human beings, more precisely young children. The classical sources are filled with references to this practice, which is generally ascribed to the Phoenicians, but specifically associated with the Carthaginians." He goes on to say "the Greek historian Diodorus . . . relates that they were enacted publicly in response to a military crisis. According to his account, the Carthaginian aristocracy, under siege, . . . offered up two hundred of their noble born in an effort to appease a Carthaginian deity whom they had offended through neglect and ritual abuse: in place of their own offspring they had wrongfully substituted children surreptitiously purchased from commoners."[26]

Xella writes: "Even today, some scholars claim that no real human sacrifice was performed in the tophet, but that it was a special necropolis used to receive children who had died of natural causes. In fact, both direct—strictly archaeological, epigraphic, osteological . . . and indirect sources—biblical and Classical texts—consistently indicate the bloody nature of the sacrifices and the function of the victims as offerings, children and animals alike."[27]

The sacrificing of children to appease the gods during a time of national crisis will be encountered again in chapter 15, during the siege of Tyre.

EIGHT

THE SHIPS
OF PERSIA

The land along the Phoenician coast was hemmed in to the east by the
Lebanon mountain range, with peaks reaching as high as eleven thousand feet. The coastal strip was narrow—in modern times only a mile wide
in some places and nowhere wider than four miles[1]—and so the arable land
around the coastal cities was insufficient to support a large population. Because of this the Phoenicians naturally turned to the sea—for fishing, exploration, and trade. Although the mountains were a constraint, their
proximity also endowed the Phoenicians with an abundant natural re-
source—timber—and in particular cedar logs. This wealth of timber resulted in an export trade that began early in Phoenician history, famously
with King Solomon, but also with treeless Egypt, a trade that was well doc-
umented in Egyptian records. In addition to cedar, other tree species such
as fir abounded, providing wood suited for a variety of purposes.[2]

This ready access to high-quality timber resulted in the Phoenicians
being the finest shipbuilders in the ancient world. Their warships formed

the bulk of the fleet of the Persian Empire, and, according to Harden, "as explorers, in antiquity, the Phoenicians were second to none." In addition to exploring, the Phoenicians were famous as merchants, and their cargo ships carried not only timber but manufactured goods that were traded across the Mediterranean, returning with hulls full of food products, raw materials, and precious metals.[3] To supply their extensive metalworking factories, Phoenician ships carried ores from as far away as Spain. In addition to metalwork and dyed cloth, pottery and glassware were important exports.

Duane W. Roller writes that "Phoenician seamanship and exploration would already have been well established when Solomon of Israel commissioned Hiram of Tyre to construct a fleet for him on the Red Sea, sometime in the second half of the tenth century." By the Early Iron Age, ships from Phoenicia had crossed the Mediterranean and, after passing Gibraltar, turned south to explore the western coast of Africa. Archaeologists suggest that Phoenicians had reached the coast of what is now Portugal shortly after the year 1000. According to Greek sources, Phoenicians had sailed beyond Spain around the time of the Trojan War, or nearly the same time as Hiram was building ships for Solomon. The fact that Solomon wanted these ships suggests there were existing trade routes he wanted to exploit, and using Phoenician-built ships was the best way of doing so. Keith DeVries and Michael L. Katzev write: "It is not particularly surprising that the Phoenicians should have surpassed the Greeks in reaching distant places for trade and colonization. There is much evidence that until the fifth century they were the better sailors."[4]

Scholars have debated whether Phoenicians, sailing north along the coasts of Spain and France, reached Cornwall and traded for Cornish tin. Evidence for this was based on obscure references in ancient accounts by the geographer Strabo and the historian Diodorus. A painting by Frederic Leighton (AD 1830–1896) titled *Phoenicians Bartering with Ancient Britons* was commissioned for the Royal Exchange in London. Timothy Champion writes of this painting, "The richly clad Phoenicians are presented as the bringers of civilization, learning and technical skill to the mostly fur-clad Britons, with whom they traded textiles and high-quality manufactured goods in exchange for furs and metal." At one point the connection between Cornwall and Phoenicia was thought to be so important that in AD 1906, the president of the Royal Institution of Cornwall wrote that Cornish clotted cream had been "introduced to us by those navigators from Syria." However, modern scholars are skeptical that the Phoenicians ever reached

Cornwall. Champion writes, "The direct archaeological evidence for the presence of Phoenician or Carthaginian traders as far north as Britain is non-existent, and the most recent review of Phoenician activity in the west does not even bother to consider the question."[5]

An amazing example of Phoenician seafaring prowess—the circumnavigation of Africa—is recounted by Herodotus, a journey that was only seen to be feasible, according to Roller, "because it was believed that Africa was much smaller than it was."[6] Herodotus's story begins: "Necos king of Egypt . . . when he had made an end of digging the canal which leads from the Nile to the Arabian Gulf, sent Phoenicians in ships, charging them to sail on their return voyage past the Pillars of Herakles till they should come into the northern sea and so to Egypt."[7] The ships of this expedition made their way through the canal from the Nile to the Red Sea, and from there sailed south down the east coast of Africa. At the end of the first year the expedition found a suitable spot on the African shore and beached their ships, built shelters, sowed grain, and waited for it to ripen. When the grain was ripe they harvested it, launched their ships, and kept sailing down the coast. They repeated this pattern—building shelters, sowing, and reaping grain—at the end of the second year. In the third year the expedition reached the Strait of Gibraltar (Herodotus's Pillars of Herakles) and sailed into the Mediterranean (Herodotus's northern sea), finally returning to Egypt.

Herodotus concludes his story, "they said (what some may believe, though I do not) that in sailing round [Africa] they had the sun on their right hand." In the Southern Hemisphere, the sun would be on the right (north) side of a ship sailing west around the southern coast of Africa, whereas in the Northern Hemisphere, a ship sailing west would have the sun on the left (south) side of the ship. Herodotus thus finds the claim in this story that the sun was on the right side of the ship as it sailed west to be unbelievable. Donald Harden writes, "Most modern commentators accept this story as genuine on the basis of their statement—which Herodotus says he did not believe—that, as they sailed round [Africa] they had the sun on their right hand (as would occur during such a journey)."[8]

In commenting on the seafaring skill of the Phoenicians, Roller writes that "the Phoenicians were able to make such extensive journeys because of their skill in shipbuilding: they were preeminent in this for hundreds of years. Long after Phoenician political power had declined, their reputation as sailors was still so strong that Alexander the Great took their shipwrights on his expedition, making use of them on the Indus." The Phoenicians are also thought to have made important discoveries related to navigation, allowing them to use the positions of stars in the night sky to find their location.[9]

As well as being craftsmen, explorers, and traders, the Phoenicians were fighters. For over a century, the ships, sailors, and marines from the cities of Phoenicia made up a large part of the Persian fleet. The Phoenician city of Sidon was well known for its warships. John W. Betlyon argues that the importance of warships to the Phoenicians was reflected in their coins: "The most consistent elements on the Sidonian coins were representations of the warships—the galleys—of Sidon. First depicted with unfurled sails, then the partially furled sails, and finally without sails in full military splendor, the galleys are shown above waves with oars, and with a battering ram on the bow, as the vessels race into battle—presumably with the Greek navies."[10]

The incorporation of the ships of the Phoenician cities into a Persian fleet went back at least as far as 526 and the reign of the Persian king Cambyses, son of Cyrus the Great, who in that year combined the Phoenician ships into a fleet to join his expedition against Egypt.[11] Llewellyn-Jones writes, "It was typical of the Persians to use this type of recruitment system; from the empire's inception to its final sharp demise, this was the method used by all Great Kings. Soldiers, cavalrymen, and sailors came from every part of the empire, bringing with them their diverse weapons and fighting styles." Tarn writes that Phoenicia was not forced into the Persian Empire by conquest but "came in of her own free will; on what terms we do not know, but the acquisition of the Phoenician fleet without fighting for it was so tremendous a gain to Persia that the terms for Phoenicia must have been good ones." Tarn speculates that the cities of Phoenicia (and also those of the province of Cilicia) had enough leverage that they could bargain with the Persian king to limit the length of time they were required to provide ships for the fleet.[12]

Jidejian explains that Persia "was not a sea-power. To obtain a fleet the Mediterranean seaboard had to be occupied and an understanding reached with the city-states of Phoenicia to furnish ships and crews. An arrangement was reached whereby the city-states placed their fleets at the disposal of the Persian monarch in return for which Persia did not occupy the cities and allowed them to retain their native kings." While the ships of the Phoenician cities were serving as part of the Persian fleet, they were commanded by their own kings and treated as allies of Persia rather than subjects. The Phoenicians did not seem to have been forced to serve the Persian king but rather appeared to do so willingly.[13] Perhaps, like so many subject peoples throughout history, the Phoenicians simply tried to make virtue out of necessity. Or perhaps they just hated the Greeks and were happy to fight them, regardless of whom they had to serve to do so.

When Xerxes decided to invade Greece in 480, he took along an enormous fleet. Herodotus says there were 1,207 triremes, of which 300 were furnished by the Phoenicians, together with "the Syrians of Palestine."[14] However, this large number of 1,207 triremes is questioned by scholars.[15] Llewellyn-Jones says Herodotus "widely exaggerated his calculations" and "the actual number of triremes supplied by Ionia, Phoenicia and Egypt [essentially everyone but Cyprus, with 150 ships] was closer to 500."[16]

Herodotus implies that in 480 the best triremes in the Phoenician fleet were those of Sidon, and he gives two examples of Sidonian ships being singled out for excellence. The first is a race between the ships of the various cities that was ordered by Xerxes prior to the start of the invasion of Greece. Herodotus writes: "Xerxes sat, and looked down on the sea-shore, viewing his army and his fleet; and as he viewed them he was fain to see the ships contend in a race. They did so, and the Phoenicians of Sidon won it; and Xerxes was pleased with the race, and with his armament." The second example occurs when Xerxes and his army reached the border of Thessaly in northern Greece and were looking for a route through mountainous country. Xerxes decided to personally reconnoiter the mouth of the river Peneus where it empties into the Aegean, since the river gorge may have offered a possible way through the mountains, and he wanted to observe the mouth of the gorge from the sea. Herodotus offers this insight: "As [Xerxes] desired, so he did; embarking in a ship of Sidon, wherein he ever embarked when he had some such business." In other words, the Persian king always chose a Sidonian trireme as his personal flagship.[17]

When the Greeks defeated the Persian fleet at the Battle of Salamis in 480, most of the enemy ships they faced were from Phoenicia or Cyprus, although the decks of these ships would have been filled with soldiers and archers from across the Persian Empire. Scholars don't know much about the Greek and Phoenician triremes that fought at Salamis—modern knowledge of ancient warships comes from a later period. Barry Strauss writes: "Our information about the trireme is plentiful if incomplete. Unfortunately for the student of Salamis, most of that information comes from the period ca. 430-320 BC, that is, at least fifty years after the Persian Wars." In other words, scholarly descriptions of the triremes used by Xerxes's sailors in the Persian Wars are more applicable to the ships of the Persian fleet that Alexander faced in 332. According to Strauss, the triremes of the Phoenicians differed in subtle ways from those of the Greek city-states. "The Phoenicians prided themselves on being the greatest sailors in the Mediterranean and followed their own boat-building tradition." Although the Phoenician triremes were probably about 130 feet long, the same length as the Greek ships, scholars think that the Phoenician triremes were wider and higher.[18]

The Greeks relied on ramming as their primary method of attacking enemy ships, using a bronze-sheathed wooden ram with three blades extending out in front of the ship's bow, while the Phoenician ram was longer and tapered. Phoenician ships may have carried more marines than Greek ships, perhaps Persian allied soldiers from throughout the Empire, and therefore had wider decks to hold the additional men and higher sides to screen them from arrows. Because of the large number of soldiers on board, the Phoenicians may have favored boarding and capturing enemy ships in hand-to-hand combat. Boarding not only required less technical sailing skill compared with ramming, it also left the successful attacker with an undamaged prize.

For Alexander, fighting against the Persian Empire meant fighting a powerful fleet made up primarily of ships from Phoenicia and Cyprus. As will become clear in chapter 12, these Phoenician and Cypriot warships would play a crucial role in Alexander's conquest of Asia, not in any sea battle, but in the siege of Tyre.

NINE

SURRENDER

The ancient city of Arados (modern Arwad) occupied a small rocky island off the Phoenician coast, opposite the mainland city of Marathos, where Alexander had received the peace messengers from Darius.[1] Fuller writes that Arados, although small, "was immensely strong, for it was situated on an island of rock, 800 yards in length and 500 in breadth, two and a half miles from the shore." The city was surrounded by an imposing wall made of large, squared-off stone blocks (ashlars), some of which were as long as eighteen feet. The blocks were cemented together, creating a wall so strong that parts of it still survive, with some of these remaining sections reaching as high as thirty feet.[2] The size and construction of this wall was probably similar to those of other Phoenician port cities, such as Tyre.[3] The wall likely served to protect the city from enemy attack and to shield it from high waves caused by storms at sea.

At Arados, Alexander's strategy of defeating the Persian fleet from the land began to show promise. The king of Arados, Gerostratos, was absent. Like the kings of the other Phoenician cities, he was in the Aegean with the

Persian fleet, commanding the city's contingent of warships. In the king's absence his son Straton was ruling in Arados, and as Alexander approached the city, Straton met him on the mainland at Marathos. At this meeting, Straton presented Alexander with a golden crown, surrendering to him not only the city of Marathos but all the other cities over which his father ruled, including the island fortress of Arados.[4] Despite its small size, Arados was an important city with a good harbor, controlling much of the land along the northern Phoenician coast. Lane Fox calls it a "small land empire." Romm writes, "The surrender of Arados by Straton thus marks the beginning of what was to become a crucial turning point in the Perso-Macedonian war: the defection to Alexander of the Phoenicians serving in the Persian navy."[5] Although Arados likely retained a few warships to defend the city in the absence of its fleet, there is no mention in the ancient sources of Alexander taking ships from Arados at this time.

Moving south down the coast road from Arados, Alexander negotiated the surrender of Byblos, another important Phoenician port. Byblos was reputed to be the oldest city in the world,[6] and was known for importing papyrus from Egypt in exchange for timber. The Greek word *byblos* (βύβλος) means "papyrus," suggesting to scholars that the city may have been an important source for the Greeks of imported Egyptian papyrus. The word also means a roll of papyrus—a "book" to the Greeks—and thus the city's name eventually ended up reflected in the English word "bible."[7]

Continuing south from Byblos, the next major port was Sidon, which had an uneasy relationship with Persia, having rebelled against King Artaxerxes III in the 350s and as a result been crushed by the Persian army in 345.[8] Although the Sidonians had put up a fierce resistance in defense of their city, the Persian forces arrayed against them were reported to be three hundred thousand men and eight hundred ships. In the end, the city was betrayed by the Sidonian king, Tennes, who allowed the Persians inside in exchange for a guarantee of his own safety. It is reported that forty thousand Sidonians were killed in the ensuing bloodbath, some choosing to burn to death as they set fire to their own homes rather than submit to the Persians.[9] Diodorus gives this graphic description: "When they saw the city and the walls captured and swarming with many myriads of soldiers, they shut themselves, their children, and their women up in their houses and consumed them all in flames."[10]

Although these events occurred thirteen years before Alexander's arrival, the memory was still painful for many Sidonians, and as a consequence they welcomed the chance to sever ties with Persia. The Sidonian king, Straton II, a friend of Darius's, was overthrown by his subjects, and the city surrendered to Alexander.[11] Arrian writes that "the Sidonians who loathed Persia and Darius called [Alexander] in themselves."[12] For the first time in Phoenicia, Alexander faced the need to install a new king in a surrendered city.

Curtius tells a fascinating story about how the new king of Sidon was selected.[13] Alexander tasked one of his generals, Hephaestion, with choosing a king from among the Sidonians. Hephaestion initially offered the position to two of the leading citizens who told him they must decline since the kingship could only go to someone of royal blood. When pressed by Hephaestion to provide him with the name of someone suitable, the two men told him the best candidate was a man named Abdalonymus, who was distantly related to the royal family. Although Abdalonymus was a poor man who made his living by tending a garden, his poverty was put down to his honesty, and because his work in the garden took up all of his time, he was unaware of the arrival of Alexander and the Macedonian army.

When Hephaestion's two advisers went to tell Abdalonymus the news, they found him pulling weeds in his garden. The two men told him to wash up and put on the royal clothing they had brought for him. Abdalonymus at first thought the men were playing a joke on him and wondered whether they were in fact sane. The men then gave him some advice: when he became king, they said, and had the power of life and death over all the people of Sidon, he should remember that he had once been a poor gardener and that his poverty was one of the reasons he had been chosen as king. Eventually he washed off the garden dirt, put on the purple robes of the king, and entered the palace.

The news that Abdalonymus had been chosen as king spread quickly throughout the city, pleasing some citizens while angering others. The wealthiest men tried unsuccessfully to lobby Hephaestion to change his mind and choose someone else. When Alexander met with the new king, he praised Abdalonymus for the cheerful and honorable way the man had dealt with his life of poverty. The former gardener replied that his hope was to rule as king with the same honor and humility as he had shown as a gardener. He told Alexander that, poor as he had been, he had lacked for nothing in his life. The words so impressed Alexander that he ordered all of the property of the deposed king to be handed over to Abdalonymus, as well as some of the Persian treasure looted after Issus. He also enlarged Abdalonymus's domain by giving Sidon control over some nearby territory.

This same story—the gardener chosen to be a king—is also told by Justin, so it must come from a common source. Interestingly, Diodorus also tells this story in his history but places the timing seven months later, *after* the fall of Tyre, and he moves the location; in Diodorus's telling, the gardener is chosen to be the king of Tyre, not Sidon. Although Diodorus was confused as to the when and where of the story, it was apparently too good a tale for him not to include it somewhere in his narrative.[14]

In January 332, Alexander left Sidon, still heading south.[15] On the road he was met by a large group of envoys from Tyre who had been sent to tell Alexander that the city was willing to do whatever he ordered. The delegation impressed Alexander since it consisted not only of Tyrian noblemen but also the son of the king of Tyre. The king, Azimilkos, was away from the city commanding the contingent of Tyrian ships serving the Persians in the Aegean.[16] Of the Phoenician cities providing ships for the Persian fleet, Tyre was the only one that Alexander had still not occupied. Thus, everything seemed to be falling nicely into place for his strategy of defeating the Persian fleet from land.

But then things began to go wrong.

Alexander told the Tyrian envoys that he wanted to make a sacrifice to Herakles—whom the Greeks associated with the Tyrian god Melqart—at Melqart's great temple in Tyre. Xella explains that "Melqart was identified with Herakles, the Greek deified hero and founder of colonies. Indeed, both the Phoenician god and the Greek hero have a mythological background . . . that certainly favored the convergence of the two deities and their perception in the popular imagination."[17] Alexander's arrival seems to have corresponded to an important annual Tyrian festival dedicated to Melqart-Herakles. Burr C. Brundage writes, "Josephus, quoting a Greek source, tells us that it was Hiram of Tyre who instituted the rite of the 'Awakening of Herakles,' celebrated probably in January, thus connecting him with the sleeping winter-god who returns with the northering sun."[18] Legend had it that the temple of Melqart at Tyre was the oldest temple of Herakles in the world.[19]

There are at least two possible explanations for why Alexander insisted on making this sacrifice. The first is that Alexander honestly believed he was descended from Herakles-Melqart. According to Curtius, an oracle had told Alexander to make this sacrifice at Tyre because the Macedonians kings were descended from the god.[20] N. G. L. Hammond writes that there is no doubt that Alexander, "as a deeply religious king, believed in the divine nature of dreams and omens, and in the interpretation of diviners."[21] So Alexander may have had a strong religious reason for wanting to make the sacrifice at the world's oldest known temple to his ancestor. However, Arrian spends considerable time going over the ancestry of the Tyrian Herakles, demonstrating that this is a different god from the one worshipped by the Greeks, and thus is not Alexander's ancestor. He also mentions an Egyptian Herakles who is distinct from both the Tyrian and Greek gods.[22]

The second reason Alexander may have asked to make the sacrifice is that he did not entirely trust the surrender offer made by the Tyrians. The timing of the sacrifice created a problem for Tyre. Bosworth writes, "It so happened that [Alexander's] presence coincided with the main festival of Melqart, in February 332, and a sacrifice at that time would have been a striking display of his sovereignty. So the Tyrians seem to have interpreted his request."[23] Romm writes that Melqart "was the focus of a yearly state-sponsored ritual occurring at about the time of Alexander's arrival." His request to make the sacrifice was thus "a challenge to national sovereignty. The Tyrians would have lost autonomy symbolically if they allowed Alexander to dominate this important ritual."[24]

The importance of this ritual for the kingship of Tyre is explained by Xella: "It was an important public event celebrated by the king himself, where the god's tragic vicissitudes, followed by his reawakening, was the focus of the ritual. . . . This complex tradition concerning Melqart is of fundamental importance for understanding Tyrian and, generally speaking, Phoenician royal ideology. It deals with the hypostasis—both at mythical and ritual level—of the royal figure, projected into the divine sphere."[25] By making the sacrifice, Alexander would be asserting his kingship over Tyre. It is unlikely he was unaware of this fact.

The envoys who returned from Tyre with the city's answer tried to walk the fine line between giving up what they perceived to be royal sovereignty and incurring Alexander's wrath. Perhaps they hoped they could simply remain neutral in the struggle between Macedonia and Persia. The Tyrians said they were willing to obey all of Alexander's other commands, but they refused to allow any outsiders, either Macedonians or Persians, into the city, at least during the festival of Melqart. This decision seemed to them the safest course, since the outcome of the war was still in doubt.[26] If they gave in to Alexander now, they worried about how that decision would look to Darius should the Persian king ultimately prevail. The envoys helpfully explained that on the mainland, across the channel from the island city of Tyre, was another city called Old Tyre, which had a temple to Melqart that was also quite old.[27] The Macedonians were more than welcome to sacrifice at the temple in Old Tyre. Needless to say, this response did not satisfy Alexander.

Lane Fox writes that this response "exposed the Tyrians' offer and revealed that at heart, they wanted to remain neutral." Diodorus expresses the view that by opposing the Macedonians, the Tyrians were trying to curry favor with Darius. By forcing Alexander to undertake a long and—in the view of the Tyrians—futile siege of the island city, the Tyrians would be gaining for Darius the time he needed to assemble a new army at Babylon. They hoped that by doing so they would ultimately be rewarded by the Persian king.[28]

Events began to quickly spin out of control. Curtius writes that Alexander sent his own heralds back to Tyre in a last effort to negotiate a peaceful surrender. The Tyrians killed the heralds and threw their bodies into the sea.[29] This was a shocking breach of Greek law that naturally infuriated Alexander and his men. Heralds were protected under Greek laws of war and religious custom.[30] In the *Iliad*, Homer has Achilles receive Greek messengers with the words: "Greetings, heralds, messengers of Zeus."[31] Adriaan Lanni explains that "violations of norms arising from religious customs (which included most of the Greek laws of war) created the possibility of divine sanctions. Both Sparta and Athens were said to have suffered divine punishment for killing Persian envoys at the start of the first Persian war. . . . The Megarians were purportedly struck with an unusual form of divine punishment for killing an Athenian herald: it was said that the gods condemned the city to permanent poverty."[32] After this brutal and provocative action by the Tyrians, peace with Alexander was out of the question.[33]

The reason the Tyrians killed the heralds is unclear, but the effect on the Macedonians was to make a siege a certainty. Perhaps that was the Tyrian plan all along, if they truly wanted to help Darius by delaying Alexander. There may have been a large peace faction within the city urging surrender, and the killing of the heralds ensured that their arguments never had a chance to be heard. Atkinson points out that Curtius is the only ancient historian to relate the story of the killing of the heralds. However, Arrian writes that during the siege, the Tyrians captured some Macedonians sailing from Sidon and, making them "mount the wall, so that they might be seen from the camp, cut them down and cast them into the sea."[34] It is possible that Arrian is referring here to the killing of the heralds, although he does not refer to the captured Macedonians using that specific term.[35]

Alexander now faced a choice. One alternative was to leave Tyre unsubdued and continue moving south along the coast of Canaan, toward Egypt, his eventual short-term goal. Bosworth argues that strategically, a siege of the island city "was unnecessary. Tyre . . . could have been left supervised by a garrison on the mainland and held in check by her neighbors' enmity. Eventually she would have to make her peace with the invader." Heckel, in his commentary on Justin, disagrees, writing that "Tyre was the major port for Darius' Phoenician fleet and the capture of the city was necessary to continue the disintegration of that fleet.... The importance of Tyre should not be underestimated: one may look ahead to Saladin's failure to capture Tyre, after his victory at the Horns of Hattin and the fall of Jerusalem ([AD] 1187), which allowed the kingdom of Acre to exist for another century."[36]

Fuller also argues that Alexander "could not leave an unsubdued Tyre on his line of communications" and that "he may also have learnt that [the Tyrians] had received a promise from the Carthaginians to come to their aid with a powerful fleet." Similarly, Lane Fox writes that Alexander "could not leave [Tyre] unsubdued on his main route of communication, especially as many of Tyre's warships had remained in the city." In addition, representatives from Tyre's former colony of Carthage were in the city to take part in the Melqart festival. Alexander "would be aware of Carthage's link with Tyre and the possibility of naval help once his back was turned. It might be important to scare off this new threat from the west."[37]

Carthage, a city-state on the North African coast (in present-day Tunisia), will play a role in the siege of Tyre. The traditional date for the founding of Carthage is 814,[38] and the remarkable and entertaining story of how it was founded is told in detail by Justin.[39] The story is important because it illustrates the way the Greeks viewed the Tyrians: as deceitful people who could not be trusted. As do all good stories, this one begins with a princess, the daughter of the king of Tyre and the great-niece of Jezebel. (The same Jezebel who married Israel's King Ahab, recounted in the Bible's book of I Kings.) The princess was named Elissa, although later in the tale she is called Dido, and is known in history by both names. According to Justin she was "a maiden of extraordinary beauty." When the king of Tyre died, the throne went to Elissa's brother, Pygmalion. Elissa married her uncle, a fabulously wealthy man, who, worried that the new king would seize his wealth, buried caches of gold secretly about the city.

Hoping to get his hands on this rumored wealth, Pygmalion had Elissa's husband murdered. Elissa was afraid that her brother would murder her as well, so she devised a plan to escape from the city with the gold. She told Pygmalion that she wanted to leave her dead husband's home and move back to the palace, and the king, seeing this as a way to get access to Elissa's hidden wealth, sent his servants to help her with the move. Before the servants arrived, Elissa secretly had sacks filled with sand, and Pygmalion's servants loaded these sacks, which the servants assumed contained gold, onto a ship along with the actual gold. However, rather than rowing the gold-laden ship to the palace dock, Elissa had her rowers take the ship out to sea, where she had the sand-filled sacks thrown overboard as an ostensible offering of gold to the shade of her dead husband. She then told the king's servants, who were still on board, that her brother would be furious with them for losing the treasure and would have them executed; their only hope of survival was to accompany her into exile. The servants readily agreed, and so, together with the ships of some Tyrian noblemen who loathed Pygmalion and were anxious to escape the city, Elissa set sail for freedom.

Elissa's ship landed on Cyprus, where the priest of Jupiter, together with his wife and children, joined the expedition. Then Elissa had a stroke of luck: "It was a custom among the Cyprians to send their daughters, on stated days before their marriage, to the sea-shore, to prostitute themselves and thus procure money for their marriage portions, and to pay, at the same time, offerings to Venus for the preservation of their chastity in time to come." Elissa ordered her men to kidnap eighty of these young women and take them on board her ships. In this way she procured wives for the men who were accompanying her and ensured her newly founded city would have a stable population in the future. Meanwhile, Pygmalion was dissuaded from pursuing her by omens that were interpreted as warnings that the gods would punish him if he interfered with the founding of a future city. Elissa and her little squadron of ships left Cyprus and sailed for Africa, taking along Pygmalion's servants, the Tyrian noblemen, the priest of Jupiter and his family, and the eighty virgins.

Ultimately landing on the shore of North Africa, Elissa bargained with the local people for a plot of land on which she and her followers could settle. They agreed on a price for an amount of land that could be covered by an ox hide. Elissa then had a hide cut into one very long thin continuous strip of leather, and this ruse allowed her to encircle with the leather strip—and thus acquire—much more land than she had actually bargained for. Justin writes that "the place had afterwards the name of Byrsa." The Greek word *byrsa* (βύρσα) means "hide," suggesting the story may be of Greek rather than Phoenician origin. The thin strip of hide was long enough to encircle an entire hill, and that is where Elissa and her followers settled.

The little group of exiles prospered, and the local people asked Elissa to build a city. She agreed, and this building activity attracted more and more people from the surrounding country to move there, swelling the population until the site was transformed into the city of Carthage. Elissa's fame spread, and one day the leader of a powerful North African tribe came to speak with the city elders and demand Elissa for his wife. The elders, knowing Elissa would refuse, devised a clever trick to get her to accept. Realizing she had been tricked and unable to back out of the marriage agreement, Elissa took three months to prepare for the wedding ceremony. During that time, she had a large funeral pyre built, telling people she wanted to make sacrifices to appease the shade of her dead husband before she remarried. When it came time for the wedding, she climbed to the top of the pyre and made a speech, telling her people she would now go to her husband, just as they had asked her to. She then pulled out a sword and killed herself. Throughout Carthage's long history, she was worshipped as a goddess.[40]

To our modern eyes, Elissa may seem a hero, fighting in the only way she could against a corrupt male-dominated world out to subjugate her, bravely making her own way and founding a powerful city in a new land, refusing in the end to give in to male control, even if it meant death. As viewed by the Greeks who told this story, however, the deceitfulness of the Tyrians is evident, and Elissa's tricks are proof that Tyrians can't be trusted.

This view that the Greeks held of Phoenicians—that they were a deceitful, greedy people who could not be trusted—stretched back at least to Homer. In the *Odyssey* we are told that "an avaricious man came from Phoenicia. He was good at lying, skilled and well practiced at exploiting people." Susan Sheratt argues that in epics like the *Odyssey*, the Phoenicians are portrayed "as convenient maritime taxi drivers, willing to pick up passengers; but they are also not averse to the odd act of kidnapping, slave dealing, theft, and even murder."[41]

These traits are also reflected in the story of the founding of Carthage. Elissa tricks Pygmalion's servants by having them believe the bags of sand they have thrown into the sea are gold; she cruelly kidnaps eighty Cypriot virgins and provides them as wives for her crew; she tricks the North Africans into selling her more land than she paid for by cutting the ox hide into a thin strip. In the end, she is tricked herself by the elders of Carthage, and so for her final trick, she commits suicide rather than honor her agreement with them. Pamina Fernández Camacho writes that in the Elissa story, "Carthage is built as a result of an economic transaction marked by deceit, with the natives of the land, who had welcomed the refugees from overseas, as the duped party."[42]

The Greeks regarded deceit by non-Greeks as fundamentally different from the trickery practiced by Greek heroes such as Odysseus. Irene Winter writes, "While Odysseus has long been identified as a sort of trickster throughout the *Iliad* and the *Odyssey*, his artifice and his various stratagems do not cross the line into dishonorable deceit, as do the acts of Phoenicians." However, Mark Peacock argues that the distinction isn't all that clear, writing, "Homer's terminology suggests only a limited distinction between a disreputable Phoenician guile and a less reprehensible guile of Greeks or gods."[43]

By the year 332, when Alexander was besieging Tyre, Carthage had grown into a rich and powerful city-state that dominated the western Mediterranean with a fleet of warships. In 264, less than seventy years later, Carthage battled Rome in the First Punic War, a naval conflict that went on for twenty-three years. Carthage was therefore too strong a military power for Alexander to ignore the threat that the city posed as he contemplated marching deep into Asia in pursuit of Darius. Curtius writes that at the conclusion of the siege of Tyre, Alexander issued a declaration of war against Carthage, "although the war was delayed by the urgency of present affairs."[44] Alexander must have seen his fears of Tyrian duplicity realized when the Tyrians murdered his heralds and threw their bodies into the sea, presumably in view of the Macedonians and a clear violation of accepted Greek rules of warfare.

On the Tyrian side, Carthage represented both an inspiration and a potential source of support, which perhaps played a critical role in Tyre's decision to resist Alexander. Justin writes, "Tyrian resolve was strengthened by the example of Dido [Elissa] who had founded Carthage and gone on to conquer a third of the world. They thought it humiliating if their womenfolk had shown more courage in acquiring an empire than they themselves did in safeguarding their independence. They therefore evacuated all who were not of age for fighting to Carthage, whence they called for assistance."[45]

The depth of the paternal feeling that the Tyrians had for Carthage is illustrated by an anecdote recounted by Herodotus about a plan by the Persian King Cambyses to attack Carthage. According to Herodotus, Cambyses "bade his fleet sail against [Carthage]. But the Phoenicians would not consent; for they were bound, they said, by a strict treaty, and could not righteously attack their own sons; and the Phoenicians being unwilling, the rest were of no account as fighters. Thus the [Carthaginians] escaped being enslaved by the Persians; for Cambyses would not use force with the Phoenicians."[46]

Although Alexander was now committed to besieging Tyre, he needed to persuade his men to go along, and they had good reason to question the decision. Tyre was located on a well-fortified island half a mile out to sea. Alexander's ships were still in the Aegean, while Tyre possessed a number of warships and two excellent harbors and could easily be supplied by sea. The Tyrians were sending women, children, and old men by ship to Carthage for safety,[47] a sign they intended to hold out for a long time. Everyone knew about the thirteen-year unsuccessful siege by the Babylonians.

On the other hand, Tyre had been captured forty years earlier by a king of Cyprus named Evagorus. His story is recounted by the Greek rhetorician Isocrates:

For when his enemies permitted him to be at peace, all he possessed was his own city; but when he was forced to go to war, he proved so valiant ... that he almost subdued the whole of Cyprus, ravaged Phoenicia, took Tyre by storm, caused Cilicia to revolt from the king [of Persia], and slew so many of his enemies that many of the Persians, when they mourn over their sorrows, recall the valor of Evagorus.[48]

Other than the phrase "took Tyre by storm," nothing is known about the endeavor, but it would likely have been an event familiar to Alexander and his generals. However, Evagorus, as a king of Cyprus, would have had warships at his disposal; Alexander had none. Curtius writes that one reason Alexander sent his heralds to Tyre for one last chance at peace was "because the fleet which he had was afar off."[49]

To convince his generals of the necessity of besieging Tyre, Alexander made a speech. In it he lays out the reasons why the Macedonians cannot bypass Tyre and move on. Edmund F. Bloedow and Edmund J. Bloedow write that Alexander gives at least eleven major arguments in this speech, but "reduced to their essence, these arguments can be summarized as follows: without Tyre it will be impossible to take Cyprus and Egypt, and, in particular, without Egypt it will be impossible to pursue Darius into Mesopotamia."[50]

The reason, once again, has to do with sea power and the Persian fleet. Arrian has Alexander make the following argument to his men: Once they capture Tyre they will control all of Phoenicia, and the Phoenician ships, which were the most powerful part of the Persian fleet, would likely change sides and ally themselves with the Macedonians. With the Phoenician cities in the control of Alexander, the Phoenician sailors and marines will no longer be willing to fight for Darius. Once the Phoenician fleet is available to the Macedonians, they can use it to easily conquer Cyprus. The combined

fleets of Macedonia, Phoenicia, and Cyprus will be so powerful they will
control the Mediterranean, and the invasion of Egypt will therefore be
easy.[51]

Bloedow and Bloedow argue that "Persia was in fact no longer supreme
at sea, nor would have been, had Alexander not taken Tyre. Indeed, her fleet
was in the process of disintegrating, concerning which Alexander could have
(or should have) had some knowledge." However, it isn't at all clear that
Alexander would have known this prior to commencing the siege at Tyre.
Curtius does write that Alexander's admirals had achieved some success in
the Aegean and that "with a fleet of 160 ships had brought the islands between Achaiae and Asia under the sway of Alexander," but P. A. Brunt, in
appendix 2 to his translation of Arrian, writes that this success was "contemporary with the siege of Tyre" and argues that Alexander only heard this
news "in connection with the report he made in Egypt."[52]

Tarn argues that the speech "is short, sensible, and to the point. All the
facts about sea-power are correct, and the prophecy that the rowers in the
Persian fleet would not go on fighting for Persia once their cities were in
Macedonian hands did come true." Tarn says the speech may be genuine,
"but more probably, I think, it reflects a manifesto issued by Alexander to
the army on the eve of the great siege."[53]

Bosworth, however, says the speech seems to focus too much on the ex-
peditions to Egypt and Babylon, and "the question of Tyre is strangely sub-
sidiary." He goes on to argue that the speech fits better coming immediately
after Issus, when the decision was made to move south to Phoenicia rather
than pursue Darius. "I suspect that Arrian found in his sources a speech
in favor of conquering the Levant and turned it into a set piece before Tyre.
. . . The city [of Tyre] could have been left in check, an isolated unit on a
coast under Macedonian control. The consideration is crucial to the earlier
problem whether or not to leave the Levantine coast unpacified."[54]

Curtius does not quote Alexander's speech at Tyre verbatim but makes
several brief comments about a speech made by Alexander. He writes that
Alexander reminded his men that the Tyrians had violated the law and offended the gods by killing the heralds. He also told them that Tyre was the
only city so far that had threatened to delay their campaign by a significant
amount of time. Rather than the reasoned arguments about sea power and
Egypt, these are designed to kindle the anger of the Macedonians against
Tyre. Curtius says Alexander told his generals to stir up the courage of their
men. Perhaps strategic arguments would convince Alexander's generals, but
the common soldiers needed more motivation, given the task they were fac-

ing. Whatever Alexander said, it apparently worked. Arrian writes that Alexander's speech convinced the Macedonian generals to support a siege.[55]

Curtius also writes something odd about Alexander's speech: "Alexander, who was by no means inexperienced in working upon the minds of soldiers, announced that an apparition of Herakles had appeared to him in his sleep, offering him his right hand; with that god leading him and opening the way he dreamed that he entered the city."[56] This statement—that Alexander was "by no means inexperienced in working upon the minds of soldiers"—is quite cynical, suggesting that Alexander would play on his soldiers' superstitions and belief in omens to manipulate them and get the result he wanted. The whole story is reminiscent of the eagle omen that occurred at Miletus.

The dream of Herakles is also mentioned by Arrian, although not as part of Alexander's speech. Arrian writes that after the speech, Alexander dreamed that night he was approaching the wall of Tyre and Herakles was waiting for him, stretching out his hand and guiding him into the city. When Alexander told this dream to his seer Aristander, the seer interpreted it to mean that the city of Tyre would be captured, but the effort required would be extreme, since Herakles himself was involved.[57]

Aristander was correct: the siege of Tyre would indeed require Herculean effort. It lasted seven months and required all of the courage of the Macedonian soldiers as well as all of Alexander's military skill. The first thing he had to figure out was how to physically get at the Tyrians. The city was on an island, half a mile out to sea, surrounded by a high wall, and although the bulk of its navy was in the Aegean, it still possessed powerful warships in its harbors. Arrian writes that the Tyrians had the advantage over the Macedonians because they controlled the sea. Tyre had ships available to defend the island, while Alexander at this point had none.[58] Supplied by sea, Tyre could hold out indefinitely. No wonder the Tyrians felt secure enough to kill his heralds.

In the end there was only one solution to the problem of how to physically get at the Tyrians. Alexander would build a mole.

PART III

The Siege: Land Assault

The siege of Tyre lasted seven long months of unprecedented ferocity. It was a grandiose occasion for the Greek sources to highlight all that differentiated the local people, who had thrown themselves into a senseless resistance doomed to failure, from the Greeks, noble and clever, led by Alexander and assisted by the gods themselves (Herakles, Apollo), as if in Tyre the epic battle of Troy were playing out again.

—Corinne Bonnet, "The Hellenistic Period and Hellenization in Phoenicia" in *The Oxford Handbook of the Phoenician and Punic Mediterranean*

TEN

THE MOLE

Because he had no ships, Alexander planned to assault Tyre by first filling in the channel separating the island from the mainland. His men would demolish the walls and buildings of Old Tyre to provide a nearby source of quarried stone. Using these stone blocks, along with sand and dirt, he planned to create a dry, road-like surface for his men that would be solid enough to support catapults and siege towers. The term for a solid structure of this type that extends out into the sea is "mole."

The *Oxford English Dictionary* has twelve definitions for the word "mole," one of which is, "A massive structure, esp[ecially] of stone, serving as a pier, breakwater, or causeway." The Greek word for this structure is *chōma* (χῶμα). In the Liddell and Scott *Greek-English Lexicon*, *chōma* has several definitions, one of which is "mole or pier carried out into the sea, jetty." The equivalent Latin word is *moles*, which again has several definitions, one of which is "a dam, pier, mole."[1] In the online *Oxford Classical Dictionary*, the term "mole" is associated with structures that protect harbors from the sea.

One of the most famous moles was the one protecting the harbor at Dunkirk, which was used to evacuate British and French troops during the Second World War.

Both Arrian (2.18.3) and Diodorus (17.40.5), writing in Greek, use the term *chōma*, and it is translated in the Loeb Classical Library editions as "mole." Curtius (4.2.16), writing in Latin, uses the term *moles*, and it is translated in the Loeb Classical Library edition as "causeway." The *Oxford English Dictionary* defines causeway as "a raised road across a low or wet place, or piece of water; formerly also applied to a mole or landing-pier running into the sea or a river." The two terms in English, "causeway" and "mole," are similar, and both could be (and have been) applied to the structure envisioned by Alexander to link Tyre with the mainland.

Alexander was not the first general in ancient times to utilize a mole to besiege an island city. In 398, Dionysius I of Sicily had to rebuild a causeway to capture the fortified island city of Motya.[2] In anticipation of a siege, the people of Motya destroyed part of the causeway that connected their island to the coast of Sicily.[3] According to Diodorus, the distance from the island to the shore was "six stades," or about three-quarters of a mile. When Dionysius saw that the causeway had been destroyed, he directed his engineers to build a mole that reached across the water to reconnect Motya with the mainland.[4]

The assault on Motya by Dionysius has more in common with Alexander's siege of Tyre than just the mole. It was an example of Greeks attacking a Phoenician city, albeit in the western rather than eastern Mediterranean. Dionysius was the ruler of Syracuse, the leading Greek city on Sicily, whereas Motya was the main Carthaginian base on Sicily. By Alexander's day, Greeks had been fighting Carthaginians for control of Sicily for over a century.[5]

How big was Alexander's mole? Diodorus writes that Tyre "lay four furlongs away from the coast," and that Alexander's men began "to construct a mole two plethra in width." According to David Whitehead, one *plethron* is equal to one hundred feet, so a mole two *plethra* in width would be two hundred feet wide. Ian Worthington writes that Alexander "began construction of a causeway 25 feet or so in width," but this seems much too narrow, given the towers that will later be constructed on the mole, and Worthington provides no reference for this number.[6]

The length of "four furlongs away from the coast" is more troublesome, since a furlong is not an ancient Greek (or Roman) unit of measure but is an English word used by the translator of the Loeb Classical Library edition. The Greek word used by Diodorus that is translated as furlong is *stadion*.

Curtius writes that "a strait of four stadia separates the city from the main-land," and Bosworth also writes that the strait was four stades wide. Lane Fox writes that Tyre was "cut off from the coast by half a mile of sea." According to the *Oxford English Dictionary*, a stade (or stadium) is "an ancient Greek and Roman measure of length, varying according to time and place, but most commonly equal to 600 Greek or Roman feet, or one-eighth of a Roman mile. (In the English Bible rendered by furlong.)" So a distance of four stades would be one-half of a Roman mile. Whitehead writes that one stade is equal to six *plethra*, or six hundred feet, so four stades would equal 2,400 feet—just under half a mile.[7]

The mole planned by Alexander was therefore to be about half a mile long by two hundred feet wide. But how deep was the water? Lane Fox writes that the sea was "shallow at first but soon dropping to a depth of some 600 feet," although the exact area to which he is referring is not clear, and he doesn't give a reference for the source of the number. Paul Cartledge writes, "The sea around the island was some 100 fathoms (almost 600 feet, 200 meters) deep," but he also gives no reference for this number and may simply be echoing the figure from Lane Fox.[8] Tyre (and the whole coast of Lebanon) lies at the eastern edge of what is called the Levantine Basin, an area in the eastern Mediterranean where "the water depth averages 1600m or roughly 5250ft,"[9] so a depth of 600 feet half a mile from shore isn't un-reasonable. For another point of reference, in 2019, Lebanese underwater archaeologists reported the discovery south of Tyre of the remains of eleven ancient cargo ships at a depth of 35 meters (115 feet).[10] The ships were es-timated to be from the time of Alexander's siege and were thought to have been sunk by a sudden storm. The ships' cargo was mostly stone, which the archaeologists speculate was being carried to Tyre for use in constructing the mole. In addition to the stone, the ships were also carrying supplies.

But the water in the channel between the island and the shore was not nearly so deep. Arrian writes of the spot chosen for the mole, "The place is one where people cross over shoal-water; it has shallows and patches of mud towards the mainland; next to the city itself where the crossing is deep-est, the water is about three fathoms deep."[11] The Greek word translated as fathom is *orguiōn* (ὀργυιῶν), a unit of measure equal to six feet.[12] So the water depth starts out quite shallow near the coastline and increases to eighteen feet at the island.[13]

Using these dimensions for the mole—zero to 18 feet deep; 200 feet wide; 2,400 feet long—would mean Alexander was proposing to construct a mole containing 4,320,000 cubic feet of stone, dirt, and sand.[14] To put this in perspective, assuming a First World War trench was six feet deep and six feet wide, the mole's volume would represent a trench approximately 23 miles long. Given that First World War trench lines were mostly dug by hand and stretched for hundreds of miles, this volume of material doesn't seem extraordinary, despite the fact the Greeks had not yet invented a wheelbarrow.[15] Every foot that the mole extended above the waterline would require another 480,000 cubic feet of material.

But was the water really that deep? In a recent study, geologists argue that at the time of the siege, there may have been an underwater sand bar one to two meters below the surface, stretching between Tyre and the shore. This sand bar is called a "proto-tombolo," where a tombolo is "a bar or spit of sand or shingle joining an island to the mainland." [16] According to the study, "the leeward wave shadow generated by this island, allied with high sediment supply after 3000 [years before present], culminated in a natural wave-dominated proto-tombolo within 1–2 [meters] of mean sea level by the time of Alexander the Great." The authors attribute this to two causes: "(i) natural accretion of Tyre's early Holocene marine bottom, leeward of the island breakwater," and "(ii) formation of a wave-dominated proto-tombolo after 6000 [years before present]." They go on to write that "this shallow sublittoral spit greatly facilitated the construction of Alexander the Great's sea bridge in 332 B.C."[17]

Interestingly, these authors speculate that the formation of the proto-tombolo may have been aided by the earlier unsuccessful Babylonian siege. "Rapid spit growth may also have been amplified by earlier attempts to build a causeway on this underwater proto-tombolo, notably during the Babylonian siege of the city by Nabuchodonozor II (6th century). Like Alexander, it is probable that Nabuchodonozor II exploited the shallow proto-tombolo in an attempt to overcome the defensive bastion, although it is equivocal whether or not he completed his ambitious sea-bridge project."[18]

To the extent the depth of water around Tyre where the mole was being constructed was three to six feet (one to two meters) rather than eighteen feet, it would mean a tremendous reduction in the amount of stone, sand, and dirt Alexander's men would have had to dump into the water. One possible way to reconcile the shallow three-to-six-foot depth of a proto-tombolo with Arrian's assertion that the seabed was eighteen feet deep near the island is provided by Romm, who writes that "Arrian speaks in the present tense" when he states that "the water is about three fathoms deep." Arrian was writing in the second century AD, and Romm points out that "by

[Arrian's] time the strait described here had become silted up so that Tyre was attached to the mainland, as it is today. Alexander's mole became buried under layers of silt to form the isthmus between Tyre and the mainland."[19] Any proto-tombolo utilized by Alexander would have been completely covered with silt and sand by Arrian's day, creating an actual sand spit. When Arrian measured the depth of water near the island, but away from this sand spit, it could well have been eighteen feet.

Regardless of the mole's volume, Alexander had plenty of men available to do the work. There is uncertainty about whether the mole was constructed by Macedonian soldiers, by local civilians forced into work gangs, or both. Some historical accounts suggest the workers were soldiers. For example, as the mole neared Tyre's walls and came within catapult range, Arrian writes that the workers were attacked with catapult bolts fired from the parapet. He goes on to state that these missiles were highly effective since the men working on the mole were dressed for laboring and not dressed properly for fighting (that is, not wearing armor or carrying shields).[20] This statement suggests that the work was being done by soldiers who had armor available but were not wearing it while they worked. In another example, Arrian writes that the men worked with enthusiasm because Alexander spent a lot of time among them—directing, encouraging, and handing out rewards to those who did their jobs particularly well.[21] This also makes it sound like his soldiers were doing the work.

Alexander may even have participated in the work himself. The second century AD Greek writer Polyaenus records this anecdote: "At the siege of Tyre, Alexander having resolved to join the city, which was then an island, to the mainland, by raising a mound in the surrounding waters, himself first carried a basket of sand, which he threw into it. As soon as the Macedonians saw their king at work with his own hands, they all instantly threw aside their robes, and soon raised the ground."[22]

However, Curtius gives a different and far more pessimistic picture of the eagerness of the Macedonians to begin work on the mole, writing that the soldiers became discouraged when they saw how deep the water in the channel was. There seemed to the men no way to complete the job, even with the help of the gods, since there didn't appear to be rocks large enough or trees tall enough for such a task. And even if they scraped bare whole sections of the surrounding countryside for enough material to fill in the channel, the sea around Tyre was subject to frequent storms that would destroy their work, and these storms would become more violent the closer to the island they came.[23]

There is also a suggestion that local civilians were forced into working on the mole. In a third account of the mole's construction, Diodorus writes that Alexander conscripted tens of thousands of people from the surrounding area, using them to tear down the walls and buildings of Old Tyre and carry the stones to the channel. Because there were so many workers, progress on the mole went quickly, despite the fact that it was two hundred feet wide. Fuller suggests that both soldiers and conscripted civilians took part: "Besides the soldiers, thousands of the local inhabitants were pressed into labor gangs, stone was obtained by demolishing Old Tyre, and wood gathered in abundance from the forests of the Lebanon."[24]

Curtius, again taking a pessimistic view, writes that constructing the mole was difficult, even in good weather when the sea was calm. When southern storms blew in from Africa, however, the wind churned up waves that crashed against the mole, washing over the top and eroding the foundation. No matter how strongly the mole was built, the waves would wash away the dirt and sand from the gaps between the stones, eventually undermining the structure and turning it into a pile of rubble.[25]

How, exactly, was this mole constructed? The ancient historians mention three types of materials being used: stone, wood, and mud. Curtius writes that a large amount of stone was taken from Old Tyre and that timber was brought down from the mountains and used to make "rafts and towers." Presumably the rafts provided floating platforms from which the men could work, and the towers may have been used as derricks for lifting heavy stone or timber, or as pile drivers to set posts into the channel bed. Arrian writes that the Macedonians had access to as much stone and wood as they needed and that the wood was "heaped on to the stones." He says the men set wooden posts into the mud of the channel and that the mud made a "stable binding" for the stones.[26] Taken literally, Arrian's description makes no sense. It sounds like stone was first dumped into the water, and then wood was piled on top of the stones. This could not have been done underwater, as the wood would float. But if the level of the stone was above the surface of the water, why pile wood on top? And how could mud have been a stable binding for the stones if the stones were under the water? Fixing the wooden posts in the mud would potentially be useful. With the sea so shallow, posts could be pounded into the seabed to help stabilize the stone being dumped into the water and hold the stone in place against shifting currents and storms.

Stephen English speculates the work would have progressed in the following four-stage process: First, stone blocks from Old Tyre would be dropped into the water to form a solid foundation. Next, large wooden stakes would be driven into the seabed "on either side of what Alexander wanted to be the causeway." These helped hold the stone blocks in position. As the level of stone rose, sand would then be poured on top to sift down between the stone to provide stability. This is perhaps what Arrian is referring to when he talks about mud making a stable binding for the stones. Finally, when the stone base was higher than the level of the water, a layer of dirt would be added to the top and then compacted, forming a surface on which soldiers and siege equipment could easily move.[27]

Assuming that the mole eventually reached the base of Tyre's walls, what sort of walls would Alexander's men be facing? Arrian writes that "the walls facing the mole were about 150 feet high and of corresponding breadth, constructed of big blocks of stone fitted in mortar."[28] The notion that the walls at Tyre were 150 feet high seems implausible. The fourth century AD Aurelian walls of Rome were 52 feet high, and the inner Theodosian walls of Constantinople were 40 feet high. Why would a city like Tyre, situated on an island, need walls three times as high as these cities that were open to land attack? There is no uncertainty about the Greek measure being used, since Arrian uses the Greek word *podas* (πόδας), which literally means feet, and he clearly states there are "fifty and one hundred" (*pentēkonta kai hekaton*) of them. A Greek foot was 308 millimeters, or 12.1 inches, approximately the same as a modern foot.[29]

When writing about the 150-foot height of Tyre's walls, modern scholars seem to fall into three groups. First, there are those who say the number is clearly wrong. Bosworth writes, "This is surely a blatant exaggeration. . . . Had the walls been of the height Arrian states, it would have been quite superfluous to build wooden towers on the battlements to gain additional height." Whitehead and Blyth, commenting on the height of city walls encountered by Alexander, say "outlandish figures persisted in the historiography of the expedition." Whitehead writes about ancient city walls: "Archaeological remains, for obvious reasons, are often smaller than original heights. Literary sources, conversely, might exaggerate those heights; see for instance Arr[ian] Anab[asis] 2.21.4 (Tyre)." Duncan Campbell writes about Tyre, "Nothing now remains of the town fortifications, but Arrian's claim that the walls were 150ft (46m) high is absurd." Fik Meijer says Tyre's walls were about 25 meters high, or approximately 82 feet. Martin Hammond writes, "This figure (c.45 m) is surely an exaggeration."[30]

A second group of scholars questions whether the 150 foot figure is really correct without actually disputing it. English writes, "The walls being a reputed

45m [150 feet]. . . . The towers were no doubt huge, although 45m [150 feet] seems unbelievable." Lane Fox writes, "The wall itself rose as much as 150 feet, at least in the opinion of the besiegers."[31]

Finally, a third group of scholars accepts the 150-foot figure without comment. Kern writes that Tyre was "surrounded by high walls reaching 150 feet on the eastern landward side." Fuller writes, "The city was surrounded by a lofty wall, which rose to the height of 150 feet on its eastern side." Heckel writes of Tyre, "Its 2.75-mile circuit of walls extended to a height of 150 feet." Woolmer and Markoe say "the city was founded on an island, protected by huge walls that were an impressive 46 meters [150 feet] high in places." Tarn writes, "the top of the wall at Tyre was 150 feet above sea-level." Worthington writes that there was a "150-foot high defensive wall." Green says Tyre was "protected by great walls which on the landward side rose to a height of about 150 feet."[32]

If Tyre's walls were not actually 150 feet high, how high were they? In the third century, a Greek known as Philon of Byzantium (also known as Philo Mechanicus) wrote a treatise advising rulers on how to defend against and conduct sieges. In giving advice about the dimensions of city walls, he wrote that they should be no less than twenty cubits (30 feet) high so ladders could not reach the top. However, Whitehead gives what he calls "a credible instance" of a fortress "described as exceptionally well fortified, with a wall nowhere less than thirty cubits (45 feet) high."[33] These two numbers—30 feet and 45 feet—give what may be a plausible range for the height of Tyre's walls.

Alexander's men, and possibly conscripted locals, began dismantling the walls of Old Tyre to get stone blocks, hauled logs down from the mountains to get wooden posts, and dug up sand, dirt, and mud from the seashore to use as building materials. In the shallow water near shore, out of catapult range of Tyre's walls, the mole began to grow. Things seemed to be going well, at least for a while.

Then the Tyrians struck back.

Legato infesta Tyros Neotunia, mole
Pressa Gyganteâ nauali clade subacta

VII

Menstrua post septem redeuntis cornua lunæ
Pelleo iuueni meritas luit improba pœnas.

Alexander the Great's siege of Tyre has been a subject of fascination over the centuries. Top: Alexander attacking Tyre from the sea, from "The Deeds of Alexander the Great," Antonio Tempesta, 1608. (*Metropolitan Museum of Art*) Bottom: Alexander, wearing a crowned helmet, orders the building of the mole to besiege Tyre after the envoys he sent to make peace were killed and thrown into the sea, right. A fifteenth-century manuscript illumination from the *History of Alexander the Great*. (*Bibliothèque nationale de France*)

Relief carving showing a figure thought to be Alexander the Great fighting a Persian cavalryman at the Battle of Issus. The figure wears a distinctive lion-head helmet, evoking an image of Herakles. The carving, believed to be one of the earliest depictions of Alexander, is from the Alexander Sarcophagus, thought to have been made for King Abdalonymus of Sidon. Scholars believe the sarcophagus was originally colorfully painted. (*Istanbul Archaeological Museum*)

Relief carving of a Greek or Macedonian cavalryman on a fourth century funerary stele. The figure wears a Phrygian type helmet. (*Louvre Museum*)

Relief carving from the Alexander Sarcophagus showing one of Alexander's cavalrymen in battle. The figure carries a sword and wears a Boeotian-type helmet. Note the lack of stirrups. (*Istanbul Archaeological Museum*)

Gold stater coin from the time of Alexander the Great. On the obverse (left) is the head of the goddess Athena wearing a Corinthian-type helmet. On the reverse (right) is the winged goddess of victory with the word ΑΛΕΞΑΝΔΡΟΥ (Alexandrou), the possessive form of the name "Alexander." (*Metropolitan Museum of Art*)

Gold stater coin from the early fourth century found in the Mysia region of Asia Minor (north of Lydia). It shows a kneeling Persian archer wearing a Phrygian cap and trousers. (*Staatliche Museen zu Berlin*)

A bronze Boetian helmet of the type worn by Alexander's Macedonian and Thessalian cavalrymen. A similar helmet is depicted on the Alexander Sarcophagus. (*Ashmolean Museum*)

Illustration of Greek torsion catapults in a defensive tower. Note the vertical bundles of rope that provide the torsion force. Two of the catapults are stone throwers, as evidenced by the stacked stone shot. The other two are bolt shooters. (*F. Kirschen*, Die griechische Stadt, *1918/Wikimedia Commons*)

Seventh-century Assyrian wall-panel relief from the palace at Nineveh showing a Phoenician ship being rowed down the Euphrates River. Note the row of shields along the rail. (*British Museum*)

Photograph illustrating the way Tyre looks in modern times. Over centuries drifting sand has accumulated on Alexander's mole, turning Tyre into a peninsula on the coast of Lebanon. The southern portion of the island (bottom of photograph) is now mostly underwater. There is still a small harbor on the north side of the island. (*Wikimedia Commons*)

Fragment from a late fifth-century marble relief showing the rowers of a Greek trireme. (*Acropolis Museum*)

An illustration of the siege of Rhodes from *Cassell's Illustrated Universal History* published in 1882. The siege of Rhodes took place in 305-304 and was part of the series of wars that occurred among Alexander's generals following his death. The illustration shows a siege tower with a ram, and protective sheds for a second ram and a catapult. Note the padded leather bags lowered from the wall to absorb the blows of the rams. The siege was not successful.

"A Naval Action During the Siege of Tyre," an 1899 engraving by French artist André Castaigne. Note the mole in the background with two large towers at the end. The ships engaged in combat would have used oars rather than the sails depicted here. The image of a bull was often used for the Phoenician god El.

ELEVEN

TYRE STRIKES BACK

Tyre's initial response to the construction of the mole was to make fun of the Macedonians. Diodorus writes that while the work was just beginning, the Tyrians would sail small boats near the mole and mock Alexander, asking whether he thought he could overcome Poseidon. Curtius writes that the Tyrians in their small boats taunted the Macedonian soldiers at work on the mole, calling out that men famous for war were now being used as donkeys and mules. The Tyrians asked whether Alexander thought he was more powerful than Neptune.[1] Looking back on these accounts after twenty-three centuries, it is difficult to know if this taunting was simply the ancient equivalent of drunken frat boys hiking up their tunics to expose bare buttocks, or whether the reference to Poseidon-Neptune suggested Alexander was breaking a religious taboo by challenging a god—*Poseidōnos* in Greek and *Neptuno* in Latin—and that such massive hubris must lead to his destruction.

That the role of gods in the siege was important to the Tyrians is clear from some of the stories Diodorus preserved. In one story, a wave tosses a sea monster onto the mole without harming either the mole or the monster. The monster remained there for a long time, its body partly on the mole. Eventually it freed itself and swam away, but the occurrence had a profound effect on the Tyrians and the Macedonians. Each of the adversaries interpreted the omen as suggesting that Poseidon was surely on their side. In another story, a man in Tyre claimed to have had a vision in which Apollo said he was going to leave the city. News of the man's vision so enraged people that they wanted to stone him, and he only escaped by claiming sanctuary in a temple. However, the whole incident so worried the Tyrians that they used golden ropes to tie down their statue of Apollo and fasten it to its base, thus ensuring that the god could not leave the city. Plutarch writes that the response of the Tyrians in this incident was to treat Apollo like a deserter who gets caught trying to sneak over and join the enemy army. In Plutarch's account, the Tyrians used golden ropes and nails to fasten the statue firmly to its base, and began to refer to the statue as an Alexandrist. Curtius writes that the Tyrians used golden chains to fasten the Apollo statue to its base and attached the other end of the chains to the altar of Herakles. Their hope was that Herakles would use his powers to keep Apollo from leaving the city. According to Curtius, the Carthaginians had originally taken the statue of Apollo from Syracuse as spoils of war and had later donated it to Tyre. The Carthaginians, who viewed Tyre with reverence as their mother city, had over the years presented to Tyre's temples much of the booty they had captured in the course of their many wars.[2]

As the mole grew closer to the city, the taunting and mocking were replaced with arrows. The walls of Tyre were still too far away for bows or catapults to reach the mole, but the Tyrians had warships and Alexander did not. By putting archers aboard their ships, the Tyrians made it impossible for the Macedonians to continue working.[3] The Tyrians could row up close to the mole from any direction, fire off volleys of arrows, and then withdraw out of range before the Macedonians could reply. The work on the mole stopped as the men scrambled for protection from the attacks.[4] The range was so close, the mole was such an exposed location, and the workers were so numerous and unprotected that it was hard for the Tyrian archers to miss. Because the Tyrian ships could approach the mole from either side, it made it nearly impossible for the Macedonians to find shelter since the arrows came raining down from all directions.[5]

Although Macedonian archers could shoot back at the Tyrians, the archers on the ships were well protected while the Macedonians on the mole were exposed. Barry Strauss—applying ship data from later periods to the

480 Battle of Salamis—writes that "Phoenician triremes had wide decks, lined with a bulwark to protect the tightly packed men from falling overboard. Along the outside of the deck hung a row of shields."[6] The Macedonians did what they could to protect themselves. Screens made from hides and heavy cloth were set up along the sides of the mole to provide some shelter for the workers.[7] But at the end of the mole, where the wooden stakes were being driven into the seabed and the stone blocks were being dropped into the water, it would have been difficult to protect the workers from the barrage of arrows.

There is disagreement among the accounts of three historians—Arrian, Curtius, and Diodorus—about Alexander's next move: exactly what he did and why. As to what Alexander did next, Arrian and Curtius write that he ordered two towers to be constructed on the end of the mole. Towers would provide a platform for Macedonian catapults to fire on the Tyrian ships from above. Since the catapults outranged normal bows, the tower catapults would potentially stop the Tyrians from getting close enough for the arrows of their shipborne archers to reach the mole workers. We are told by Diodorus that the Tyrians equipped their ships with light and heavy catapults,[8] so the Tyrians may have had the ability to use ship-mounted catapults as well as archers in attacking the mole. It is thought that the Tyrian catapults were essentially large crossbows, while the Macedonian catapults used newer and more-powerful torsion technology that was based on the force generated by twisted bundles of rope. If correct, the Macedonian catapults would have outranged the Tyrian catapults.

In contrast to Arrian and Curtius, Diodorus doesn't mention towers at all but instead writes that Alexander used his own ships to counter the Tyrians. In Diodorus's account, Alexander takes command of his ships and has them row toward one of Tyre's harbors with the intention of cutting off the retreat of the ships attacking the mole. Realizing their danger, and the fact that their harbor was unguarded, the Tyrians turned and quickly rowed back to their city, reaching the safety of the harbor before Alexander could intercept them. Diodorus here is jumping ahead in the story and conflating the response to the attacks on the mole with a later event that occurred once Alexander was able to acquire sufficient ships to overwhelm the Tyrian navy. Tarn writes that the details in Diodorus's account, "like the items out of their order in the main account, shows that his whole account of the siege is merely a draft, which never had a final revision."[9] Like the story of the gardener being made king of Sidon, this is another example of Diodorus mixing up when and where certain events occurred. This unreliability will become particularly problematic later in trying to understand the sequence of events that occur at the end of the siege.

While towers with catapults make perfect sense as a defensive mechanism against the Tyrian ship attacks, what is not clear is whether the towers were installed solely as an antiship measure or were installed after the mole came within range of the catapults on Tyre's walls. Assuming a range of three hundred yards for the Tyrian catapults (less than a quarter mile), the mole would need to reach past the half-way point in the channel before it came within range of catapults mounted on Tyre's walls.[10] Curtius seems to suggest that the towers were used solely to keep the Tyrian ships at bay and not to attack the walls, writing that Alexander had two towers built on the mole and that the catapults in these towers were able to hit the Tyrian ships that rowed in to attack the workers. This view—that the towers were used only against the Tyrian ships—is echoed by English, who writes that the Macedonians constructed "two siege towers at the end [of the mole], to rain down missile fire of their own onto any naval vessels that strayed too close." Curtius says that in response to the towers, the Tyrians modified their ship-based attack by secretly rowing their ships down the coast to a spot away from where the mole was being built. Marines landed from these ships surprised the Macedonians and attacked workers carrying stone from Old Tyre, killing many of them and disrupting the supply line to the mole.[11]

In contrast to Curtius's view that the towers were solely for use against Tyrian ships, Arrian writes that once the mole reached a point near the island, the workers came under attack from catapults mounted on the ramparts of Tyre's walls. According to Arrian, the Macedonians responded to this by constructing two towers on the end of the mole to counter the wall-mounted Tyrian catapults. These towers were covered with hides to protect them from fire arrows or flaming catapult bolts and to screen and protect the men working within the towers. Because the towers were higher than Tyre's walls, the catapults on the top level could suppress the wall-mounted catapults, while those on lower levels in the towers could keep away any Tyrian ships trying to attack the workers on the mole.[12] Here Arrian presents the ability of the towers to repulse the Tyrian ships as a secondary effect. The main job of the towers, according to Arrian, was suppressing the catapult bolts being launched from atop Tyre's walls.

Arrian's view that the main purpose of the towers was related to attacks from the walls is echoed by several scholars. Fuller writes, "Only when the deeper water near the city was reached was work seriously impeded by missiles showered down on the workers from the summit of the wall. . . . To frustrate these attacks and to gain command of the wall, Alexander had two wooden towers" constructed. Tarn writes, "It was when the deep water near the island was reached and the workers came within shot of the walls that trouble began." Bosworth writes, "The construction work needed the protection of two vast siege towers which cleared the city battlements of skirmishers."[13] It isn't clear whether these scholars based their conclusion—that the main purpose of the towers was to counter missile fire from Tyre's walls—on their own analyses or if they are simply following the narrative provided by Arrian.

The story told by Curtius—that the purpose of the towers was to repulse the Tyrian ship attacks and not to attack Tyre's walls—seems the more plausible. Given the tenacity with which the Tyrians defended their city up until the very end, and given their control of the sea at this point in the siege, it seems unlikely they would allow the mole to reach more than halfway across the channel without trying to stop it. The depth of the water would not have prevented Tyrian ships from getting within arrow range of the mole; they used small boats, and even the larger triremes had a very shallow draft, estimated at 1.1 meters, or about three and a half feet.[14] As an example of the ability of Tyrian ships to sail in shallow water, recall Curtius's account of the Tyrians rowing down the coast to land marines behind the Macedonians and attack the workers carrying stone from Old Tyre. If the Tyrians were in fact attacking the mole from their ships long before it reached the center of the channel, it seems likely Alexander would come up with the idea of building the towers to repel them.

The confusion about the nature of the antiship towers likely stems from the fact that as the siege progressed and the mole approached the island, Alexander did in fact set up large siege towers that overlooked Tyre's walls and used them as platforms for his catapults in an attempt to clear the defenders from the battlements. With the benefit of hindsight there may be a tendency to assume that the two initial towers—set up to keep ships away from the mole—are the same types of towers as those large siege towers that will be set up later to clear Tyre's walls. To clarify this point, it may be useful to consider this question: what sorts of towers were potentially available to Alexander?

Siege towers have a long history. In Western culture, they are thought to have originated with the Assyrians and were adopted in turn by the Babylonians and Persians.[15] Lane Fox writes that "the Greeks had been slow to develop advanced siege equipment, drawing their knowledge of siege-towers and rams in the course of the fifth century from their contact with the

Orient; probably the techniques had passed from Assyria to Tyre, from Tyre to Carthage, from Carthage to the battlefields of Sicily, where the resident Greeks could have learnt from their Carthaginian enemies. Tyre, then, had been a vital link in the roundabout passage of siegecraft to the Greeks."[16]

Siege technology in Greece developed more rapidly when Philip established his unit of military engineers. Marsden argues that "military technology progressed in Macedonia for a period of less than twenty years with such steadily increasing momentum that we may reasonably recognize it as a situation noticeably anticipating to some degree the many examples of similar technological development in the twentieth century."[17]

The technology of Greek siege towers was based on that of Dionysius I of Syracuse. Kern writes that Dionysius was a ruler "from the fringes of the Greek-speaking world" and that "he had more in common with Macedonian princes than with the classical Greek polis." Syracuse faced "invasion by the Carthaginians, a Phoenician people who knew eastern siege methods. Threatened his entire life by Carthaginians, Dionysius learned the art of siege in this hard school." At the siege of Motya, "Dionysius built six-story siege towers to reach beyond the top of the walls and equal the height of the houses." These towers were on wheels and could be moved into place by teams of oxen.[18]

By the time of Alexander's expedition, the Macedonian unit of military engineers was under the supervision of a man named Diades, who is said to have besieged Tyre with Alexander.[19] Diades's name has become associated with something called mobile siege towers, which could be dismantled and transported in sections from place to place. Marsden writes that "Alexander and his engineers seemed to expect to be able to transport as many siege-engines as possible, normally by sea. In 334 this was arranged and carried out from Miletus to Halicarnassus."[20] It isn't clear how these mobile siege towers were transported from Halicarnassus to Tyre, since at the time the siege began, Alexander's fleet was still in the Aegean, and there would have been danger in moving the siege equipment by sea, from both the winter weather and the remaining ships of the Persian fleet.

The term "mobile" in relation to Diades's towers had caused some confusion, as it seems to imply they were on wheels and, once assembled, could be wheeled around the battlefield. The Latin word *ambulatorius* has been used by some ancient writers in referring to Diades's towers, suggesting they are movable. Whitehead and Blyth ask: "were Diades' towers [. . .] wheeled?" Their answer: "we are confident in rejecting any such inference, together with any and all evidence that appears to justify it." Apparently the same

terminology was used by ancient authors to refer to towers with components that could be transported to a siege site ("mobile") and towers on
wheels ("movable"). Whitehead and Blyth say "it is a distracting verbal co-
incidence which must not be allowed to mask a fundamental distinction of
substance and function: between towers which needed to be moved around
the streets of Alexandria, to reach where they could be deployed to best advantage, and Diadian ones erected wherever, and on whatever quality of
terrain, they were to serve their offensive purpose." Marsden writes "Diades
probably did not invent the fully mobile siege-tower mounted on a really
efficient chassis fitted with wheels, though he may have refined the detailed
design. But he certainly produced the first large towers which could be rapidly taken to pieces that would facilitate their carriage over many miles."[21]

English argues that the towers at Tyre "were fixed in position on the
mole, rather than wheeled—the risk of them being pulled or falling into
the sea would have been too great for them to have been wheeled."[22] However, he later writes, "I say the towers were presumably wheeled else they
would have to be dismantled and rebuilt every hundred meters, or probably
less, in order to maintain the protection of the forward working parties."[23]
English is likely talking about two different types of towers: the antiship
towers—which had to be moved frequently—and the larger siege towers
used later against the city walls.[24]

It is thought that Diades's mobile towers were 60 cubits (90 feet) high.
Diades is also reputed to have designed a mobile tower 120 cubits (180 feet)
high. Although this is sometimes mentioned by scholars as being used at
Tyre—Lane Fox writes "the world's largest siege towers were assembled to
a height of one hundred eighty feet, according to the technical manuals"[25]—
it isn't clear that it ever got off the drawing board.[26] To give some perspective
to tower height, consider that in 306, "a siege tower on an enormous
scale"—called a *helepolis* or "city-taker"—was used at the siege of Salamis,
a city on Cyprus. According to Romm this tower was 130 feet high.[27]

Whitehead and Blyth write that the mobile towers consisted of "timbers
precisely cut and prepared for their purpose. If building siege-towers from
scratch every time had *always* been the best policy, Diades could have spared
himself the trouble of designing 'portable' ones!" (emphasis in original)
These timber sections, at least for the 60-cubit tower, consisted of pieces
short enough to allow all the components of the tower, once disassembled,
to be transported on the backs of mules, thus avoiding the need for carts.
Whitehead and Blyth explain that "the 60-cubit size was not only the likelier
to be deployed anyway . . . but also—provided we are right to suggest that

the sections of its horizontals never exceeded 6 cubits [9 feet]—had the advantage of not needing carts at all. Whatever Diades had intended and hoped for, then, it may very well be that, once Alexander's extraordinary Anabasis was under way, only the [60-cubit tower] turned out to be [mobile] in practice."[28]

Were the antiship towers Alexander had built on the mole the same mobile towers invented by Diades? Whitehead and Blyth argue that they likely were. "We envisage that, whatever ancillary functions Diades' towers might take on in particular circumstances, . . . their main job was to house archers and light artillery." And they were likely different from the towers used later in the siege, when the mole reached the city's walls. Those later towers may have had bridges or gangways that could be lowered onto the top of the walls for assault troops to cross over, but there is no indication that Diades's mobile towers had such features. Whitehead and Blyth argue that "whether the . . . Diadian towers had any further part to play in the assault . . . is nevertheless uncertain." Bosworth seems to agree with this conclusion, writing: "Both Arrian and Curtius make it plain that the [initial] towers were designed primarily to repel counter-assaults by the Tyrians; they were not the assault towers later described by" Diodorus, as assumed by Fuller and Tarn. "Alexander was concerned to get the mole far enough advanced and stable enough to provide a platform for the heaviest engines. [As used here, "engines" is a generic term for siege machines: catapults, rams, and towers.] The measures to defend the laborers will have needed less massive preparations."[29]

It is likely, therefore, that the initial towers were assembled from precut parts that had been transported to Tyre along with other siege machines, primarily catapults. They may have come by ship, although there is no indication that Alexander's Aegean fleet had arrived at Tyre. But they may just as well have been carried overland on carts or the backs of mules, following the army's path. Alexander would later in his campaign haul siege equipment across the length of the Persian Empire and over the Hindu Kush Mountains, where no ships could transport it. In relative terms, getting it from Halicarnassus to Tyre would not have been difficult.

Regardless of the nature of the towers or how they got to Tyre, the Tyrians wanted them gone, and gone quickly. To accomplish this they came up with a remarkable plan. The Tyrian counterattack is described by only two of the five historians—Arrian and Curtius—and while their accounts differ in many details, they agree on the basic facts of the event, which are fairly straightforward. The Tyrians decided to burn down the towers that were defending the mole, and they settled on using a fireship for that purpose. (Fireships have been used throughout history to attack wooden vessels. They were famously used in AD 1588 by the English to disrupt the Spanish Armada.) Within one of their harbors, the Tyrians modified what is described by Arrian as a "cavalry transport-ship" and by Curtius as a "ship of unusual size." This would be something larger, and presumably broader, than a trireme. They built up the sides of the ship with wooden boards, making it possible to load in more flammable material. Then, according to Arrian, they filled the interior of the ship with "dry boughs and other combustible wood" as well as "chips and shavings and torches, to say nothing of pitch, sulfur, and anything else to stir a great blaze, which they added liberally."[30]

The Greek word used by Arrian to describe the dry material loaded onto the fireship—*klēmatōn* (κλημάτων)—is translated as "boughs" in the Loeb Classical Library translation by P. A. Brunt; as "vine twigs," its literal definition, in *The Landmark Arrian* translation by Pamela Mensch; and as "brushwood" by Martin Hammond.[31] English also uses the term "brushwood," and argues that "it is hard to see where such material could have come from in the island city. It is unlikely to have been specifically imported, and therefore timber from buildings was far more likely to be the primary incendiary material."[32] However, at this time Tyre was not blockaded, and ships were free to resupply the city with food, water, and other necessities, which presumably included firewood for cooking and heating. It seems likely that a supply of this firewood—including branches, sticks, vine cuttings, and other similar types of kindling ("brushwood")—would have been available to the island dwellers and that this type of combustible material may have better served the purpose of the fireship than would large beams taken from knocked-down buildings.

Arrian continues his explanation: the Tyrians "fixed two masts in the bows" of the ship. It is not clear if these masts were in addition to the ship's regular main mast, which would have been in the middle of the ship. The ship would need its main mast if the Tyrians planned to use the sail, and it is not clear whether they did so. Curtius explains that the ship was moved by oars but then writes that "its sails also had caught the wind in full force," while Arrian doesn't mention a sail, although he writes that the Tyrians "waited for a wind blowing towards the mole,"[33] so he may have had a sail in mind as well. We are also not told whether the two additional masts in the bows were set fore and aft, so that one was behind the other, or side by side, one on each side of the ship.

Arrian says the Tyrians then "lashed a double yardarm to each mast." This is confusing—what does Arrian mean by a double yardarm? Some scholars take the view that this means there were two yardarms attached to each of the two masts, a total of four yardarms. Fuller writes that "they lashed two yardarms to each of her masts," and Lane Fox writes, "to each of its two masts near the prow they lashed two beams." However, Bosworth argues that "it is most improbable that each of the two foremasts had a double yard attached." He argues instead that "two yards of normal length were passed over the foremasts and lashed together at their meeting point above the center of the vessel."[34] He seems to be envisioning the masts fixed on either side of the ship, with the distance between them being spanned by one long double-yard that has been spliced together.

Regardless of how many yardarms ended up on the masts, the Tyrians then hung cauldrons from the yardarms and filled them with highly flammable substances: "anything that could be poured or thrown on to increase the flame" writes Arrian. Finally, they loaded the stern of the ship with rocks, ballasting it in such a way that the bow came out of the water.[35] This was to ensure that the ship would ride up onto the mole rather than simply crash into it. Then they waited for the wind to blow toward the mole.

Curtius writes that they rowed the fireship out of the harbor ("drove it ahead by oars") and then let the wind catch the sail and take it toward the mole. Rowing seems unlikely, given that the ship was stuffed full of combustible material right up to the top of its extended gunwales. It isn't clear where the rowers would sit or even stand. Arrian writes that they waited for the wind and, "making fast hawsers, towed the transport astern with triremes."[36]

There is some confusion about the meaning of the Greek term used by Arrian that is translated as "towed the transport astern." This translation is from the Loeb Classical Library edition, translated by P. A. Brunt. *The Landmark Arrian*, translated by Pamela Mensch, uses the phrase "towed it behind their triremes."[37] In both of these translations, the sense is that the triremes were pulling the fireship and that the fireship was behind the triremes. However, Bosworth disagrees with this view and argues that the correct translation is: "fastening the ship with ropes, they towed it *from the rear* by means of triremes." (emphasis added) In other words, according to Bosworth, the triremes were not pulling the fireship behind them, but were pulling the fireship "from the rear," meaning that the tow ropes from the triremes were attached to the stern of the fireship, rather than the bow. The translation by Martin Hammond agrees with this interpretation, the passage reading "with ropes attached to the stern of the ship to tow it out by the rear."[38]

If Bosworth's and Martin Hammond's translations are correct, attaching the tow ropes to the rear of the fireship would help keep the fireship's bow raised out of the water, since pulling from the front would pull down on the bow. But perhaps equally important, if the fireship was in the center, with the two towing triremes flanking it on either side, it would give the triremes more time before they had to cut the tow lines and turn sharply away from the mole prior to impact. In fact, if that was an important consideration, it isn't clear that the tow ropes that were fastened to the *stern* of the fireship would not have been better fastened to the *bows* of the towing triremes. In that configuration the triremes would have actually been slightly behind the fireship, although the weight of the fireship tugging on the bows of the triremes would have made steering difficult for the helmsmen of the triremes.

Regardless of the arrangement of the tow ropes, between the wind, the rowers (in Curtius's account), and the towing triremes (in Arrian's account), the fireship made its way out of the harbor and straight toward the towers at the end of the mole. At some point Tyrian sailors on the fireship set the wood and other combustibles ablaze, and once things were burning nicely, they either jumped overboard and swam back to Tyre (in Arrian's account), or climbed into some skiffs that were trailing alongside and rowed away (in Curtius's account). Meanwhile, according to Arrian, the Tyrians "hauled with the Triremes as violently as possible and dashed the ship on to the edge of the mole." The raised bow of the ship crashed up onto the mole and buried itself in the base of one of the towers, setting it alight and perhaps causing it to collapse. The force of collision tore the yards free from the masts, pouring the flammable contents of the cauldrons down onto the burning wood and causing the fire to spread across the mole.[39] The fire would have been enormous, and both towers were set alight.

While the towers burned, the towing triremes waited alongside the mole and shot down those Macedonians rushing forward to fight the fire. The men on the mole and in the towers either jumped into the sea or remained to burn to death. Curtius writes that the Tyrians preferred to take the Macedonians prisoner rather than kill them, and so they "lacerated the hands of the swimmers with stakes and stones, until they were disabled and could be taken into the boats without danger."[40] This is an odd statement. Perhaps the Macedonians were trying to climb onto the Tyrian ships, and the Tyrians were keeping them out by pounding on their hands as they clung to the gunwales. And the Tyrians may have preferred to take them prisoner rather than kill them in the hopes they could be used in future negotiations with Alexander.

At that point something remarkable happened, which was either carefully planned in advance or was simply a spontaneous reaction that reflected the Tyrians' pent-up anger. With the towers burning fiercely, large groups of people swarmed out from Tyre's harbors in small boats, rowed across the channel, and climbed up onto the mole. There they destroyed whatever they could lay their hands on, tearing down the protective hide screens and setting fire to any catapults that were not already burning.[41]

It must have looked like a disaster to the Macedonians, standing dumbstruck on the shore, watching in anger as the wreckage of the towers burned in twin pyres at the mole's end. To the Tyrians, watching from the safety of their high walls and powerful warships, it must have seemed a remarkable victory. Perhaps now the Macedonians would come to their senses, realize the futility of attacking an island fortress with no ships, and leave Tyre in peace.

But quitting wasn't on Alexander's mind. He had more towers available in his mobile siege train, and more catapults, and if need be, his engineers could build still more. There was certainly no shortage of timber. As he had demonstrated at Issus, backing away from a fight simply wasn't in his nature, even if the odds were against him. And as bad as things looked for the Macedonians, at least the mole was undamaged.

But not for long. Perhaps Poseidon-Neptune really was angered by the hubris of the Macedonians, or perhaps it was just the weather. The brisk favorable wind that had propelled the fireship toward the mole continued to build until it blew up into a fierce storm. The wind drove waves that pounded the mole. Curtius writes that "the joints of the structure, lashed by surge after surge, loosened, so that the sea, flowing in between the blocks, broke right through the work. Therefore, when the heaps of stones which supported the earth that had been heaped upon them were demolished, the whole structure sank headlong into the deep."[42] Weeks of work by thousands of men, gone overnight.

But then, just as suddenly, none of that mattered. "Just when Alexander was feeling discouraged," writes Curtius, "and was not quite certain whether to continue the siege or to withdraw," word came from Sidon.[43]

Alexander's ships had finally arrived.

TWELVE

"THE SHIPS IN ALL
THEIR NUMBERS!"

After the storm, Alexander ordered the mole rebuilt, making it wider and stronger.[1] It isn't clear whether the mole had been two hundred feet wide and now was to be made even wider, or if it would now be widened to two hundred feet. Lane Fox argues for the latter. Arrian writes that the mole was widened to accommodate more towers, and Curtius adds that the widening was done so that towers erected in the middle of the mole would be out of range of weapons fired from either side.[2] This suggests the weapons the Tyrians were firing may have been ordinary bows or short-range catapults, while in the towers the Macedonians had catapults with a longer range. This may also have been a way to defend against future fire-ships. Diodorus writes that the strengthening was done in part by dragging large trees down to the shore—"branches and all"—and weighing them down with rocks to line the sides of the mole. It was thought these trees would break up the power of waves in any future storms.[3]

Curtius tells a slightly different story about how the trees were used in rebuilding the mole. Like Diodorus, Curtius writes that the Macedonians

used large trees, including their branches, and they threw the trees into the
water. These trees were then loaded down with piles of stone. More trees
were placed on top of the stone, and finally a thick layer of dirt was piled
on top of the trees.[4] This description seems to imply that whole trees were
incorporated into the structure of the mole itself to tie it together and brings
to mind the way steel rebar is imbedded within poured concrete.

Curtius also relates an odd story about the rebuilding of the mole. He
writes that Alexander changed the mole's direction so that its front—rather
than the side—faced in the direction of any incoming storms. By making
this change it was hoped that the force of any future storms would be borne
by the smaller surface area of the mole's face rather than the long exposed
sides.[5] But it isn't clear how this would be possible. The island of Tyre and
its high walls protected the mole from wind and waves coming from the
west. For the front of the mole to face the direction of a storm would mean
that the mole would have to face either north or south. However, a mole
that began on the mainland and faced either north or south would miss
the island completely, unless it began at a place on the mainland far to the
south or north of the island and was angled toward Tyre. But in that case
the mole would, for part of its length, lie beyond the shelter provided by
the island and thus be exposed to wind and waves from the west. Also, such
a north-south mole would be very much longer than one running directly
west from the mainland, requiring much more time and material to complete. One possible explanation for this account is that the force of the
storm may have shifted the underwater sand bar upon which the mole
rested—the proto-tombolo discussed in chapter 10—and this shifting may
have required a change in the mole's orientation to keep it over the shal-
lowest part of the seabed. Atkinson argues that the redirection of the mole
"is probably a fiction." He suggests that Curtius may have "misinterpreted
a Greek phrase."[6]

According to Arrian, Alexander also ordered his engineers to build more
siege machines.[7] It isn't clear whether this meant assembling more of Diades's mobile towers or building completely new towers from scratch. It is
likely that the catapults that were destroyed with the towers represented a
small part of those available in the mobile siege train, so building more siege
machines may also have meant assembling mobile catapult components
rather than building catapults from scratch. In any event, there was plenty
of timber available nearby if new construction was required, and metal
components could have been salvaged from the ashes of the towers and
reused, unless they were washed away by the storm.

Meanwhile, the Tyrians were not idle. Curtius tells another rather odd story of them attacking the mole using divers who could swim long distances underwater. Starting from boats that were apparently out of range of the Macedonian catapults, these men were able to swim underwater to the mole, where they attached ropes to the trees that had been incorporated into the rebuilt structure. When the Tyrians pulled on the ropes, presumably with their triremes, it dislodged the trees, thus undermining the whole foundation of the mole and causing it to collapse. A lack of ships to keep the Tyrians away from the mole made it difficult for the Macedonians to counter this strategy, although the whole story seems implausible.

Prior to rebuilding the mole, Alexander received news that ships from the Phoenician cities to the north were beginning to return from service with the Persian fleet. The disaster with the fireship had shown him that to be successful at Tyre he was going to need his own ships to counter the Tyrian navy. He was hopeful that with the Phoenician cities as his new allies, their ships would be made available to him. In a hurry to find out, he left Tyre accompanied only by a cavalry escort, the Shield Bearers, and some light troops—javelin men and archers—and headed north to Sidon, where the Phoenician ships had been reported.[8]

What he found there was the vindication of his strategy to defeat the Persian fleet from the land. As soon as they learned that Alexander had control of their cities, Gerostratos, king of Arados, and Enylos, king of Byblos, withdrew their ships from Persian service and sailed from the Aegean to Phoenicia. Once back home they agreed to join Alexander. The ships of Sidon had also returned from the Aegean, and their newly installed gardener-king made them available to the Macedonians. All together these totaled eighty Phoenician warships that Alexander could use against Tyre. In addition, there were nine ships from the island of Rhodes, three from Soloi and Mallos (cities in southern Asia Minor), ten from Lycia (a region of southwest Asia Minor), and a fifty-oared ship from Macedonia.[9] This latter ship likely carried news of the Spartan king's attempt to ally himself with the Persians. Alexander's Macedonian and allied Greek ships would have to remain in the Aegean for the time being to counter this potential threat.[10]

For Alexander, more good news soon arrived from an unexpected source. The kings from several cities on Cyprus sailed into the harbor at Sidon, bringing with them 120 warships that they pledged to Alexander. These cities had long been unhappy under Persian rule, and according to Arrian, once the Cypriot kings heard about the victory at Issus, they became concerned that all of Phoenicia would soon fall under Macedonian control. Their best option now was to abandon the Persians and switch sides. Alexander in turn recognized how important these new allies could be to his campaign, despite the fact that the Cypriots had just returned from fighting his fleet in the Aegean.[11] He therefore "absolved all these kings of any blame for their past actions."[12] In other words, Alexander "let bygones be bygones."[13] With the Cypriot force, Alexander suddenly found himself in possession of a fleet of over two hundred powerful warships, complete with trained rowers and marines, more than enough to defeat the Tyrian navy.

William M. Murray argues that rather than responding to news of Issus or the surrender of their home cities, the Phoenician and Cypriot ships gathered in response to messages sent out by Alexander early in the siege requesting their aid. In Murray's view, Alexander recognized early on that he could not take Tyre without naval superiority, and the gathering of this combined fleet, including the ships from Cyprus, was part of his siege planning.[14] This argument is inconsistent with Arrian's statement that the Cypriots came after hearing the news of Issus.

In addition to the ships, reinforcements arrived in the form of four thousand mercenary infantry sent from the Peloponnese in Greece to join the expedition.[15] Greek mercenaries were considered well-trained, reliable soldiers and had been employed in Persian service at the Battles of Issus and the Granicus, as well as serving with the Persian fleet in the Aegean. Alexander also used them to augment his own forces. Matthew Trundle writes of the widespread use of Greek mercenaries in the ancient world, "Sicilian tyrants, Alexander, the Athenians, the Persians, and Egyptian pharaohs all went to the Peloponnese for their mercenaries."[16] He says "Alexander might have used as many as 100,000 mercenary auxiliaries in support of his conquests. . . . The Macedonian phalanx and cavalry spearheaded the major battles, but the mercenaries and auxiliaries conducted specialized campaigns and manned the garrisons and new colonial cities sprinkled throughout the growing empire."[17]

While waiting for his newfound fleet to refit and prepare for battle, Alexander decided to deal with another problem that had plagued his army during the siege. Feeding the Macedonian army and its horses, mules, and oxen at Tyre would have been a huge logistical problem. Engels calculates the army would have needed 28,172 tons of grain for the seven months of the siege, including grain for the cavalry horses.[18] Since cavalry would be useless during the siege, it is likely that most of the cavalry units were posted farther inland and closer to food supplies. Requisitioning supplies from the surrounding countryside may have been delegated to the cavalry during

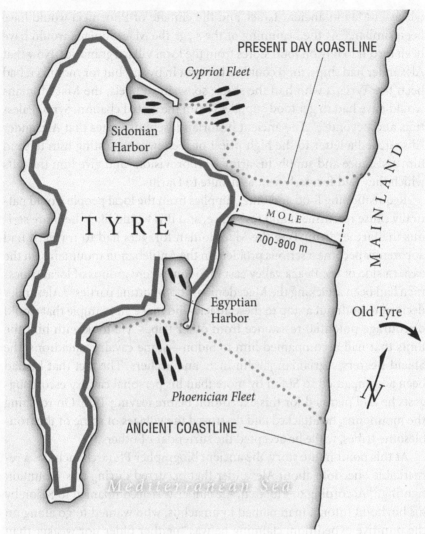

MAP 4. Tyre and Alexander's mole.

this time, while the infantry was kept busy building the mole. The agricultural land around Tyre was insufficient to supply the needs of tens of thousands of occupying soldiers. Even in normal years the city of Tyre had to import food for its population.

The siege began during the winter, either January or February, prior to any local harvest. Bible scholars think barley was harvested in April and wheat in May in ancient Israel, and the climate of Phoenicia would have been similar.[19] At the beginning of the siege the Macedonians would have been forced to rely on food stores from the local village granaries. Now that Alexander had ships, food could be brought in by sea, but for months it had been the Tyrians who had the ships, so, writes Engels, the Macedonians would have had to get food supplies "from the Anti-Lebanon, Syria, Palestine, and beyond."[20] The ancient historian Josephus writes that Alexander "dispatched a letter to the high priest of the Jews, requesting him to send him assistance and supply his army with provisions and give him the gifts which they had formerly sent as tribute to Darius."[21]

Requisitioning food and other supplies from the local people would naturally cause resentment and resistance, and this would likely be more serious the farther from Tyre the Macedonian foragers had to travel. It had apparently become a serious problem in the Antilebanon mountains on the eastern side of the Bekaa valley east of Sidon, where groups of local tribesmen had been attacking the Macedonian wood-cutting parties.[22] Alexander decided to both put a stop to these attacks and make an example that would discourage potential resistance from other tribes. He took with him the units that had accompanied him to Sidon—some cavalry squadrons, the Shield Bearers, Agrianian javelin men, and archers. The fact that he had been accompanied to Sidon by more than his personal cavalry escort suggests he had planned for this expedition before leaving Tyre. On reaching the mountains, he attacked and destroyed the villages of some of the troublesome tribes, while he accepted the surrender of others.[23]

At this point in the story, the ancient biographer Plutarch includes a remarkable anecdote about Alexander that occurred during this mountain fighting.[24] According to Plutarch, Alexander was accompanied to Sidon by his boyhood tutor, a man named Lysimachus, who wanted to go along on the punitive expedition, claiming he was "neither older nor weaker than Phoenix," a reference to the boyhood tutor of Achilles.[25] Lysimachus would have known that Alexander claimed descent from Achilles through the family of his mother Olympias,[26] and that Alexander liked to compare himself to, and measure his achievements against, his famous ancestor. By couching his request in a reference to Phoenix, Lysimachus could reasonably anticipate it would be viewed favorably by Alexander. The old man's participation in the expedition is not implausible.

When the Macedonian task force reached the mountains, the rugged terrain forced the cavalry to dismount, and the men all proceeded on foot. As they climbed higher, the veteran soldiers soon outdistanced the elderly Lysimachus, and Alexander, reluctant to abandon the old man, hung back with him, concerned because it was getting dark and there were enemy soldiers nearby. Although Alexander tried to hurry Lysimachus along, they soon found themselves far behind the main force, with only a few bodyguards to accompany them.

Eventually darkness forced them to stop for the night. They were high up in rugged mountains, the night was bitter cold, and they had no way of making a fire. Alexander began to worry about the old tutor. As it grew darker, Alexander could see through the trees the lights of several campfires burning in the distance. He couldn't tell whether these were his own men or the tribesmen they were hunting, but he set off into the trees to find out. "Since he was confident in his own agility, and was ever wont to cheer the Macedonians in their perplexities by sharing their toils, he ran to the nearest campfire," where he found two tribesmen sitting unaware. Using his dagger he quickly killed the two men, took a burning branch from their fire, and carried it back to where he had left Lysimachus. The Macedonians were thus able to make their own fire and warm themselves. After that they were able to either kill or frighten off other groups of tribesmen who came to investigate their fire, and they eventually ended up spending the balance of the night warm and safe.

This story seems like the sort of apocryphal tale people would come to tell about Alexander after his death, as the myths began to grow and spread about the new Achilles who conquered the world like a god.[27] For example, Lane Fox writes that in the medieval *Romance of Alexander*, the king is "thought to have soared to heaven in a basket which was raised by flying griffins" and to have "scoured the floor of the ocean for pearls in a shining barrel of glass." But Lane Fox argues that Plutarch's story of Alexander and Lysimachus is authentic, as it was "only proper" that Alexander should have "risked himself in the manner of his hero for the tutor."[28]

Having dealt with the troublesome tribesmen, Alexander returned to Sidon, where he gathered up his new fleet and sailed for Tyre. Both the number and variety of ships under his command were truly impressive, perhaps bringing to mind images of the Greek fleet at Troy, and words from the *Iliad*: "The mass of troops I could never tally, never name, not even if I had ten tongues and ten mouths. . . . Now I can only tell the lords of the ships, the ships in all their numbers!"[29]

In general, the Greeks recognized two categories of ships, and both types would have likely been available to Alexander. "Long ships" were warships that, as the name implies, were long and narrow and designed to be fast and maneuverable. "Round ships" were merchant vessels, broad and tublike, their holds designed to carry a large volume of cargo.[30] The long ships could utilize a sail if the wind was favorable but relied on oars for propulsion in calm weather or in combat. The round ships relied on sails or, in the event they carried soldiers, horses, or military supplies, could be towed by the oar-powered warships. Long ships were sometimes converted into transports by removing some of the oars and rowing benches and fitting them out to carry infantry or horses.[31] To the extent that Alexander's siege machines—the disassembled catapults, towers, and rams—were being transported by ship from Halicarnassus, they would have been carried in either round ships or these specially converted transport ships.

Alexander's campaign took place during a time of rapid innovation in warship design across the Mediterranean world, and the variety of types of long ships that accompanied him from Sidon would have reflected this innovation. From at least the sixth century, the warship design that dominated Mediterranean navies was the trireme (Greek: *triērēs*, literally "three-rowed"), a long, narrow ship with three levels of oars running along each side, each oar manned by a single rower.[32] The lowest level of oars projected through holes in the hull just above the waterline. Leather sleeves around the oars (Greek: *askōma*) kept water from splashing in through the oar holes.[33] A middle level of rowers sat just above (and slightly in front of) the rowers on the bottom level, the middle level oars extending through holes in the hull above those of the bottom level. The top level of rowers was just below deck level, above (and slightly in front of) the middle level rowers, and the top level oars extended through the top of the ship's hull. In Greek triremes, a wooden projection called an outrigger (Greek: *parexeiresia*) ran along the outside of the hull, providing support for the top level of oars and allowing the top level rowers to sit close against the side of the ship.[34]

According to Strauss, "a Greek trireme was about 130 feet long and about 18 feet wide (or about 39 feet wide with the oars extended) and sat about 8 1/2 feet above the waterline." A typical trireme would carry 170 rowers, distributed as 26 on each side on the bottom level (Greek: *thalamioi*), 29 on each side on the middle level (*zygitai*), and 30 on each side on the top level (*thranitai*).[35] Rowing a trireme at speed or over long distances was a tough, exhausting job, and the rowers were crowded together almost on top of each other in the narrow hull. To cool the rowers and provide them with fresh air, the sides of the ship were open. To protect the rowers against arrows during combat, screens of leather or heavy cloth could be lowered to cover the side openings. On some ships these screens were replaced with wooden louvers that provided more protection.[36]

Each ship had a pictorial representation of human eyes on the bow to help guide and protect the vessel. These eyes were either painted on the wood of the hull or, in the case of some Greek ships, were carved as marble plaques that were attached to the hull.[37] The ships were also given names by their crews.[38]

The trireme's principal weapon was a bronze ram that jutted from the front of the ship at the waterline. In battle, the attacking ship would attempt to drive this ram into the side or stern of an enemy ship, tearing a hole in the wooden hull and allowing water to flood in. The ramming attack had to be carried out at high speed to be effective, but at the same time the attacking ship needed to stop quickly before penetrating too far and becoming caught up in the wreckage. Carrying out a ramming attack required great skill on the part of the attacking ship's captain, its helmsman (who manned the steering oar), and its rowers. During the ramming attack, the marines and archers on deck would sit down to avoid being thrown off their feet with the impact. Although the rammed ship would flounder and be unable to continue fighting, it rarely sank because of its wooden construction.[39]

Triremes could also attack enemy ships by coming alongside and boarding them with marines. At the time of the Battle of Salamis in 480, the Athenian ships had no decks, and the marines and archers occupied a narrow gangway running down the center of the vessel between the rowers. This was done to minimize weight and make the ships as fast and maneuverable as possible, but it left little room for marines or archers, so the Athenians relied on ramming to defeat the Persian fleet.[40] In contrast, Phoenician and Cypriot triremes in the Persian fleet (and later Greek triremes) were fully decked, providing space for more marines and archers. The ships had shields hung along the deck railing for additional protection.[41] For these ships, boarding was a viable alternative to ramming.[42]

Although triremes dominated naval combat in the Mediterranean for hundreds of years, that began to change in the fourth century. New, larger warships began to appear, called quadriremes (Greek: tetrērēs, "four-rowed") and quinqueremes (Greek: pentērēs, "five-rowed").[43] As with other military technological innovations, these new ships seem to have arisen from the wars between the Greeks and Carthaginians on Sicily, although it isn't clear which of the two antagonists first developed the idea.[44] One argument is that Dionysius of Syracuse (the same man who built a mole and used towers at the siege of Motya) came up with the design, and it was later copied by his Carthaginian adversaries. But Meijer writes that "Pliny, the Roman encyclopedist, credits the Carthaginians, and not the Syracusans, with the invention of the quadriremes."[45] Another argument is that the idea was developed at Tyre (or Cyprus) and then traveled west to Carthage, where it was seen and copied by the Sicilian Greeks.[46] Whatever their origin, by Alexander's day quadriremes and quinqueremes were in the fleets of the eastern Greeks, the Cypriots, and the Phoenicians.[47]

The idea behind these new ships was to add a second rower to one or more of the oars, thus providing more power. It is thought that the impetus for this design change may have been the inability to hire experienced rowers in the western Mediterranean.[48] To propel a trireme in a ramming attack required highly skilled rowers, and as the wars in Sicily continued, it may have been increasingly difficult to find such men. Adding a second rower to an oar would have substituted power for skill. In addition, adding a rower meant widening the beam of the ship, thus making it more stable in the water. A wider beam also meant a wider deck, and thus these ships could carry more marines and archers.[49] Although the extra rower added power, the larger size slowed the ship and made it heavier and less maneuverable, so although these larger ships also carried rams, their primary method of attack became boarding.[50] The skill of the rowers was therefore of less importance.

We don't know exactly how the rowers and oars were arranged on these larger ships. For the quadriremes ("four-rowed"), there are two likely possibilities. First, the extra rower may have been added to the top level of oarsmen, keeping a single rower on the middle and lower levels of oars. This would have kept the ship the same height as a trireme, with three levels of oars, but would have resulted in a wider beam and deck. A second possibility, which seems more likely, is that these ships had only two levels of oars, with two rowers manning each oar. This would have widened the ship but would also have allowed its sides to be lower, since only two levels of oarsmen needed to be accommodated within the hull. A wider and lower ship would have been extremely stable in the water, providing an excellent fighting platform. The use of two levels of oars with double rowers may also have reduced the total number of oarsmen on each ship.[51]

Although a lower deck height of a quadrireme would have made the ship more stable in the water, it would have put the marines and archers aboard it at a disadvantage when trying to board—or defend against being boarded by—a ship with a higher deck. This meant that ships with higher decks and three levels of oars would have had an advantage. To overcome the disadvantage of a lower deck but keep the wider beam and more rowers per oar, a quinquereme ("five-rowed") kept the three levels of oars of the trireme, as well as the wider beam and deck of the quadrireme, and added a second rower to both the top and middle levels of oars.[52] These ships could hold as many marines and archers for boarding as a quadrireme. Although their higher decks meant they were not as stable in the water as quadriremes, they were likely more stable than the narrow triremes, although slower and less maneuverable. The quinquereme became a popular type of warship and was used extensively in the later Punic Wars between Rome and Carthage. Tarn writes, "There can be no doubt that, for the Roman navy of the third and second centuries B.C., at any rate, the quinquereme was the standard warship, quite apart from the first Punic war. . . . It was the typical Roman ship."[53]

When Alexander set sail with his fleet, heading south from Sidon, he would have known that the Tyrian ships in Persian service would also have returned from the Aegean, and so he would have been prepared for a naval battle. The 120 Cypriot ships were divided into two wings. Alexander, aboard what Curtius refers to as the royal quinquereme,[54] commanded the right (seaward) wing, which consisted of all of the ships from Cyprus except those under King Pnytagoras as well as all of the Phoenician ships.[55] The remaining Cypriot ships, under Pnytagoras, formed the left wing, which was commanded by the Macedonian general Krateros.[56] Not knowing what type of battle it might be—ramming or boarding—Alexander loaded the decks of his ships with as many of the Shield Bearers as they could carry.

As Alexander's fleet approached Tyre, all the Tyrian warships were waiting for them, their decks full of marines and archers, anticipating a sea battle. We don't know the exact number of ships available to the Tyrians for this battle. Diodorus writes that the Tyrians had eighty ships at the start of the siege, although it isn't clear if he is including those away in Persian service, all of which would have returned by the time of Alexander's approach.[57]

Herodotus describes the armor and weapons of the Phoenician marines at the time of the Battle of Salamis in 480, writing that they had bronze helmets of the same type as the Greeks, wore cuirasses made of layers of heavy linen fabric, and carried round shields. He says their shields were without metal rims, which would have made them lighter. The men were armed with javelins.[58]

The Tyrians would have known about the return of the Phoenician fleets and the capitulation of the Phoenician cities to the north. It is likely they were expecting Alexander to be accompanied by ships from Sidon, Byblos, and Arados, and perhaps some Macedonian and Greek ships that joined him from the Aegean. Tyre didn't yet know that the 120 ships from Cyprus had joined him. As the Tyrians watched Alexander's ships fill the horizon, it became clear that they were heavily outnumbered.

Here Arrian writes that Alexander tried some sort of ruse to tempt the Tyrians into fighting. While they were still some distance away, Alexander ordered his ships to stop and back away from the Tyrians, hoping this would cause them to attack. While we don't know exactly what else this strategy entailed, it didn't work. The Tyrians, seeing that the odds were heavily against them, decided to avoid battle, and their whole fleet turned and headed back to the safety of their two harbors. Diodorus records what happened next, although he has placed this account out of order, inserting it earlier at the time of the fireship. According to Diodorus, when Alexander saw the Tyrian ships withdrawing he ordered his own ships to row as fast as they could to try to reach the harbors first and block them, forcing the Tyrian ships to remain at sea where they could be attacked and overwhelmed by Alexander's greater numbers. When the Tyrian sailors saw what was happening they panicked, realizing their city was practically defenseless with all the fighting men aboard ships. Both fleets thus found themselves in a desperate race, their oars churning the sea into foam as they rowed as hard as they could for the harbors. The Tyrians got there first, making it into the harbors just ahead of Alexander's ships and blocking the entrances against their pursuers. A few of the slower Tyrian ships were caught outside the harbors and either captured or sunk.[59] It was a near-run thing.

During the race for the harbors, the Tyrians had three of their triremes take up a position outside the city to try to delay the pursuit. According to Curtius, Alexander personally rammed and sank these three ships. This seems unlikely since Alexander was not an experienced sailor, was on board a quinquereme (which would not have been as maneuverable, and perhaps not as fast, as a Tyrian trireme), and would have been outnumbered three ships to one. In a retelling of this same incident, Arrian writes that "the Phoenicians"—meaning ships from the allied Phoenician cities like Sidon and Arados—rammed the three Tyrian ships moored farthest out and sank them.[60] This seems more likely since the crews of the allied Phoenician ships were every bit as skilled as those of Tyre, and their numerous triremes could have overwhelmed the three Tyrian ships. The crews of the rammed ships managed to swim back to the harbor and safety.

The Tyrians sealed the openings to both of their harbors using their triremes, jamming as many ships together side-by-side as would fit into the harbors' entrances.[61] This is similar to the tactic used by the Macedonians when defending the harbor at Miletus from the Persian fleet—anchoring their triremes tightly together in the harbor mouth with their bronze rams facing out toward any potential attacker. The only way the Macedonians could break into Tyre's harbors would be to board and capture the Tyrian block ships in hand-to-hand fighting, with the attackers leaping across the narrow bows of the ships while Tyrian archers shot down at them from the city walls. Given the strength of the Tyrian position, Alexander decided not to attempt an assault.

Although this naval encounter was brief and inconclusive, it changed the nature of the siege dramatically. It was now the besieger who controlled the sea around Tyre and whose ships could strike anywhere without warning. The Tyrians were trapped on their island, and without help from Carthage they would eventually starve. But starvation wasn't a likely outcome. Alexander was too impatient for that. Starving Tyre would take too long.

Alexander now had under his command modern warships, experienced crews, and powerful siege machines. If he could find a way to effectively bring those weapons to bear against the walls of Tyre, he might be able to capture the city quickly. It would not be easy, but if anyone could do it, it was the man who thought he was a god. Was he greater than Poseidon? the Tyrians had taunted him. In Alexander's mind the answer may well have been yes.

PART IV

The Siege: Sea Assault

Apart from his considerable skills as a commander of infantry and cavalry forces, Alexander also ranks among the great naval innovators of antiquity. This surprising fact stems from his development of the first naval siege unit worth the name and his effective use of it against the Phoenician city of Tyre in 332 BCE.

—William M. Murray, "The Development of a Naval Siege Unit under Philip II and Alexander III," in *Macedonian Legacies: Studies in Ancient Macedonian History and Culture in Honor of Eugene N. Borza*

THIRTEEN

BY LAND AND SEA

By gaining control of the sea around Tyre, Alexander was able to push the mole forward without opposition until it came within catapult range of the city's walls. We are told that the Tyrians had catapults and that they used them to attack the workers on the mole, but we don't know exactly what types of catapults they were.[1] Diodorus writes that the Tyrians had a great many catapults and other types of siege machines and that they were able to construct as many catapults as they needed because the city was home to skilled engineers and craftsmen. In addition to the catapults, these engineers devised a number of defensive measures to either keep the Macedonians at bay or kill them—often in gruesome ways—if they ventured too close. According to Diodorus, the walls of Tyre were full of catapults and other devices, particularly on the side where the wall faced the mole.[2]

As with so many military innovations in the ancient Mediterranean world, it is thought that the first catapults originated in Sicily in the wars between the Greek cities and Carthage in the early fourth century.[3] The first catapults were essentially large crossbows small enough to be held and used by a single soldier. Later, as the size and power of the bows increased, the catapults were mounted on wooden stands that allowed them to be swiveled from side to side and elevated for greater range. These larger catapults generated greater power and range, but their bows were much too stiff to be drawn back by hand. Instead, the arms of the bow were pulled back using a winch at the rear of the weapon. When the bowstring was drawn all the way back, it was engaged by a lever that held it in place until the weapon was fired. The projectiles for these machines—called bolts—were essentially large arrows that rested in a groove on the wooden stock until they were shot out by the release of the bowstring. The weapon's power came from the tension generated by drawing back the arms of the bow.

The effective range of these catapults is unclear, and efforts using modern re-creations have provided mixed results. Marsden writes, "No satisfactory results have ever been obtained by those who have tried to calculate the ranges of catapults theoretically."[4] He says, "We may guess, as intelligently, we hope, as possible, that these advanced non-torsion catapults, discharging bolts or shot, could achieve a maximum effective range of about 300 yards."[5]

The Macedonians countered the wall-mounted Tyrian catapults by rebuilding their towers on the reconstructed mole, making them higher than Tyre's walls and mounting their own catapults on the towers. It is thought that the Macedonians had an advantage in that their catapults—called torsion catapults—utilized a relatively new technology developed in Macedonia by Philip's military engineers,[6] although Fuller argues that "the torsion catapult was invented by the Phoenicians." Tarn writes that "whether the utilization of the *principle* of torsion . . . was discovered in Phoenicia, or Sicily, or where, cannot be said; all we can say is that it was known before Alexander."[7] (emphasis in original)

Torsion catapults used the force generated when tightly twisted bundles of rope—made from animal sinew, horsehair, or even human hair—were twisted even tighter as the catapult's arms were drawn back with the bowstring.[8] When suddenly released, the arms snapped forward—in the same way that twisting a coiled spring generates a force when released—and the bowstring shot the projectile out with tremendous force. According to Tarn, the best material for the catapult springs was human hair, and women in the ancient Mediterranean world cut their long hair and sold it for this purpose, creating a huge market for hair in the third century.[9]

The torsion catapults of the Macedonians could easily outrange the older technology of the nontorsion catapults of the Tyrians. Hanson writes of torsion catapults that "such machines might hurl stones or specially crafted bolts over 300 yards as efficiently and accurately as seventeenth-century gunpowder artillery." Marsden estimates that if "the catapults were pulled back to their full extent" and "laid at an angle of elevation of 45 degrees, their missiles would have achieved a range of about 400 yards."[10] This greater range allowed the Macedonians to potentially clear Tyre's ramparts of defenders and forced the Tyrians to erect wooden screens to protect their catapults and crews.

Alexander's Greek engineers could compute the diameter of the rope bundle that was needed for a given size catapult. They found that they could make catapults that were large and powerful enough to hurl not just bolts but heavy stones as well. The siege of Tyre may have been the first time that these stone-thrower catapults were used against the walls of a fortified city.[11]

This battle of catapults became part of the cat-and-mouse struggle between the attacking Macedonians and the defending Tyrians that would continue right up until the end of the siege. For every tactic the Macedonians used to gain an advantage, the Tyrians devised a countermeasure to thwart them. For example, to counter the superior height of the towers on the mole, and the bolts and stones from their torsion catapults, the Tyrians added wooden towers to the ramparts on their wall where it faced the mole, both to increase the wall's height and to protect men and catapults from Macedonian missiles.[12] And as the mole and its towers drew closer to Tyre's walls, the range advantage of the torsion catapults no longer mattered.

Although Alexander may have been the first besieger to use stone-thrower catapults against fortified walls, it isn't clear how effective the catapults were in damaging—let alone destroying—Tyre's walls. This is partly because there isn't a consensus about exactly what type of stone throwers Alexander was using. It is thought that the initial torsion stone throwers would be two-armed machines, similar to the nontorsion bow catapults, but utilizing the torsion power of bundles of sinew or hair rope. These machines, while more powerful than the bow-type nontorsion catapults, would likely not have been powerful enough to bring down the massive stone blocks that made up the walls of Tyre.

Campbell writes, "It is extremely doubtful whether stone-projectors could ever have demolished masonry walls." Marsden writes, "At Tyre, in 332 Alexander actually employed stone-throwers with some effect against the walls. These engines were almost certainly torsion stone-throwers, because I doubt whether even the most powerful non-torsion machines would have been worth using for this purpose." He adds, "Since the first half of

Philon's seventh book is devoted almost exclusively to wall-building with a view to withstanding stone-throwers, it seems that their blows were not to be despised." Tarn writes of the stone thrower "it was no good against a first-class wall, but it was effective against other machines or groups of men, and would breach any improvised wall."[13] From these statements it seems that Alexander's stone throwers could have done some damage to the walls but were not powerful enough to destroy them.

English seems to disagree with this view, writing of Alexander's catapults, "The attackers now had the very real possibility of punching a hole through the defenses of a besieged fortress, or of bringing down stretches of walls from a distance."[14] This assertion is apparently based on English's view that Alexander possessed what is known as a one-armed stone thrower, called a *monankōn* by the Greeks and (later) an *onager* by the Romans. The 1996 edition of the Liddell and Scott *Greek-English Lexicon* defines a *monankōn* (μονάγκων) as "a one-armed engine to throw projectiles."[15] These one-armed machines had a single vertical arm that was pulled back into a horizontal position against the torsion force of a twisted rope bundle. When the arm was released it sprang back up to vertical with a great crash, and a sling on the end of the arm hurled a stone up into the air toward the target. According to English, "Alexander's single-armed stone-throwing catapults ... would have been similar in design, although perhaps less powerful, than the better known, but rather later, Roman *onager*."[16]

Marsden argues against Alexander having the powerful one-armed *monankōn*, writing, "There is little evidence for the employment of [one-armed stone throwers] before the fourth century A.D."[17] He criticizes an 1885 book by George Rawlinson, saying, "Rawlinson saw, in an Assyrian relief, what he thought was a representation of two one-armed stone-throwing engines (μονάγκωνες, *onagri*) ... in the complete absence of even the slightest additional evidence, it is unjustifiable to transform the straightforward, innocent beams into the arms of *onagri* and, solely by vivid imagination, to surround them with all the essential major and minor components which make up these relatively complicated machines."[18] Whitehead also argues against one-armed stone throwers appearing at the time of Alexander. Commenting on the appearance of the term *monankōn* in Philon's early third century treatise on siegecraft, he writes that "experts have been rightly troubled by an apparent mention of *monagkōnes*, a.k.a. *onagers* ... so long before they are referred to again ... and even there in material very likely to be a later addition.... The whole phrase has the appearance of an intrusive gloss on τοῖς πετροβόλοις; I follow Lawrence in rejecting it."[19]

English is likely basing his assumption that Alexander possessed powerful one-armed stone throwers on arguments made by T. E. Rihll in her book
The Catapult: A History, since he cites Rihll in his notes as the source of his
information about torsion catapults. Rihll examines archaeological findings
of catapult components, and she focuses on discoveries made since Marsden
wrote *Greek and Roman Artillery: Historical Development* in 1969. Rihll argues that the first torsion catapults to be developed were, in fact, one-armed
monankōnes, and that the two-armed torsion machines, both bolt shooters
and stone throwers, developed from the one-armed model.[20]

In a critical review of Rihll's book, Campbell disagrees with many of her
conclusions, writing, for example, that "her startling conclusion, that 'the
Phokians or the Thessalians independently invented the torsion one-armed
stone-thrower', may as well have been drawn from a conjuror's hat." While
Campbell does not dispute the possibility that the first torsion catapult may
have been the one-armed *monankōn*, he points out that Rihll is not the first
person to make that argument.[21]

The idea that the first torsion catapult was the one-armed stone throwing
monankōn was put forth in a 1920 article in the journal *Classical Quarterly*
by E. P. Barker. If correct, that would imply that the *monankōn* would have
been available to Alexander at Tyre. In the article, Barker argues that the
one-armed torsion machine must have come first because "great inventions
are never such leaps as they look: there has always been a tentative stage—
preliminary tinkering, perhaps for a generation or so, perhaps more," and
that "before its complex application to the double-spring, torsion power
must have been showing itself effective in simpler devices." In other words,
a machine with a single spring must have come first, since it is less complicated than one with two springs.[22] Barker argues that the double-armed torsion catapult was a combination of the earlier bow machines and the
one-armed torsion machine, and writes, "We do not know when or by whom
it was seen that two adapted μονάγκωνες [*monankōnes*], placed edgeways
up, coupled and working in opposite directions, could be made to work a
cord like the elastic bow, and so combine the force of the torsion-piece with
the bow's precision, but this, or something very like it, must have been the
course of development, and would lead to the first double-spring pieces."[23]

Barker says, "It seems unnecessary now to combat the old view . . . that
the μονάγκων [*monankōn*] was a late invention: it is accepted now as
known in all periods of ancient artillery."[24] Regardless of how accepted that
view is among scholars, the question relevant to this book is this: were
Alexander's stone throwers powerful enough to destroy Tyre's walls? English

seems to equate them with the much later Roman *onager*, although he does state that Alexander's machines were "perhaps less powerful" than the *onager*. However, he adds that Alexander's stone throwers had "the very real possibility of punching a hole through the defenses of a besieged fortress, or of bringing down stretches of walls from a distance." But Barker states that the first one-armed machine was an "inaccurate lobber, in some rather crude form."[25]

Would a crude, inaccurate lobber be powerful enough to bring down sections of Tyre's walls? And this raises another question: if the first crude, inaccurate one-armed machines led to the development of double-armed torsion machines shooting both bolts and stones, doesn't that imply that the new double-armed machines were better? If so, then even if Alexander's engineers were aware of primitive one-armed "inaccurate lobbers," would they have used them at Tyre if they had available newer state-of-the-art double-armed machines?

With respect to the siege of Tyre, Rihll writes, "The first use here of stone-throwing catapults against walls, rather than people, did not have a dramatic impact, because ultimately the walls collapsed under the impact of good old-fashioned rams." She continues, "Ineffectiveness against well-built walls might explain why, despite the number of battles and sieges that occurred while Alexander's marshals, generals, and assorted other subordinates fought among themselves and with others for control of parts of his empire, the next explicit reference to stone throwers concerns events some twelve years later." Tarn writes of the *monankōn*: "This form is never actually described till Roman times, though it was certainly Hellenistic. . . . It would throw a considerable distance, but had no pretensions to accuracy, and probably played little part in Hellenistic warfare."[26]

Regardless of whether Alexander could break through Tyre's walls with his stone-throwing catapults, he certainly could do so with his rams, and so the Tyrians wisely began taking countermeasures to reinforce the section of wall opposite the mole. Diodorus writes that the Tyrians were concerned about whether their wall at this point was thick enough to withstand Alexander's rams, so they built a second wall behind the original one. This second wall was fifteen feet thick, and the space between the two walls— about seven and one-half feet—was filled with dirt.[27] It was clear that regardless of how many rams Alexander put on the mole, he was never going to break through Tyre's wall at that point. The narrow, two-hundred-foot frontage was simply too restrictive, and the Tyrians knew exactly where the blow was coming.

Once Alexander realized his mole was unlikely to lead to success, he turned to his newly acquired navy for a new strategy. His first action was to establish a naval blockade of Tyre's two harbors, preventing food and supplies from reaching the city. He assigned the ships from Cyprus to blockade the northern (called "Sidonian") harbor, and the ships from the Phoenician cities to blockade the southern (called "Egyptian") harbor. (A small northern harbor still exists at Tyre. The southern harbor is gone.) Because the mole bisected the channel between these two harbors, it acted as a barrier between the two blockading squadrons, whose ships could only interact by sailing completely around the island. Diodorus writes that Alexander made a show of taking his ships on a slow cruise around the entire island, looking for weaknesses but also making clear to the Tyrians that his assault on their city would not be confined to just the two hundred feet at the end of the mole. Curtius writes that the Tyrians were beginning to feel encircled by the Macedonians, with the mole reaching nearly to the wall and Alexander's ships prowling all around the island. Tyre now faced assaults from land and sea.[28]

In deciding on his next steps, Alexander had available to him a wealth of technical advice from a wide range of talented military engineers. Arrian writes that engineers came from Cyprus and the cities of Phoenicia to help with building catapults and other siege machines.[29] These engineers would be in addition to the corps of Greek military engineers that had been assembled by Philip and traveled with the Macedonian army. The men used their combined expertise to do something extraordinary: they mounted Alexander's powerful siege machines—the catapults and covered rams—on the decks of ships. This was likely the first time that stone-throwing shipborne catapults had been used.[30] As Tarn points out, these ship-mounted catapults were only used against the city walls and their defenders, and not against other ships. "There is no recorded case in the Hellenistic world of catapults being used in a naval battle; that first came in with the Roman civil wars."[31]

Commenting on this use of ships as platforms for siege machines, William H. Murray asks: "Since all this activity required specialized hardware operated by specially trained crews, one wonders how Alexander and his men learned these new skills so quickly. Four years earlier, when he came to the throne, the young king had shown no particular interest in his navy, and yet at Tyre we see him as a master of naval innovation, presiding over an engineering corps of great sophistication that provided him with all kinds of siege machinery used to great effect by his men. How was this possible?"[32]

Murray's answer to his own question is that Philip may have developed a "naval siege unit" in anticipation of having to use siege machines against either a fortified island or harbor.

The exact nature of these floating platforms for the siege machines is unclear, since the ancient historians are not consistent in their explanations. Whitehead argues that one drawback of the ancient accounts is the vagueness of their vocabulary with respect to siege engines: "Occasionally there is a mention of (e.g.) catapults or rams or towers, but mostly the talk is of these indeterminable *mēchanai*." Diodorus simply writes that they "lashed triremes together," while Arrian writes that they used "horse-transports" or "slower triremes." The horse transports may have been cargo ships (round ships), or triremes specially modified as transports. The slower triremes were either heavy ships with wider decks to carry extra marines, or waterlogged ships that rode low in the water and needed to be hauled on shore to allow their hull timbers to dry out. Curtius goes into more detail about the type of ship that was used, writing that two quadriremes were firmly fastened together at the bow, while the sterns of the two ships remained far apart. The triangle-shaped space between the ships was then covered over with large beams and planks, fastened together to make a solid platform upon which catapults or rams could be mounted and the crews that operated the machines could stand.[33]

Using quadriremes as platforms for the siege machines was a good choice, because these ships were broader and lower than triremes, making them more stable in the water. And lashing two ships together not only increased the stability but provided the width needed for both a massive ram and a covering shed to protect the ship and crew from anything dropped on them from the walls. However, the idea that the bows were lashed together, with the sterns wide apart, seems unlikely. Atkinson views it as improbable, writing that "Curtius' picture of the quadriremes as linked at the bows, with their sterns wide apart is at variance with D[iodorus]. . . . Ships linked in this way would not have been maneuverable."[34]

Once the catapults and rams were mounted on the ships, the Macedonians immediately began attacking the walls of Tyre. Curtius writes that as the ships approached the city and fired catapults at the defenders on the ramparts, the crewmen on the ships were protected by the ships' prows.[35] However, Atkinson points out that "breastworks built up from the prows would not have afforded much protection against missiles fired from the top of the city walls."[36] The ships must have been protected by roofs of thick timbers, proof against heavy rocks dropped by the Tyrians, and these timber roofs would be protected against fire with wet hides. However, once the ships got near Tyre's walls, they would have been safe from catapult fire because although catapults could be elevated for long-range firing, they could not be depressed below a few degrees, so firing down at targets near the walls would have been impossible. This same effect would have occurred when the mole neared the base of the wall—the Tyrian catapults on the walls could not be depressed enough to target Macedonians standing on the mole. Marsden calculated that a catapult fired from atop a forty-two-foot-high wall would not have been able to reach a target nearer than seventy-eight yards.[37] On the other hand, since catapults on the Macedonian ships could be elevated quite high, they would have been able to target Tyrians manning the ramparts, while the Tyrians could only reply with arrows from ordinary bows.

At this point in their stories, both Diodorus and Curtius—who may have been relying on Diodorus's account—report that the ram ships breached Tyre's walls. Curtius writes that Alexander brought his ships up close to the walls and shattered them with catapults and rams. But the breach was quickly blocked up with stone by the Tyrians, who also began building a second wall behind the breach. Diodorus writes that the Macedonians mounted siege machines on ships and knocked down one hundred feet (one *plethron*) of the wall. Some attackers entered the city through this breach but were quickly driven back by a shower of missiles fired from the walls. During the night, the Tyrians rebuilt the collapsed portion of the wall.[38]

In contrast to the other two historians, Arrian writes that when the mole reached the wall, the Macedonians brought up rams on the mole and on their ships. As the rams on the mole began pounding at the base of the wall, making little progress, the ship-mounted rams began probing at several places around the island looking for a weakness. However, the men on the ram ships soon discovered a problem. The Tyrians had dropped large stones into the water at the base of the walls, making it impossible for the ram ships to anchor close enough to do any damage.[39] To be highly effective, the ram ships would need to anchor close to the base of the walls. Even then it would be difficult to work the rams effectively from ships.

To clear the area at the base of the walls, the Macedonians used their ships to pull the stones out of the water. Arrian makes it clear that this was a difficult and time-consuming job, especially since rocks, missiles, and all manner of flaming material were being hurled down from the ramparts onto the ships while the men worked. The Macedonians must have used some sort of ship-mounted cranes, which, like the rams, would require a stable platform to work effectively. Their ships would have been securely anchored to keep them from shifting as the rocks were pulled up. While this was going on, the Tyrians struck back by protecting some small fast ships with armor. Fuller writes that protecting them "with armor" likely meant protecting them "against arrows and catapult projectiles by fencing in their decks."[40] These armored ships then rushed out of the harbor and cut the anchor ropes before the Macedonians could respond. Alexander countered this by armoring some of his own ships and setting them in a defensive picket line around the anchored ships, keeping off the fast-moving Tyrians.[41]

Undaunted, the Tyrians simply shifted their strategy: they sent divers to swim underwater and cut the anchor ropes. Alexander responded by using chain rather than rope to secure the anchors to the ships. This apparently worked, as we are told that the attacks by divers stopped. Once free of interference, the Macedonians used ship-mounted cranes to lift the stones away from the base of the wall and drop them into deeper water where they would not impede the work of the ram ships. A passage in Arrian stating that the stones were lifted high with "engines" (μηχαναῖς; mēchanais) has been interpreted by some scholars as meaning that the stones were flung away using stone-throwing catapults. For example, Lane Fox writes, "Alexander's men replied by hauling up the rocks on rope lassoes, loading them into their stone-throwers and hurling them far out of harm's way." Martin Hammond translates the phrase in Arrian as "lifted on the catapults."[42]

Commenting on the possible use of catapults to dispose of the stones, Bosworth writes: "Arrian adds that the salvaged stones were loaded on to the siege engines and shot out into deep water. Now the maximum recorded weight of a catapult shot is 3 talents . . . and the catapults involved were specially designed by Archimedes, certainly much larger than Alexander's artillery. If Arrian's description is correct, the stones of Tyre's outer defenses were surprisingly small." The Oxford English Dictionary reports that the weight of the later Attic talent was 57 pounds, so a shot of 3 talents would weigh 171 pounds. By way of comparison, a one-cubic-foot block of limestone weighs 169 pounds. Romm writes that at the siege of the Cypriot city of Salamis in 306, the besiegers had catapults that "could fire two-hundred-pound stones to break down walls." But these massive catapults were used on land and were likely much too heavy to mount on a warship. Murray provides data on the weight of stone shot used by ship-mounted catapults, showing that the heaviest shot weighed 26.2 kilograms (58 pounds). Tarn writes of Hellenistic stone throwers, "The heaviest stone thrown was a talent—between 50 and 60 pounds."[43] If Alexander's men used torsion catapults to fling away the stones, then either the stones were small or the catapults had a capacity far beyond what seems probable.

There is an alternative explanation. According to *The Cambridge Greek Lexicon*, the word Arrian used that is interpreted here as catapults—*mēchanais* (μηχαναῖς, plural of μηχανή)—has several meanings, one of which is "siege-engine" but another of which is "crane." It is possible that in using the term here, Arrian was referring to some type of ship-mounted crane rather than to the stone-throwing catapults.

According to Curtius, while the ram ships were working to clear the base of Tyre's walls, a fierce storm came up, although neither Arrian nor Diodorus mention it. Large waves began to form, stirred up by a strong wind, and soon the Macedonian ships began to break loose from their anchors and crash against one another. The ropes holding the platform ships together didn't hold, the paired ships separated, and the platforms spanning the gap between them fell into the sea, taking the siege machines and their crews with them. The ships that remained tied together in pairs were difficult for the helmsmen and rowers to control. Panic set in among some of the crews—rowers abandoned their oars and tried to flee, interfering with soldiers trying to save the machines. Yet Alexander's luck still held, and the battered ships eventually made it safely back to shore.[44] It could have been much worse.

The siege now settled down into a sort of stalemate. The Tyrians were bottled up in their harbors and, because of the strength of Alexander's fleet, were unable to break out. On the other hand, because of the strength of Tyre's walls, the ingenuity of its engineers, and the courageous resistance of its soldiers, the Macedonians were unable to break in. The siege had been going on since January, and it was now summer. Eventually Tyre would either have to be relieved, by Persians or Carthaginians, or it would starve. But that could take a long time.

In the meantime, while the siege was in progress, another letter arrived from Darius proposing peace.[45] According to Arrian's version of the letter, Darius proposed giving Alexander 10,000 talents in exchange for the release of his family. The mother, wife, and children of the Persian king had been captured following the battle of Issus, and although they were treated with great respect by Alexander, he still held on to them as valuable prisoners. Darius also offered to give Alexander the part of his kingdom west of the Euphrates River—which included Asia Minor, Syria, Phoenicia, and

Egypt—and to give Alexander his daughter in marriage. The two kings would swear to be friends and allies.[46]

When Alexander disclosed the contents of this letter at a meeting of his generals, it led to one of the best-known anecdotes in the Alexander saga. Arrian writes that the Macedonian general Parmenion, second in command of the army, told Alexander that if he (Parmenion) were Alexander he would accept Darius's terms and end the war immediately without further fighting. Alexander answered that he (Alexander) would also accept Darius's terms if he were Parmenion. But since he was Alexander and not Parmenion, he was making a different decision. The same story is told by Plutarch. Bosworth writes, "This is the most famous of the exchanges between Alexander and Parmenion . . . and is reproduced by virtually every source for the history of Alexander."[47]

In Arrian's account, Alexander replies to Darius that he was not in need of money from Darius, nor did he want part of his kingdom. In Alexander's view, all of Darius's money and his entire kingdom now belonged to Alexander. He would marry Darius's daughter if he chose to, with or without Darius's permission. If Darius wanted to be treated favorably by Alexander, he needed to come to him. Arrian writes that when Darius received this reply from Alexander, he gave up any hope that he could come to terms with the Macedonian. Instead, he "began to prepare again for war."[48]

FOURTEEN

SHIPS AND LADDERS

B oth Diodorus and Curtius describe the use of an odd weapon by the
Tyrians: red-hot sand. Diodorus writes that the Tyrians made contain-
ers of iron and bronze, filled them with sand, and heated them for a long
time over an intense fire until the sand became red hot. They then used a
special device to pour the sand over the attacking Macedonians. The hot
sand worked its way under the armor and clothing of the soldiers and
caused terrible burns. We are told that the men who received these burns
screamed in agony as though they were being tortured. Driven mad with
pain, they eventually died.[1]

While the pouring of red-hot sand on unsuspecting attackers makes for
a dramatic story, it seems implausible in the context of the siege of Tyre.
The technique could only be effective on soldiers standing very near the
walls, since the farther the sand was thrown out from the walls, the less its
effect would be when it finally hit the ground forty or fifty feet below. This
raises questions: why would Macedonian soldiers be standing at the base
of Tyre's walls? And if they were, wouldn't it have been easier to simply drop

rocks on them? The men on ships would be protected by roofed sheds, as would anyone working rams on the mole. Tarn writes that pouring the sand down on the attackers "could only be done if the enemy were right under the walls, not on shipboard." He goes on to argue that Curtius copied the story of the red-hot sand from Diodorus, and, as will become apparent later in this chapter, he views much of what Diodorus has written about the siege as essentially made up.[2]

English suggests one possible reason for the use of red-hot sand, writing that "this boiling hot sand was then dropped upon the attackers as they attempted to scale ladders. . . . One can only imagine how agonizing this must have been, especially when halfway up a ladder."[3] The problem with English's view is that nowhere in any of the Loeb Classical Library translations of the three accounts of the siege of Tyre—by Arrian, Diodorus, or Curtius—is the word "ladder" mentioned. The Greek engineer Philon, in his treatise on sieges, writes that a city's walls should be no less than twenty cubits (30 feet) in height so that ladders cannot reach the top.[4] While the walls of Tyre were likely not the 150 feet given by Arrian, they must have been incredibly high to warrant such an extreme estimate, certainly more than the 30-foot minimum suggested by Philon, thus calling into question the idea that ladders could have reached the top.

Were ladders used at Tyre? English apparently based his view—that the Macedonians used ladders to scale Tyre's walls—on his interpretation of a section in Bosworth's *A Historical Commentary on Arrian's History of Alexander*. In that book, Bosworth writes that the Macedonian ships "were equipped with *a type of scaling ladder* which Arrian calls γέφυρα [*gephura*] and Diodorus ἐπιβάθρα [*epibathra*]." (emphasis added) Bosworth argues that "the two expressions [*gephura* and *epibathra*] were synonymous as is proved by Arrian's description of the siege of Massaga (iv 26.6, 27.1)."[5] Massaga (spelled Massaka in *The Landmark Arrian*) is a fortress thought to have been located near the Indus River in the northwest of modern Pakistan.

While the terms *gephura* and *epibathra* may in some settings be synonymous, it isn't clear that those settings deal with a type of scaling ladder. Table 1 shows how the two terms are defined in three ancient Greek lexicons.[6]

It seems clear from these definitions that the term *gephura* means "bridge." It also seems clear that while one definition of the term *epibathra* is a scaling ladder, the term can also refer to a structure similar to a gangway or gangplank. One of the definitions of "gangway" in the *Oxford English Dictionary* is "A plank or ramp used as a temporary walkway to enable people to board or disembark from a ship or boat; a gangplank." Therefore, if

TABLE 1.

Source	Definitions	
	γέφυρα (*gephura*)	ἐπιβάθρα (*epibathra*)
Liddell and Scott Greek-English Lexicon	bridge	ladder or steps to ascend by: scaling ladder; ship's ladder, gangway
Brill Dictionary of Ancient Greek	bridge; causeway	ladder (portable, for sieges); small set of steps; gangplank (for a ship)
Cambridge Greek Lexicon	structure affording a passage across water, bridge	(figuratively referring to a place) means of approach, stepping-stone (to another place)

Bosworth is correct, and the two terms can be used interchangeably, the physical structure being referred to by both terms would seem to be similar to a bridge or gangway rather than a ladder.

At least that is how the translators of Arrian and Diodorus view the two terms. Table 2 shows translations of the terms as they relate to both the siege of Tyre (from Arrian Book 2 and Diodorus Book 17) and the siege of Massaga (from Arrian Book 4).[7]

The translators refer to both terms as bridges, gangways, ramps, or gangplanks as opposed to ladders, the only exception being the P. A. Brunt translation of *epibathra* for the siege of Massaga. However, Bosworth argues that since both *gephura* and *epibathra* are synonymous, both are a type of scaling ladder. The reason this is important will become clear in chapter 16, which discusses differences between Arrian and Diodorus in their descriptions of the final assault on Tyre. Arguing that both *gephura* and *epibathra* refer to a type of scaling ladder will allow Bosworth to argue that the two accounts are in fact consistent.

The translation of the text in Arrian just prior to that referred to by Bosworth, 2.23.1-2, reads, "First, [Alexander] battered down the wall for a good space. But when the breach seemed wide enough, he ordered the engine-carrying ships to back water; and sent in two others, carrying his gangways [*gephuras*], which he intended to let fall where the wall was breached." Arrian is using the term *gephuras* to refer to the bridge or gangway the Macedonians would use to get from their ships onto the breach in Tyre's wall. The translation of the text in Diodorus referred to by Bosworth, 17.45.5, reads that the Tyrians "left the shelter of the walls and their positions within the towers to push out onto the very bridges [epibathras]." This seems to suggest that Diodorus is referring to bridges from the mole towers to the walls, rather than scaling ladders. In 17.46.2 Diodorus writes that Alexander "flung a bridge [epibathran][8] across from the wooden tower to the city walls and crossing by it alone gained a footing on the wall." Again, this seems to suggest a bridge from the mole towers to the walls. Diodorus uses the same term (epibathra) in 17.43.10 for bridges used by the Macedonians to get from the mole towers to the walls; these clearly would not have been scaling ladders.

More evidence suggesting that epibathra could refer to a gangway comes from the first century Roman architect and engineer Vitruvius. In his book On Architecture, written in Latin, Vitruvius records the following about Alexander's military engineer Diades: "Concerning the Climbing Machine, which in Greek is called epibathra and concerning the use, in naval engineering, of such a machine for boarding a ship he just made mention." Here Vitruvius has the understanding that an epibathra could be used in naval warfare for boarding an enemy ship during combat, suggesting a device more similar to a gangway than a ladder. The Loeb Classical Library edition of On Architecture contains an "Index of Technical Terms" in which epibathra is defined as "gangway."[9]

There are numerous additional examples suggesting that epibathra can be translated as "gangway" or "bridge." In the Oxford Classical Dictionary, Whitehead writes that Diades provided Alexander with "an assault-bridge (epibathra)." Jan Stronk's translation of Diodorus's account of the siege of Tyre says "the Macedonians moved up towers of the same height as the walls and from them fastened assault-bridges to the walls." Stronk adds in a footnote: "See also Vitruvius . . . on the assault-bridges (epibathra), which Vitruvius calls both ascendens machina ('climbing machine') and an accessus ('entry'): Vitr. 10.13.3, 8." A passage from Plutarch's Life of Demetrius (8.2) translated by Bernadotte Perrin reads, "one of his friends said to Antigonus that they must keep [Athens], if they took it, in their own hands, since it was a gangway [epibathran] to Greece. But Antigonus would not hear of it; he said that the goodwill of a people was a noble gangway [epibathran] which no waves could shake." In describing Byzantine siege towers, Christos Makrypoulias writes, "The middle platform (or top one, if the tower was level with the enemy wall), was equipped with a drawbridge (epibathra or diabathra) over which assault troops would storm the battlements." Fred-

TABLE 2.

Source	Translations of	
	γέφυρα (*gephura*)	ἐπιβάθρα (*epibathra*)
Arrian 2.23.4 (Siege of Tyre)		
Arrian (P. A. Brunt, trans.)	gangways	
Martin Hammond	ramps	
James Romm	gangways	
(Pamela Mensch, trans.)		
Diodorus 17.45.5 (Siege of Tyre)		
Diodorus of Sicily		bridge
(C. Bradford Welles, trans.)		
Arrian 4.26.6 (Siege of Massaga)		
Arrian (P. A. Brunt, trans.)	bridge	
Martin Hammond	drawbridge	
James Romm	bridge	
(Pamela Mensch, trans.)		
E. J. Chinnock	bridge	
Arrian 4.27.1 (Siege of Massaga)		
Arrian (P. A. Brunt, trans.)		step-ladder
Martin Hammond		drawbridge
James Romm		gangplank
(Pamela Mensch, trans.)		
E. J. Chinnock		bridge

erick Winter writes, "The engineers of Dionysios I 'invented' the non-torsion catapult, and later, during the siege of Motya, almost fortuitously developed the combination of wheeled siege-tower, or *helepolis*, and boarding-bridge, or *epibathron*." In describing the siege towers of Dionysius, Whitehead writes, "They were equipped with gangways (*epibathrai*), allowing troops to cross into the city." In discussing the work of the first century AD architect and engineer Apollodorus of Damascus, Whitehead translates *epibathra* as "flying bridges." In discussing the lack of detail in the ancient sources about any of Alexander's siege engines, Campbell writes, "Nor are there any instructions regarding the gangplank or boarding-bridge (*epibathra*) that must have been extended from the tower to carry the storm troops across to the enemy battlements."[10]

Bosworth goes on to argue that the *epibathra* "looks like an anticipation of the famous *sambycae* [*sambucae*] which were later used by Marcellus against Syracuse and by Mithridates against Rhodes.[11] These were large scaling ladders, carried between two vessels lashed together and raised by a pulley system on the mastheads." Bosworth says, "Alexander's ἐπιβάθραι [*epibathrai*] seem to have been raised from a specially constructed wooden turret (Diod. 45.2; cf. Athen. Mech. 10.10, 15.5) not from masthead pulleys. The principle, however, seems to have been the same—ship-borne ladders raised mechanically to the height appropriate for storming the walls."[12] The reference Bosworth gives for the "specially constructed wooden turret" (Diodorus 45.2) reads: "Alexander mounted the stone-throwing catapults in proper places and made the walls rock with the boulders that they threw. With the dart throwers on the wooden towers he kept up a constant fire of all kinds of missiles and terribly punished the defenders of the walls." It isn't clear from this reference where Bosworth's idea of wooden turrets comes from. It seems likely that he is referring to the "wooden towers," which he is assuming are located on the ships.

Whitehead and Blyth disagree with Bosworth's interpretation. They consistently translate *epibathran* as "assault bridge," and argue that Bosworth "may not be correct" in combining Arrian 4.26.5 with what follows "into a description of a single machine." Heckel refers to them as "landing ramps" and says they were similar to the "crows" (*corvus*) "later used by the Romans against Carthaginian ships." Tarn writes that "the first boarding-bridges known are those used by Alexander at Tyre. Alexander's bridges were carried on two merchant ships, which could stand the weight, and were lowered on to the wall where part of it had been breached, thus enabling picked troops to assault."[13]

Based on Bosworth's argument that ship-mounted siege ladders in wooden turrets were used at Tyre, English writes: "Alexander apparently also had triremes lashed together and siege towers built on their decks. . . . These would have been equipped with scaling ladders that were raised from a turret, not unlike the larger naval siege towers, the intention being that the artillery would lay down a suppressing fire against the defenders and allow the marines to climb the walls unhindered."[14] This all seems quite speculative and is based on the interpretation of a single Greek term as either a gangway or a siege ladder.

However, there are two more problems with the idea that red-hot sand was poured down on soldiers climbing up ship-mounted scaling ladders. If, as Bosworth suggests, these ladders came not from the ships' decks but from wooden towers, then it is likely they would have reached across from the tops of the towers to the wall (or to the pile of rubble filling the breach

in the wall), in effect more of a gangway or bridge than a ladder. Any climbing that would have to be done by the soldiers would be up the ship-
mounted siege tower, rather than up a scaling ladder. All of the ancient
accounts seem consistent with men scrambling across a bridge to reach the
wall rather than climbing a ladder.

The second problem with the idea of pouring red-hot sand on men
climbing scaling ladders is this: even if the ladders were, as Bosworth argues,
proto-*sambucae*, and rose from the ships' decks rather than from atop a
tower, the *sambuca* that Polybius describes provided quite a lot of protection
for the men using it. Polybius writes:

> These engines are constructed as follows. A ladder was made four feet broad
> and of a height equal to that of the wall when planted at the proper dis-
> tance. Each side was furnished with a breastwork, and it was covered in by
> a screen at a considerable height. . . . At the summit of the ladder there is a
> platform protected on three sides by wicker screens, on which four men
> mount and face the enemy resisting the efforts of those who from the bat-
> tlements try to prevent the *sambuca* from being set up against the wall. As
> soon as they have set it up and are on a higher level than the wall, these
> men pull down the wicker screens on each side of the platform and mount
> the battlements or towers.[15]

In other words, if Alexander's men had an actual *sambuca* as described
by Polybius, the top of the ladder would have been above the wall, and protected by screens, preventing red-hot sand from being poured down on the
men climbing up.

One final concern about Bosworth's proposed ship-mounted siege ladders is worth noting. Bosworth bases much of his analysis on Diodorus's
account of the siege. There is some question about the reliability of
Diodorus's explanation of the final assault on Tyre, particularly on the issue
of whether the final attack, led by Alexander in person, was from the sea,
via breaches made in the wall by ship-mounted rams, or from the mole, via
bridges from the towers to the wall.

Tarn argues that Diodorus's account of the siege poses a problem in that
it combines the actual events, which Tarn refers to as the "good" account,
with events taken from stories of other sieges, which Tarn calls the "land
siege" account. In the good account, Tarn writes, "Alexander, working from
ships, throws down part of the wall and breaks in, which is near enough to the
truth; here the main account stops, but is taken up again and supplemented."

Later, Tarn continues, "Diodorus has begun a quite different story." In this second account we get a land siege "with a description of all the wonderful machines proper to a land siege which the Tyrians used or invented." Tarn argues that the "good" account "has had dovetailed into it an account which does not belong to Tyre at all. At the end, the two accounts are contaminated." In the new account, "the boarding-bridge [Alexander] enters by is not borne on shipboard, as in the 'good' tradition, but starts from a wooden tower up against the wall . . . the fall of Tyre is duplicated to get in the boarding-bridge as part of the [land siege]."[16]

Bosworth dismisses Tarn's concerns, arguing that Tarn's view is "a bizarre hypothesis and is based on misconceptions." According to Bosworth, the tower from which Alexander attacks the wall in Diodorus's narrative is located on a ship rather than on the mole, and thus is not part of any "land siege."[17]

On the question of whether Alexander's assault ships carried gangways or ladders at Tyre, Murray takes the position that both were used, writing that Diades demonstrated the ability at Tyre "to fit catapults, *landing bridges, ladders, and assault towers* to the decks of warships."[18] (emphasis added) Murray's support for this statement is his own 2008 paper in which he writes about Diades's "known ability to fit catapults, landing bridges, ladders and assault towers to the decks of warships at Tyre."[19] Murray gives no specific example of a ladder or assault tower being used on the deck of a warship at Tyre, and his statement may just reflect what we know about subsequent Hellenistic siege techniques, such as Bosworth's mention of the later *sambuca*. Murray also writes that based on the ancient authors Athenaeus and Vitruvius, we know about Diades's "'so-called drill,' his 'raven,' his assault bridge, his covered battering ram mounted on wheels, and his portable siege towers."[20] In listing Diades's known inventions, Murray mentions an "assault bridge" but does not mention a ladder.

Murray may simply be repeating Bosworth's argument: that Diodorus's *epibathra* represents a shipboard tower or turret with a siege ladder. Murray argues that Alexander "started with a core of warships whose crews and commanders knew . . . how to attack city walls from ladders mounted on the bows of their ships."[21] However, the suggestion by Murray that both "landing bridges" and "ladders" would be used on assault ships at Tyre seems puzzling, since the landing bridges would be used to allow the assaulting infantry to get from the ship onto the rubble of a breached wall, whereas the ladders would be used to scale a still-intact wall. It is possible that Murray is basing his argument—that Alexander's commanders knew how to attack city walls from ladders mounted on the bows of their ships—on a statement by Arrian concerning events following the siege of Miletus. Arrian writes, "With [Miletus] now under control, Alexander sailed in person against those who had fled to the islet, ordering ladders to be brought to the bows of the triremes, so as to disembark from the ships on the cliffs of the island as if on a city wall."[22] The word translated here as "ladders" is *klimakas*, Greek for "ladders," rather than *epibathra*. The fact that Alexander's men might have used ordinary ladders to get from their ships up some steep cliffs along the shore of an island doesn't suggest they could do so against the high walls at Tyre.

In his book *The Age of Titans*, Murray also argues that there is evidence that catapults were placed "on shipboard wooden towers" at Tyre in 332, citing Diodorus 17.45.2.[23] However, Diodorus 17.45.2 (in the Loeb Classical Library edition) reads "Alexander mounted the stone-throwing catapults in proper places and made the walls rock with the boulders that they threw. With the dart throwers on the wooden towers he kept up a constant fire of all kinds of missiles and terribly punished the defenders of the walls." There is no mention that the towers are on a ship. In fact, just prior to this passage, Diodorus seems to make it clear that the towers are on the mole, writing (17.43.5), "Now the causeway had reached the wall and made the city mainland, and sharp fighting took place along the walls." He adds (17.43.7), "When the Macedonians moved up towers as high as the walls and in this way, extending bridges [*epibathras*], boldly assaulted the battlements, the Tyrians fell back on the ingenuity of their engineers and applied many counter-measures to meet the assault." As with his statements about shipboard ladders at Tyre, Murray seems to be following the argument made by Bosworth that towers with "bridges" (*epibathras*), the term that Bosworth translates as siege ladders, would be located on a ship. In my own research, I have found no evidence that towers were used on ships at Tyre.[24]

Adrian Goldsworthy also argues for both boarding bridges and scaling ladders. He writes that "a breach was made, and an assault launched from scaling ladders and ramps mounted on a ship," adding that "the main assault was ... spearheaded by two ships mounting ladders (like those on fire engines)."[25] This adopts Bosworth's *sambuca* argument, although Bosworth suggests that the breach may have simply been to knock the parapet away from the top of the wall.

The question remains: did the Macedonians use ladders at Tyre—not boarding bridges or gangways, but ladders that would allow the Tyrian defenders to pour red-hot sand down onto soldiers as they struggled to climb

up to the top of the wall? The ancient Greeks had a word for ladder—
κλῖμαξ (klimax)—defined in *The Cambridge Greek Lexicon* as "ladder (esp.
for ascending to a roof, scaling city walls, descending fr. a ship)." This is the
word Arrian uses in describing the final Macedonian assault on the wall at
Gaza, which was besieged and captured by Alexander shortly after leaving
Tyre. Arrian writes about the siege of Gaza, ". . . battered as [the wall] was
with his engines, so that it was not hard to make the assault with ladders
[*klimaxin*] over the fallen parts. So the ladders [*klimakes*] were set against
the wall."[26]

Since Arrian never uses the term *klimax* in connection with the assault
on Tyre's walls, it seems clear that these ladders used at Gaza were different
from the boarding bridges and gangways required at Tyre. At Gaza, the
Macedonians were attacking from atop a large mound, making the use of
ordinary scaling ladders practicable. Had the Gazans possessed red-hot
sand, they would doubtlessly have poured it down on the Macedonian soldiers as they climbed up the scaling ladders, as English suggests. This seems
unlikely to have happened at Tyre.

In the end, the only certainty about the use of ladders at Tyre is this: a
great deal of uncertainty has been caused by the scholarly interpretation
(or misinterpretation) of two obscure words from ancient Greek, γέφυρα
(*gephura*) and ἐπιβάθρα (*epibathra*). As will be clear in the next few chapters, Alexander's soldiers were somehow able to get from their ships onto
the rubble of a breach in Tyre's wall by the use of a *gephura* and/or *epibathra*.
Whether these are called gangways, boarding bridges, or ladders made little
difference to the men who had to scramble across them into battle. Whatever they are called, it seems unlikely that red-hot sand would have played
much of a role in defending against the final assault on Tyre.

FIFTEEN

DESPERATE MEASURES

Tyre was now completely blockaded, cut off from outside aid, and under constant attack from the mole and the ship-borne siege machines. The Tyrians fought back with great skill and courage. Diodorus, and to a lesser extent Curtius, spend much of their siege accounts discussing the varied and novel defensive tactics used by the Tyrians. Diodorus writes that the Tyrians relied on their engineers to come up with a variety of clever devices to counter whatever the Macedonian tried. Curtius writes that the Tyrians were able to develop many new and unusual methods of defending the city due to "necessity, more inventive than any art." The fact that both authors attribute many of the same defensive tactics to the Tyrians may mean the accounts were based on common source material. However, Tarn argues that Curtius used Diodorus as a source for his account of the siege of Tyre, writing that "Curtius has introduced from Diodorus an isolated statement which in Diodorus makes sense but in his own account makes no sense of any kind." Tarn adds (somewhat awkwardly), "If then, as seems certain, Curtius read and used Diodorus, how much did he use him? ... The conclusion must be that Curtius can only have used Diodorus much as he did so many writers—just as and when, and as much or as little as, he chose."[1]

Some of the Tyrian defensive measures seem conventional. We are told that the Tyrians (1) poured flaming liquid, dropped stones, and hurled javelins; (2) attached sharp concave blades to the ends of long poles and used them to cut ropes supporting Macedonian rams; (3) modified catapults to allow them to throw out pieces of red-hot metal; (4) dragged Macedonians over the edge of their towers using things called crows, ravens, and iron hands; and (5) fastened sharpened blades and hooks to wooden beams that they then dropped onto Macedonian ships.[2]

Diodorus writes that the Tyrians also sewed up leather sacks using hides and animal skins, filled them with seaweed, and hung them over the wall to cushion it against Macedonian stones and missiles. In this way it was able to absorb the force of the stones from the Macedonian stone-throwing catapults and prevent damage to the wall. This use of hides stuffed with seaweed apparently caught the attention of the Greek writer Philon, who included it as advice in his third-century treatise on siege tactics, telling his readers to protect their walls by using "nets woven out of ropes and filled with seaweed." Seaweed had the double benefit of cushioning the blow and protecting against fire. Concerning this advice, Whitehead writes, "Since [the use of seaweed] acquired such celebrity in the telling, it may well be that the maritime defenders' use of seaweed—where others would have naturally turned to chaff, wool or the like . . . gave rise to the generic advice in the Hellenistic and later theoretical literature."[3]

Diodorus discusses other Tyrian responses that seem puzzling. He writes that they made large, metal, barbed tridents, and they used these at close range to throw at the Macedonians in their towers.[4] These tridents had ropes attached, and they stuck in the shields of the Macedonian defenders, forcing them to either abandon their shields or be pulled off the towers to their deaths. That these weapons were used at close range suggests that the towers were so close to the wall that the Tyrians could throw the tridents by hand with enough force to have them penetrate the shields of the Macedonians. We know that this occurred with the *pila* of Roman legionaries, where the head of a *pilum* would bury itself in an enemy shield, and a barb prevented it from being pulled out. But why would the Macedonians on the towers have to rely on individual shields for protection from Tyrian missiles? Wouldn't there have been wooden screens to shield the men working the catapults? The tridents seem like a lot of effort just to remove Macedonian shields, and it seems inconceivable that a soldier would refuse to relinquish a shield and be pulled to his death. Perhaps the Macedonians were taken by surprise, and the trident ropes were jerked back so suddenly there was no time to let go of the shields?

Another puzzling story told by Diodorus is that the Tyrians threw fishing nets over the Macedonians as they were attacking across the assault bridges. These nets entangled the attackers, and the Tyrians were able to pull them off the bridge to their deaths. It is difficult to imagine this scene—a group of Macedonian soldiers running across a bridge connecting a tower to the wall, and the Tyrian defenders throwing fishing nets at them. Wouldn't the bridges have had some sort of railing to keep the men from falling off the side, similar to the railings on both sides of the Roman *corvus*, which was used as a bridge to board enemy ships? Campbell writes that "the troops crossing the bridge required protection along the flanks, and a waist-height wickerwork fence would have had the added benefit of preventing men from stumbling off the edge."[5] And to the extent Tyrian defenders had the time to throw nets at the attackers, wouldn't shooting arrows be more effective? It is possible this story became garbled over time and originally referred to nets that the Tyrians strung across the top of the wall as a way of delaying the attackers, similar to the way nets were used to repel boarders on the wooden ships of the eighteenth-century AD British Royal Navy.

Tarn has a theory about why many of the stories Diodorus tells about the siege of Tyre seem to be out of place or to not quite fit with the rest of the accounts. In Tarn's view, Diodorus has combined two accounts, one that corresponds with Arrian's and a second, which Tarn calls the "land siege account." In this second account, writes Tarn, "we get a land siege . . . with a description of all the wonderful machines proper to a land siege which the Tyrians used or invented." The real account "has had dovetailed into it an account which does not belong to Tyre at all." N. G. L. Hammond disagrees with Tarn's view and argues "the account of D[iodorus] is continuous and coherent (its historical truth is not under consideration) and comes from one source."[6]

By far the most implausible defensive measure described by Diodorus has to be the marble wheels. He writes that "the Tyrians rigged marble wheels in front of the walls and causing these to rotate by some mechanism they shattered the flying missiles of the catapults and, deflecting them from their course, rendered their fire ineffective."[7] In another place he writes, "Against the projectiles from the catapults they made wheels with many spokes, and setting these to rotate by a certain device, they destroyed some of the missiles and deflected others, and broke the force of all."[8] It is difficult to even imagine how these wheels could be made of marble, be large enough to provide some meaningful protection, and be rotated fast enough to break up the bolts and stones fired from the Macedonian torsion catapults.

If we drop the idea they were made of marble, then perhaps something along the lines of a giant chariot wheel could have been rigged up, turned by a large crank and pulley mechanism, and speeded up using gears. Spinning fast enough, it might have allowed the Tyrians to look through the spinning spokes, as through an aircraft propeller, while breaking up any missiles that tried to penetrate the wheel. However, once again the effort involved would not seem to justify such a device, as a wooden screen with viewing ports would have worked just as well.

English explains what he sees as a possible reason for this device. The Tyrians "set up what would have looked like windmills along some stretches of the walls; these continuously rotating devices would act as anti-catapult weapons. . . . This was an extremely clever device and was in some ways more effective than a simple screen as it would allow the defenders to fire when the gaps between the blades were in front of them." English seems to envision something similar to the synchronization gear on World War I aircraft that allowed the machine gun to shoot through the airplane's spinning propeller blades. However, if the Tyrians' wheel was spinning fast enough to prevent the Macedonian missiles—fired at a high velocity from torsion catapults—from penetrating the spinning spokes of the wheel, it isn't clear how the Tyrians would be able, absent a synchronization gear of their own, to time their return fire to miss the same fast-spinning spokes. Patrick Romane suggests the wheels may have been "mounted on the front of catapults, allowing the projectiles to shoot through the hub, but protecting the engineers manning the machine."[9] Opening a hatch to fire through a wooden screen seems a lot easier.

However, English isn't the only scholar to accept Diodorus's spinning marble wheel story. Bosworth seems to think the revolving wheels are plausible. Lane Fox also accepts without further comment that the Tyrians "set up large wheels of marble which they revolved with an unspecified mechanism; their whirring spokes were enough to break the missiles' course." In contrast, Fuller suggests "most of the remarkable devices attributed to [the Tyrians] by Diodorus are fictitious." None of these devices are mentioned by Arrian. Tarn argues that "among the devices the Tyrians use in the land siege account are some things which, so far as I know, are never mentioned in any Hellenistic siege." He mentions the fishing nets, the marble wheels, and the red-hot sand. "All these, indeed, may be only suggestions made in technical literature." Tarn argues that Diodorus's account of the siege reads as if he "were copying, as he probably was, from some text-book on Hellenistic siege warfare at large."[10]

Regardless of how clever and inventive their defenses were, the Tyrians kept looking for outside help. They had been holding out for months. Surely someone—Carthage or Persia—would come to their aid. Curtius writes that thirty envoys from Carthage arrived at Tyre but provided no help, nor could they promise any in the future. Apparently Carthage was fighting its own war in the western Mediterranean and was unable to spare any ships or men for Tyre. According to Curtius, Syracuse had invaded Africa, and the Syracusan army was besieging Carthage.[11] The story of the arrival of the Carthaginian envoys is clearly out of order here, since they would not have been able to get past the tight blockade of the harbors, and there was no other way into Tyre.

With respect to the Carthaginians' excuse—that the city was under siege by Syracuse—Atkinson points out that the Syracusans' campaign against Carthage was not begun until 310, and therefore could not have been the reason for Carthage not sending aid to Tyre during Alexander's siege in 332. "Curtius frees himself from chronological constraints in order to explain Carthage's failure to send military assistance." In another out-of-order passage, Curtius writes that despite the knowledge that no help would be coming from Carthage, the Tyrians didn't despair but instead had the Carthaginian envoys escort Tyrian wives and children to safety back in Carthage.[12] Atkinson points out that had Carthage been undergoing a siege at the same time, it would have made little sense for Tyre to send its women and children to that city.[13]

Interestingly, the siege of Carthage by Syracuse in 310 serves to illustrate the strong bond that existed between Carthage and its mother city Tyre. Manuel Alvarez Marti-Aguilar writes that during that later siege, the Carthaginians attributed their misfortune to the anger of Herakles, "since after the growth of the city they had abandoned the ancient custom of sending a tenth of the public revenues to [Tyre]." To attempt to placate the god, the Carthaginians sent money and other offerings to Tyre.[14]

To show how desperate the Tyrians were becoming, Curtius writes that some of them began proposing a renewal of the practice of sacrificing children to the god Saturn, the Roman name for the Phoenician god Moloch, a practice that had been discontinued for many years. Curtius explains to his readers that he personally thinks this practice of sacrificing children is displeasing to the gods and that he views it as a sacrilege and not a sacrifice.

He also writes that the practice of sacrificing children continued in Carthage until that city was destroyed. A footnote in the Loeb Classical Library edition of Curtius states that the practice "was continued in Roman Carthage in spite of the opposition of the Romans." Atkinson writes that "the immolation of children had been a common practice amongst the Phoenicians" but that opposition "had built up in the late eighth and early seventh centuries and may, as Curtius writes, have stopped the ritual." The sacrifice of children by Phoenicians, both eastern and western, to the extent it occurred, "was the *extrema ratio* chosen in critical situations or to prevent or ward off future dangers."[15] The situation at Tyre may have seemed appropriate. We don't know whether any children were actually sacrificed at Tyre.

At this point, Curtius chooses to include the story of the sea monster that was told earlier by Diodorus. Atkinson writes that the story "has more to do with romance than history." In Curtius's version of the story, the largest sea monster anyone has ever seen leaps out of the water and flops up onto the mole, where the Tyrians and Macedonians could see it. The monster then plunges back into the sea and disappears beneath the waves. This event was interpreted by both sides as a reason for rejoicing. The Macedonians saw it as a sign that their mole was heading in the right direction and they should keep going. The Tyrians thought it was a sign from Neptune that the mole would soon be destroyed.[16]

Then Curtius writes something quite odd. The Tyrians were so smitten by the idea of the sea monster as an omen of impending victory that they used it as an excuse for a celebration, and they began eating and drinking to excess. When sunrise came, and they were still drunk, they decorated their ships with flowers and rowed them out of the harbors.[17] That the Tyrians would take their ships out of the harbors at this time makes no sense, since they were blockaded by Alexander's fleet. However, in the next section of his account, Curtius describes a naval sortie made by the Tyrians that caught the Macedonians and their Phoenician and Cypriot allies literally napping. The story of Tyrians celebrating and feasting may simply be Curtius's way of leading into the naval encounter that follows, although perhaps with more romance than history.

Because the mole bisected the channel between Tyre and the mainland, the two squadrons of Alexander's fleet—the Cypriots in the north and the Phoenicians in the south—were effectively separated from one another. Each was unable to quickly support the other in the event of an attack. The Tyrians, of course, noted this, and they also noted a curious regularity in the Macedonian routine: every midday, the crews of the blockading ships would row to shore for rest and a meal. The procedure for anchoring a trireme on shore in this manner is described by Harrison: "Triremes were almost certainly brought to shore stern first, the very manner in which smaller boats had been brought to land in earlier times. . . . It is evident from representations of triremes in ancient art that the curved stern was well suited to easing up against a beach; the prow, with its projecting ram was not."[18] While the crews of the ships were eating their meal and resting on the beach, Alexander would retire to his tent, which was on the shore south of the mole.

The Tyrians decided to exploit this opportunity and attack the ships while they were anchored on shore. The plan was to secretly assemble an attacking squadron in the north harbor and to quickly sally out against the ships from Cyprus, destroying them on the beach. To screen their intentions, the Tyrians raised sails on the masts of the triremes blocking the harbor mouth. At midday, with the Cypriot ships anchored on the beach, and Alexander retired to his tent, the Tyrians struck. Their squadron consisted of three quinqueremes, three quadriremes, and seven triremes, thirteen ships in all. Only the most-skilled rowers manned the oars, and the well-armed marines on deck were the best fighters in the fleet. Relying on stealth to take the Cypriot ships unawares, the Tyrians rowed quietly out of the harbor in single file, with no one calling out the strokes for the rowers. Bosworth argues that this silent rowing was a technique requiring great skill on the part of the rowers, and that the lack of these specially trained men was the factor that limited the size of the squadron sent out by the Tyrians.[19] This may be what Arrian means when he writes that the rowers were the most skilled in Tyre.

Once clear of the harbor, the ships all turned as one and raced for the shore, oars moving with a quick rhythm, men now shouting and calling out the stroke. The attack was so sudden and unexpected that it caught some of the Cypriot ships unmanned, while the crews of others scrambled back onto their ships in confusion. The Tyrians sank three quinqueremes and drove the rest of the Cypriot ships onto the shore, where they broke apart.[20]

The attack was a brilliant success, but unfortunately for the Tyrians, the goddess Fortune intervened—or perhaps it was Neptune-Poseidon. Instead of taking his usual midday rest in his tent, Alexander had decided to return early to the ships. As soon as he spotted the Tyrian attack, he gave orders to quickly man the Phoenician ships anchored on the shore south of the mole. As each ship was manned, he sent them racing off. The first ships he directed to the southern harbor to make sure no Tyrians sallied out in another attack.

Once the southern harbor was blockaded, he assembled a small squadron of quinqueremes and triremes, quickly got their crews on board, and set out to sail around the island to reach the Tyrians fighting on the north side of the mole.[21]

The Tyrians continued to attack the Cypriot ships, unaware that Alexander was hurrying around the island to intercept them. The men on the city walls tried to signal their comrades and alert them to the danger, but they were too far away to be heard above the din of battle. The Tyrian ships only spotted Alexander's squadron as it rounded the north end of the island and came bearing down on them, at which point the Tyrians broke off their attack and turned back, rowing fast for the safety of the harbor. Most of them didn't make it, as Alexander's ships tore into them, ramming and disabling some and boarding others. A quinquereme and quadrireme were boarded and captured just outside the harbor. Although their ships were sinking, most of the Tyrian sailors and marines were able to swim safely back to the harbor.[22] Curtius writes that Alexander pursued the Tyrian ships, but although he captured or sank almost all of them, the volume of arrows and catapult bolts from Tyre's walls prevented his ships from entering the harbor.[23] Without the presence of their own ship-mounted catapults, the Macedonians would have no way to counter the missile fire from Tyre's walls and would have no protection on the open decks of the warships.

Like the fireship attack on the mole, the Tyrians had once again caught Alexander unprepared and made him pay a heavy price for his inattention. But the loss of so many Tyrian ships was a disaster for the defenders. Alexander had plenty of ships to replace his losses, and he would continue his strategy of using the ship-mounted siege machines to probe Tyre's defenses for a weak point.

There had to be one. With Fortune's favor, Alexander would find it.

SIXTEEN

THE BREACH

Day after day, Alexander's catapults worked to keep the battlements of Tyre clear while his rams relentlessly pounded the city's walls. The attacks came from rams at the end of the recently completed mole, from catapults and archers atop the great mole towers, and from ships converted into floating platforms supporting rams and catapults. But nothing the Macedonians could do seemed to be having any effect. It was now high summer, and the siege had been going on for seven months. The Tyrians may have been getting low on food, but they had water enough stored in underground cisterns carved into the island's rock. Sometime after the beginning of the Iron Age, writes Stanley Gevirtz, "slaked lime plaster came to be employed as an effective seal in the lining of cisterns for the collection and storage of rain water." Without that development "the island of Tyre, dependent upon outside sources for the bulk of its drinking water," would have been vulnerable to a siege.[1]

The Tyrians must have been hoping that help would eventually come from Carthage, notwithstanding the questionable story told by Curtius that

Carthage was under siege by an army from Syracuse. Or perhaps Darius would come with a Persian army. Or a plague would sweep through the Macedonian camp. Or another sea monster would destroy the mole. There was always hope. Tyre was not nearly ready to give up.

Both Diodorus and Curtius (who may have used Diodorus as a source) write that Alexander became discouraged. Curtius says Alexander's distress was due to weariness. He was tired of the siege and eager to get on with the conquest of Egypt. The lack of progress at Tyre was in sharp contrast to the speed with which he had conquered Asia Minor, and by languishing in Phoenicia, he was wasting the opportunity for greater glory elsewhere.[2] Diodorus writes that the only thing preventing Alexander from abandoning the siege was the realization his reputation would be tarnished if he left Tyre unconquered. The Tyrians would be seen to have defeated him—and that, for Alexander, the new Achilles, was unthinkable. When the question of abandoning the siege was discussed by a council of Macedonian generals, only one man supported Alexander's decision to continue. But apparently one was enough; the siege would go on.[3]

From this point in the siege, the accounts of Curtius and Diodorus diverge from that of Arrian in ways that make it difficult to reconcile the three narratives. Llewellyn-Jones, writing about contradictions in the Alexander histories in general, points out that "Arrian and Diodorus in particular seem to disagree on every detail." The Arrian narrative is often the one followed by modern scholars, such as Fuller and Lane Fox, in their histories of Alexander. However, Bosworth argues that there are times Arrian—in an attempt to minimize the difficulties faced by the Macedonians in the final assault—may have combined events that are reported separately by Curtius or Diodorus.[4] Because Arrian's account is so different from the other two and seems to be less problematic, the rest of this chapter is based on Arrian. The narratives of Curtius and Diodorus will be covered in the next chapter. (For a line-by-line comparison of the three end-of-siege accounts, see appendix B.)

After the surprise sortie by the Tyrian ships had been beaten back, the Macedonians continued their assault from the mole, but with no success— the wall at that point was simply too strong for either rams or high towers to overcome. At the same time, the ship-mounted rams worked their way steadily along the wall to the north of the mole, on both sides of the harbor entrance, probing for weak points. They found none. If Alexander was discouraged, as claimed by Curtius and Diodorus, he didn't show it. The ship-mounted rams rowed around the island to the south side of the mole and began again, testing each point along the wall for weakness.[5] It was tedious, dangerous work, and the men must have hated it, never knowing when arrows, rocks, sharpened blades, or flaming objects would shower down on them from the high walls, to say nothing of red-hot sand.

Then, suddenly, all that changed. In P. A. Brunt's translation, Arrian writes that along one section of the south wall, near the harbor entrance, "the wall was first badly shaken and in part broken down by a rent." Pamela Mensch's translation of this same event reads, "the wall crumbled and was even breached in a small part." Martin Hammond's translation reads, "a large expanse of the wall was first shaken loose, and a part of it broke off and collapsed to the ground."[6] After seven months, Tyre's mighty wall was broken.

The rams that caused this breach were mounted on ships, an engineering achievement about which we know little. Although rams had been used by ancient armies long before Alexander, the first century Roman architect Vitruvius attributes their invention to a Tyrian engineer named Pephrasmenos during a siege of the Spanish city of Gadis (Cadiz) by the Carthaginians. The writings of later Roman historians—Josephus (first century AD) and Procopius (sixth century AD)—provide us with descriptions of Roman rams that are likely similar to those used by Alexander. Josephus writes that the ram was "an immense beam, like the mast of a ship, reinforced at its extremity with a mass of iron," while Procopius writes that the end of the ram is covered "with a large iron head, precisely as they cover the round point of a missile, or they sometimes make the iron head square like an anvil." These iron (or possibly bronze in Alexander's time) ram heads would have been carried in the engineering siege train along with the component parts for catapults and towers. The ram would have been suspended from a framework of heavy wooden beams, roofed over to protect both the ram and the men working it from missiles, rocks, and fire. Josephus explains that the ram "is suspended at its middle point by ropes, like the beam of a balance," while Procopius writes that the ram is suspended "from the top by means of chains which swing free."[7] The heavy ropes (or possibly chains) used to suspend the rams may have been carried in Alexander's siege train.

By constantly pounding the iron head of the ram against the same spot on the wall, the attackers could crack the stone blocks at the point of impact. Eventually, when enough of the stone had been reduced to rubble, the upper part of the wall would give way and collapse, which is apparently what happened at Tyre. Josephus states "there is no tower so strong, no wall so thick, as, even though it sustain the initial impact, to withstand the repeated assaults of this engine," and Procopius writes that the ram "by frequent blows is able quite easily to batter down and tear open a wall wherever it strikes."[8]

Alexander, never one to waste time, acted immediately, launching a quick assault on the breach. Arrian writes that he went so far as to "throw gangways [*gephuras*] over the broken part of the wall," but the Tyrians easily repulsed this weak attack.[9] This failure is understandable, since the breach must have come as a surprise to the Macedonians. They would not have had assault troops ready and waiting aboard ships, day after day. The spontaneous attack must have been by whatever nearby troops Alexander could scrape together to throw into the breach. The Tyrians could easily bring superior numbers to bear on the narrow space, and they held the high ground. But for Alexander it was a start.

The weather imposed a two-day delay on further attacks, which gave the Tyrians time to shore up the wall. But Alexander's rams returned and soon made short work of the repairs, enlarging the breach and battering down a large stretch of the wall. As soon as the breach was wide enough, the ram ships backed away and two assault ships surged forward.[10] These were specially modified and would have been roofed over to protect the soldiers from anything thrown or shot from Tyre's walls. The ships carried portable boarding bridges to allow the men to get quickly and safely from the ships and up onto the pile of rubble that would have filled the spot where the wall had collapsed. Arrian again refers to these boarding bridges as *gephuras*, translated in both the Loeb Classical Library edition and *The Landmark Arrian* as "gangways" and by Martin Hammond as "ramps." Like the later *sambucae* (see chapter 14) described by Polybius, they would likely have been protected along the sides by a screen or breastwork.[11] When the assault ships were anchored close to the pile of rubble, the gangways were lowered onto the remains of the wall, and the men on board charged up the ramp to confront the Tyrian defenders.

Bosworth takes a different view of the breach, arguing that it "need not imply that the wall was breached from top to bottom. Once the parapets had gone with their defenders . . . the ἐπιβάθραι [*epibathrai*] could be brought to bear on the walls without facing the gauntlet of red-hot sand, and the assault party could gain a foothold on the walls themselves."[12] It isn't clear why the defenders had to be "gone" along with the parapets. If there was no place for defenders to stand once the parapets were gone, how could the assault party "gain a foothold on the walls"? Furthermore, how would ship-mounted rams, which would be close to the level of the ship's deck, be able to destroy the parapets atop a wall that was likely over thirty feet high?[13] Finally, if Bosworth is correct, and the wall wasn't breached, Arrian's account of the first weak unsuccessful attack following the initial breach makes no sense. If the initial breach came as a surprise, the specially equipped assault ships with the siege ladders (Bosworth's *epibathrai*) would not have been standing by at the ready; if they had been, the first assault would not have been the weak and tentative attack that was beaten back. How the Macedonians would make the weak initial attack after merely knocking down part of the parapet is unclear.

Bosworth's theory requires the belief that either (1) the rams were mounted on the ships in such a way that they could reach the top of a very high wall, which seems implausible, (2) the pounding of the rams at the base of the wall would cause the parapets at the top of the wall to crumble and fall away, beyond the ability of the Tyrians to repair them, or (3) the stone-thrower catapults were powerful enough to destroy the parapets beyond the ability of the Tyrians to repair them, which seems inconsistent with the views of other scholars (discussed in chapter 13).

Bosworth's view is that Alexander's assault was from ships (as in Arrian) but was accomplished using siege ladders rather than bridges or gangways, consistent with his argument that Arrian's *gephurai* is the same as Diodorus's *epibathrai* and that both refer to an early example of the later *sambucae* described in chapter 14. Bosworth writes that Arrian's account, in his section 2.23.4, "is decisive that the object of the final assault was to gain control of the top of the wall, not pour through a breach from top to bottom by means of 'drawbridges.'" Bosworth's use of quotation marks around drawbridges seems to indicate that he views the word as a mistranslation. The account in Arrian 2.23.4 on which Bosworth bases his argument—that the Macedonian soldiers went up siege ladders to capture the top of a still-intact wall—reads as follows in *The Landmark Arrian* translation by Pamela Mensch: "When Alexander's ships approached the city and the gangways were thrown onto the wall from their decks, the shield-bearers used them to climb boldly onto the wall."[14] The Loeb Classical Library translation of this account by P. A. Brunt reads that the gangways "were let down on the wall" and the Shield Bearers "went down them gallantly on to the wall."[15] Bosworth views the soldiers as climbing to the top of an intact wall rather than onto a pile of rubble that was the remains of the wall.

Bosworth also argues that the account in Diodorus is not from a separate "land siege" story, as Tarn suggests. If correct, this means the account in Arrian must be the same as that in Diodorus, who writes that Alexander "flung a bridge [*epibathran*] across from the wooden tower to the city walls and crossing by it alone gained a footing on the wall." To reconcile the two accounts, Bosworth must argue that the "wooden tower" from which Alexander crosses to the wall is not located on the mole but is in fact on a ship or ships, and he states this explicitly, writing, "It is clear that towers could be transported on ships."[16] According to Bosworth, the two accounts—Arrian and Diodorus—are not describing different sieges, as argued by Tarn with his "land siege" hypothesis. However, it seems clear that in Diodorus's account something is "flung" across from "the wooden tower to the city walls," and it seems likely that whatever was flung would be more similar to a bridge than a ladder, since it is connecting a wooden tower to a wall. Everything about Bosworth's argument seems to relate back to his contention that (1) the word *gephurai* in Arrian has the same meaning as the word *epibathrai* in Diodorus, and (2) the word *epibathrai* in this context means a ladder and not a "drawbridge."

There are two additional problems with Bosworth's view that the final assault on Tyre was accomplished using *sambucae*-like siege ladders raised from shipboard turrets. If ship-mounted siege ladders were used to scale the wall—rather than ship-mounted rams battering it down—then (1) why did the siege take so long, and (2) why did the stones at the base of the wall need to be removed? Considering the first question—why did the siege take so long?—Murray writes that "the city fell to Alexander after a siege of only three to four months once his navy had been transformed." By the phrase "once his navy had been transformed," Murray seems to mean once the siege machines had been mounted on the ships. He explains "it was possible to shorten the siege of a coastal city by using the awesome new power of a naval siege unit against its harbor defenses." But if the Macedonian assault troops were able to scale Tyre's wall using shipboard siege ladders, why did that take three to four months? That long time would have been required for the ship-mounted rams to find and exploit a weak point in Tyre's wall. Arrian writes that the rams first tried the wall on the north side of the mole and then shifted to the south side, "testing the work at every point. It was here that the wall was first badly shaken and in part broken down by a rent."[17] Testing the work at every point was time consuming. But if, as Bosworth suggests, siege ladders were used to scale an intact wall, it isn't clear why that couldn't have been done anywhere along the wall.

The second question is: why did the stones at the base of the wall need to be removed? Using a ram against the wall would require the framework from which the ram was suspended to be as close to the wall as possible. The length to which the head of the ram could swing out from the framework (and out from the bows of the ships) was limited, and this meant that clearing away the stones at the base of the wall was necessary to allow the ram ships to anchor as close to the wall as possible. But if siege ladders were used instead, it was not necessary to anchor close against the wall. The ships could be several yards away from the base of the wall and still extend siege ladders—at an angle—up to the top of the wall. In fact, having the ladder set up at too vertical an angle would make it harder for the soldiers to climb, so reducing the angle of ascent would be beneficial regardless of the existence of a stone barrier at the base of the wall. The fact that the stones had to be removed before the shipboard siege machines could work effectively, and the fact that the siege continued for three or four months after the siege machines were installed on the ships, both argue for the idea that it was ship-mounted rams, rather than scaling ladders, that allowed Alexander's men to gain access to Tyre.

Considering the two accounts of the assault on the breach/wall in Arrian and Diodorus, and the arguments made by Tarn and Bosworth, it appears that the following are possible interpretations of the event:

1. (The Arrian-Tarn version) The wall was breached, creating a pile of rubble and an opening, and some sort of bridge or gangway was used by the soldiers to get from the ship onto the top of the rubble pile; no ship-mounted wooden tower was used; Diodorus's account of flinging the bridge from the wooden tower to the wall refers to the mole towers, and is from a different "land siege" story, following Tarn's hypothesis.

2. (The Arrian-Diodorus-Bosworth version) The wall was not breached, but the parapets were knocked away; a *sambuca*-like siege ladder extended from a tower (turret) on the assault ship to the top of the intact wall, and the soldiers climbed up the ladder to capture the wall; Diodorus's and Arrian's accounts agree, and there is no separate "land siege" account.

The balance of this chapter assumes that the first interpretation is correct, following the narratives in both Fuller and Lane Fox.[18] The second interpretation, based on the account in Diodorus and the use of a tower, will be dealt with in the next chapter.

According to Arrian, the ram ships made a breach in the wall near the southern harbor, and the Macedonians assaulted that breach from ships. Alexander appears to have hand picked the units to go in on the first wave from the assault ships. A unit of the Shield Bearers, commanded by a man named Admetos, manned one of the assault ships, while a unit from the phalanx, named by Arrian "the so-called *asthetairoi*," from the battalion of Koinos, manned the other, presumably armed with conventional spears rather than the long and unwieldly sarissa. Alexander was in the lead ship with the Shield Bearers.[19]

The meaning of "the so-called *asthetairoi*" in reference to the unit chosen from the phalanx is unclear. Romm writes: "The term *asthetairoi* has drawn much comment among scholars. It is found only in Arrian's *Anabasis Alexandrou*, in six passages . . . all of which clearly refer to some sort of elite infantry status. But just what troops fell under the heading *asthetairoi*, or what the term means, is unclear. Some editors of Arrian's text believe that in all these passages the word *asthetairoi* arose through scribal error and should be replaced."[20]

In order to draw Tyrian defenders away from the breach, Alexander ordered his triremes—presumably full of Phoenician or Cypriot marines and Macedonian soldiers—to row to the entrances of the harbors and attempt to force their way in while the Tyrians were busy fighting off the assault at the breach. He also ordered triremes with catapults and archers on board to circle around Tyre's walls to confuse the Tyrians as to where the Macedonians were going to strike. These ships were to stand by within catapult range and to "run ashore wherever possible."[21]

As soon as the assault ships were anchored close to the breach and the gangways from the ships were lowered onto what remained of the wall, the Shield Bearers went up the gangways and onto the wall, accompanied by Alexander. Admetos, the commander of the unit of Shield Bearers, was first off the ship and was killed while urging his men up onto the wall. Alexander and the men around him, whom Arrian calls "Companions" and which likely refers to the Shield Bearers, were able to capture part of the wall. Arrian attributes their success to the fact that their access to the wall was secure for the first time.[22] *The Landmark Arrian* translation by Pamela Mensch reads, "for the first time the Macedonians had an approach that was sturdy and not too steep." Commenting on this passage, Bosworth writes that the Macedonian catapults had cleared the wall of defenders but had also "loosened the masonry, making large strips dangerous for the attackers even to gain a foothold."[23]

The Macedonians cleared the wall of defenders, seized some towers, and descended into the city. Arrian writes that it "appeared that the descent into the city was easier" this way, which suggests that climbing down the pile of rubble filling the breach may have been difficult, particularly if under fire.[24] Given what we know about Tyrian defensive tactics, it is also likely that the Tyrians had constructed a second wall behind the breach and that to avoid this the Macedonians moved out along the wall and used stairs and towers to descend into the city at various points. Arrian's account suggests there was some way for the Macedonians to gain access to the top of the wall, and this is perhaps what led Bosworth to his view that the wall remained intact, and the attackers used either a ship-borne tower or a *sambuca*-like siege ladder to reach the top. However, it may simply be that the mound of stone and rubble filling the breach provided a way for the soldiers to scramble to the top, or that stairs remained intact on a portion of the wall near the breach.

As the Macedonians were capturing the wall at the site of the breach, Alexander's allied Phoenician ships assaulted the entrance to the southern harbor and forced their way inside, destroying a barrier boom and battering the Tyrian ships. At the other end of the island, the northern harbor, which did not have a boom, was captured by the ships from Cyprus. It isn't clear why the harbors were so easily captured at this point in the siege. It may be that most of Tyre's defenders had gone to the site of the breach, leaving the harbors weakly defended. Or it may be that once the Macedonians captured part of Tyre's wall, the defenders lost heart and abandoned the harbors. Arrian writes that most of the Tyrians fell back from the wall once they realized that the Macedonians had captured it.[25]

As Macedonian troops poured into the city, resistance collapsed, and Tyre was taken. After seven long months the siege was over. Somewhat ironically, the mole—which plays such a prominent role in the legend of the siege, and which still survives after twenty-three centuries as part of the isthmus linking Tyre and the mainland—played no part in the final capture of the city, at least in Arrian's account. The siege towers, thought by some to be among the tallest ever built, in the end weren't needed. Or were they? Diodorus and Curtius seem to tell a different story, one covered in the next chapter.

SEVENTEEN

THE LAND SIEGE

I n the account of the siege of Tyre written by Diodorus, many of the important events described by Arrian are omitted. There is no mention of the Tyrians attacking the mole towers with a fireship. There is no trip to Sidon by Alexander to gather a fleet from Phoenicia and Cyprus. And the Tyrians never sortie from their harbor and make a daring naval raid, catching the Macedonians napping. In this less-detailed account, the partially completed mole does get wrecked by a storm but is rebuilt stronger. When the mole comes within catapult range of the city, Alexander brings up stone throwers, light catapults, archers, and slingers to attack the walls. The Tyrians respond with what Diodorus describes as rotating spoked wheels to deflect and break up missiles, and the defenders catch the stones from the catapults in leather cushions hung from the walls. The Tyrians build a second wall five cubits behind the first, just in case the Macedonians break through.[1]

Following this description of Tyrian defensive measures, Diodorus writes that Alexander joined ships together to make floating platforms, mounted his siege machines on the ships, and with these managed to knock down a one-hundred-foot section (a *plethron*) of Tyre's wall. The Macedonians were able to gain access to the city through this opening, but their initial assault was beaten back by the Tyrians, who were able to shower the attackers with arrows, bolts, stones, and other types of missiles. During the night the Tyrians managed to rebuild the portion of the wall that had been knocked down. This seems to correspond with Arrian's account of the initial breach, in which Alexander's first weak and tentative attack was overcome by the Tyrian defenders.[2] If this initial breach was in fact one hundred feet long, it is inconsistent with Bosworth's argument that the later, successful breach involved knocking down only the parapet atop the wall. And the statement by Diodorus that "through this breach the Macedonians burst into the city" is also inconsistent with Bosworth's argument that the later, successful breach was exploited using ship-mounted siege ladders that reached the top of the wall.[3]

It is at this point that things diverge, both in the narratives of Arrian and Diodorus, and in the opinions expressed by modern Alexander scholars. Tarn has the view that at this point "Diodorus has begun a quite different story" from that of Arrian, "which I will call the land siege account."[4] By "land siege" Tarn apparently means that the story told by Diodorus (and Curtius to the extent he follows Diodorus) after this point appears to reflect the siege of a city that is not located on an island. Put another way, Tarn seems to be saying that this part of the story is a generic siege account that might apply to any city. Tarn goes on to express his opinion that "Diodorus personally, apart from his sources, was not a good historian; but that is well-known. Left to himself, he can say the most extraordinary things."[5]

Bosworth disagrees, writing that in his opinion Tarn's "land siege" view "is a bizarre hypothesis" and asserting that Tarn is basing his view on "misconceptions." In particular, Bosworth disagrees with Tarn's view that the wooden tower from which Diodorus has Alexander launch his attack was located on the mole; in Bosworth's opinion the tower was on a ship.[6] Bosworth considers the wooden tower to be a "wooden turret" from which a siege ladder can be raised from the ship to the wall.[7] N. G. L. Hammond also rejects Tarn's "land siege" view, arguing that "the account of D[iodorus] is continuous and coherent."[8]

According to Diodorus, following the failed assault on the breach, the Macedonians completed the mole and moved up "towers as high as the walls" and "extending bridges, boldly assaulted the battlements." Diodorus then lists more countermeasures devised by the Tyrians to meet this attack from the mole: tridents, fishing nets, and red-hot sand. They used javelins, stones, and flaming materials, let down long poles with cutting edges to cut the rams' ropes, discharged red-hot masses of metal, and used "crows" and "iron hands" to drag the Macedonians off the towers. Diodorus again mentions here the wheels and cushions that he had written about earlier, adding such details as that the wheels were made of marble and the cushions were made of hides and skins stuffed with seaweed.[9]

Diodorus then describes hand-to-hand fighting between the Tyrians and Macedonians that seems to clearly take place on bridges connecting the mole towers to the wall. The Tyrians "left the shelter of the walls and their position within the towers to push out onto the very bridges and match the courage of the Macedonians with their own valor. They grappled with the enemy and, fighting hand to hand, put up a stout battle for their city. Some of them used axes to chop off any part of the body of an opponent that presented itself."[10]

The last sentence seems odd and out of place—"used axes to chop off any part of the body." However, it leads to the next sentence, in which Diodorus writes that one of the Macedonian commanders, a man named Admetos, a strong and brave soldier, "died heroically, killed instantly when his skull was split by the stroke of an axe."[11] Recall that in Arrian's account, Admetos is the name of the commander of the unit of Shield Bearers that make the assault with Alexander against the breach in the wall, and he is killed leading that assault, not by an axe but by a spear. While it seems natural that Arrian would name the leader of the Shield Bearers who was killed leading the assault, it seems odd for Diodorus to throw out the name of a random Macedonian commander whose head was split by an axe while he was fighting from a bridge on a mole tower.

Bosworth, as with many other details in Diodorus's account, has a different opinion. "Either Diodorus has misplaced Admetos' death, or Arrian has fused together two actions in one. The latter is the more likely." Bosworth argues that there is no reason for the source used by Diodorus to add an "extra vivid detail," and that "Arrian does seem deliberately to minimize the difficulties of the final assault and the magnitude of Tyrian resistance." It would seem from Bosworth's statement that there is no reason for Diodorus's source to add an extra vivid detail that Bosworth does not consider red-hot sand causing Macedonians to shriek "supplications like those under torture" and to die with "excruciating agony" to be examples of added extra vivid detail. N. G. L. Hammond writes that "the description as a whole is highly colored and sensational."[12]

Goldsworthy, in his book *Philip and Alexander*, seems to combine episodes from both Arrian and Diodorus with no attempt to address the differences in the two accounts. For example, he writes that "a breach was made, and an assault launched from scaling ladders and ramps mounted on a ship." Here he accepts the idea of a breach in Tyre's wall but suggests that both scaling ladders *and* ramps were used to assault it. He is also unclear about exactly what Alexander's role was in the final assault, writing, "Alexander watched [the ship-borne assault] from a high tower, presumably on the causeway, but quickly joined the assault as rapid progress was made."[13] The idea that Alexander led an attack from a tower on the mole is consistent with the accounts of Diodorus and Curtius but not with the ship-borne *sambuca* argument made by Bosworth. It is also not consistent with Arrian's account of Alexander going in with the first wave from the assault ships. And it isn't clear what Goldsworthy means when he writes that Alexander "quickly joined the assault," since the assault described by Goldsworthy is taking place from ships.

Campbell seems to argue that the final assault took place simultaneously from both the assault ships—through a breach in the wall—and from the mole towers—onto the top of Tyre's wall. Campbell writes, "Troops were finally able to enter the town on its seaward side through breaches in the wall, while others crossed on gangways extended from the siege towers on the causeway."[14]

Goldsworthy also avoids dealing with differences in the accounts of the death of Admetos. Arrian writes that the Macedonian commander was killed with a spear while leading the Shield Bearers in their ship-borne assault on the breach. Diodorus describes fighting that occurs when Tyrians "push out onto the very bridges" (presumably bridges from the mole towers) to engage the Macedonians, and writes that the head of Admetos was split with an axe. Goldsworthy writes that "the officer leading the hypaspists was killed on top of the wall—either by a spear or when his head was split open by an axe, depending on the account." But the account of the axe in Diodorus makes no mention of Admetos leading the *hypaspists* in their assault on the breach and takes place prior to Tyre's wall being breached. Green also has Admetos killed with an axe while leading the attack from the assault ships, writing, "The commander of the spearhead, Admetos, had his skull split by an axe."[15]

At this point in his narrative, Diodorus writes that Alexander became discouraged but decided to press on with the siege. "Fitting out all his ships for fighting, he began a general assault upon the walls by land and sea. . . .

He saw that the wall on the side of the naval base was weaker than elsewhere and brought up to that point his triremes lashed together and supporting his best siege engines." This seems consistent with Arrian's account and not part of the "land siege" account of Tarn's hypothesis. However, in the next sentence things become confused again. We are told next that Alexander "performed a feat of daring which was hardly believable even to those who saw it. He flung a bridge across from the wooden tower to the city walls and crossing by it alone gained a footing on the wall." This is the assault that, in Bosworth's view, takes place from a ship rather than a mole tower, and the "bridge" that Diodorus mentions is in Bosworth's view actually a siege ladder that projects from a ship-mounted wooden turret onto the top of the still-intact wall.[16] Nowhere here does Diodorus write that a breach was made in the wall, or even that the wall's parapets had been knocked away, as Bosworth suggests. Diodorus writes that Alexander "saw that the wall on the side of the naval base was weaker than elsewhere," and in the next sentence he writes about Alexander crossing a bridge that had been flung from "the wooden tower to the city walls." It seems rather a stretch to view Alexander's crossing of a bridge from a tower to the wall as being somehow connected with a weaker wall near the naval base.

Following Alexander's crossing of the bridge to the wall, Diodorus writes, "*Simultaneously in another part of the city* the battering ram, put to its work, *brought down a considerable stretch of wall*; and *when the Macedonians entered through this breach and Alexander's party poured over the bridge on to the wall*, the city was taken."[17] (emphasis added) This sentence seems to make clear two points. First, an actual breach was made in the wall, in "another part of the city" from where Alexander was fighting on a bridge. Second, the Macedonians who "entered through this breach" were a different group from "Alexander's party" that "poured over the bridge on to the wall."

In the end, Bosworth's view reflects his attempt to reconcile the account of the capture of Tyre given by Diodorus with the way that Arrian describes the event, which is:

... by Alexander leading an assault from ships (perhaps equipped with towers)

... using gangways or boarding bridges (or perhaps siege ladders)

... through (or perhaps over) a breach (perhaps small);

... in Tyre's wall (or perhaps only the parapet);

... created by ship-mounted rams (or perhaps stone throwers).

The view that Alexander led an assault from the sea at the site of a breached wall seems to be the consensus of almost all Alexander scholars. The argument between Tarn and Bosworth is simply over whether Diodorus's account of the final assault is consistent with this story or reflects stories taken from another land-based siege in which towers and bridges play an important role.

N. G. L. Hammond has an interesting and slightly different interpretation of Diodorus's phrase "simultaneously in another part of the city." In Hammond's view, "from his ships A[lexander] fought his way onto the wall" while "'simultaneously in another part,' i.e., by land on the mole, the ram breached a piece of wall. . . . A[lexander]'s force and the Macedonians who used the breach [on the mole] both entered the city." Hammond argues that the ram on the mole succeeded in breaching Tyre's wall, and this allowed a force of Macedonians to enter the city at the same time as Alexander's seaborne assault.[18] As with Bosworth's view, this is an attempt to reconcile the words from Diodorus with Arrian's account of the assault.

Romane takes Diodorus and Curtius at face value, arguing that the final assault on Tyre was led by Alexander from the mole towers and that Alexander led his men across a bridge to capture the wall. This conclusion seems to be based on the idea that the two accounts must be correct and therefore Arrian's account has been misinterpreted by scholars. According to Romane, when Arrian writes that the Shield Bearers went up the gangways from the ships and onto the wall and that "Alexander too was there with them," Arrian is referring to Alexander being "there" on the mole tower fighting his way onto the wall at the same time. Romane writes: "The logic of the situation is plain: The main assault, the one in which the most labor and material were expended, was from the mole, through the towers, over the city wall. . . . Both Quintus Curtius and Diodorus are precise: Alexander fought from the tallest siege tower, and led the attack across a bridge to the city wall."[19] Most Alexander scholars do not agree.

The account of Curtius contains some of the elements from Diodorus, in particular the use of red-hot sand, "ravens" and "iron claws," and the idea that Alexander became discouraged and considered abandoning the siege.[20] Curtius also has the Macedonians making an early breach in Tyre's wall that gets quickly repaired, writing that on the day following the arrival of the Cypriot ships and the retreat of Tyre's ships into their harbors, "Alexander, bringing his fleet up to the city's defenses, shattered the walls on every side with artillery, and in particular by the battering of rams. The Tyrians hastily repaired the breaches by blocking them with rocks, and began also to build an inner wall." There is no mention of a Macedonian assault on the breaches. At this point, Curtius describes the sortie by the Tyrian ships from the north harbor and the sea battle that took place after Alexander raced around the island to cut them off from the city, although the details of this battle differ from Arrian's account.[21]

Two days later, writes Curtius, the Macedonians "were ordered to bring up both the fleet and at the same time the [siege] machines, in order that Alexander might terrify the enemy by an attack on all sides."[22] Arrian's account has the Macedonians waiting two days following the initial breach due to weather. According to Curtius, the two-day delay is to allow the soldiers time to rest.

After this, the account in Curtius diverges from Arrian and seems to follow Diodorus. Curtius writes that Alexander "himself mounted a very lofty tower." The fact that the tower is described as "very lofty" suggests it is on the mole, since the extraordinary height of both Tyre's wall opposite the mole and the towers necessary to overlook it are well-commented on by scholars. While towers on ships may have been possible, as Bosworth argues, it seems unlikely they were "very lofty." Bosworth considers the ship-mounted towers to be wooden turrets serving as bases for siege ladders. Concerning the "very lofty" tower in Curtius, Tarn writes, "This is the tower of Diodorus' land siege account; but Curtius, who has throughout been talking of an attack from on shipboard, gives not the least explanation of how that tower got there, as Diodorus does; in Curtius it is a sudden bit of pure nonsense."[23]

Curtius writes that Alexander mounted the very lofty tower

> with great courage and still greater danger; for being conspicuous for his royal garb and gleaming arms, he more than any other was a special target for missiles. And his exploits were well worth beholding; many defenders on the ramparts he ran through with his spear, some he attacked hand to hand with sword and shield, and hurled them headlong from the parapet. For the tower from which he was fighting was almost joined to the enemies' walls.[24]

Parts of this statement are clearly inconsistent with Bosworth's argument that Alexander attacked a breach from atop a siege ladder extending from a wooden turret on board a ship. Curtius writes that the Tyrians were hurled from the parapet, so clearly this isn't the damaged section of wall missing a parapet that Bosworth argues is what Arrian means by a breach. And the fact that the tower was "almost joined to the enemies' walls" makes it doubtful this was Bosworth's ship-mounted wooden turret that served as the base of a siege ladder. Curtius's account seems consistent with a "land siege" view of Diodorus and inconsistent with Bosworth's arguments.

Curtius continues his account, "And now, after the blows of many rams had loosened the structure of the stones, the fortifications had begun to give way."[25] This makes it clear that as with Diodorus's account, a breach made by ship-mounted rams occurs at a different location from Alexander's attack from a tower, since the Macedonians would hardly undermine with rams the section of wall on which Alexander was fighting.

As the account by Curtius continues, the Macedonian ships fight their way into the harbors, and the soldiers take over the towers that have been deserted by the Tyrians. The Tyrians essentially give up at this point. Curtius writes that some take refuge "as suppliants in the temples," some barricade themselves in houses and commit suicide ("anticipated the enemy by a death of their free choice"), some rushed at the Macedonians and were killed, but many of them "manned the roofs of their houses and showered stones and whatever chance had put into their hands upon the Macedonians as they came up."[26]

In this way, according to Diodorus and Curtius, Tyre was taken, after a siege of seven months.

PART V

Afterword

γλυκὺ δὲ πόλεμος ἀπείροισιν (*gluku de polemos apeiroisin*): Sweet is war to those without experience.*

—Pindar, *Nemean Odes. Isthmian Odes. Fragments,*
ed. and trans. William H. Race

*Source of the Latin phrase *Dulce bellum inexpertis*

EIGHTEEN

THE UNCHAINED GOD

Once the Macedonian soldiers were inside the walls of Tyre, a slaughter began. Arrian writes that "the rage of the Macedonians was indiscriminate," in part due to the length of the siege and in part to avenge the heralds who had been killed early on by the Tyrians. Arrian gives the number of Tyrians killed in the final assault as eight thousand, and Macedonians killed in the entire siege as four hundred. Diodorus puts the Tyrian dead at "more than seven thousand," while Curtius says six thousand.[1]

As the Macedonian soldiers stormed into Tyre, many of the Tyrians sought sanctuary in temples. The temple of Herakles was crowded with terrified asylum seekers, including the king of Tyre, Azemilkos, and some envoys from Carthage who had come to Tyre in January for the religious celebration and become trapped during the siege. Alexander, always careful in matters of religion, ordered everyone within the temple spared.[2] Curtius writes that this amnesty was scorned by the Tyrian soldiers: "not a single armed man could bring himself to seek aid from the gods; boys and maidens had filled the temples, the men stood each in the vestibule of his own house, a throng at the mercy of the raging foe." Phoenician marines and sailors manning the ships from Sidon, who had participated in the capture of the southern harbor, "mindful of their kinship with the Tyrians . . . secretly protected many of the Tyrians and took them to their ships, in which they were hidden and conveyed to Sidon." Curtius writes that fifteen thousand were saved in this way, a likely exaggeration.[3]

Alexander's rage seemed to match that of his soldiers. He had two thousand Tyrian men crucified on the mainland, lining the shoreline with their crosses. Diodorus writes that these were all of the remaining men of military age.[4] As was the practice in antiquity for inhabitants of cities captured by siege, Alexander had the remaining Tyrians, mostly women and children, sold into slavery, thirty thousand of them according to Arrian. If this number is correct, it would suggest that most of the women and children had not, in fact, been sent to safety in Carthage at the start of the siege. However, Markoe suggests that the population of the city during the siege may have been swelled by "an influx of refugees and soldiers from the mainland."[5]

Although the ancient historians do not mention rape at Tyre, it undoubtedly occurred.[6] Kathy L. Gaca writes, "Even though it is rather common knowledge that women and girls were conquered and subjugated as one basic purpose of ancient warfare, the practice is still downplayed in our historical consciousness."[7] Jennifer Martinez Morales writes:

> Just as in the modern world, ancient women endured rape and sexual violence in the aftermath of their cities being captured. . . . The psychological impact of seeing your city destroyed, your crops decimated, your property being taken by the enemy, your fellow women and girls losing any rights they had as freeborn women, and your men dying trying to protect all of this, must have been unbearable for women throughout the ancient world. No modern scholarship can ever get close to what it must have felt like for women to experience this."[8]

Jonathan Gottschall argues that Greek soldiers were motivated to fight at Troy by the prospect of claiming the women of the defeated enemy as prizes. In the *Iliad*, Nestor tells the Greek soldiers, "let no man make haste to depart homewards until each has lain with the wife of some Trojan, and has got requital for his strivings and groanings over Helen," and Achilles states, "bloody days I passed in battle, fighting with warriors for their women's sake."[9]

A lavish funeral was held for the Macedonian dead, and rewards were handed out to those men who had distinguished themselves in the assault.[10] Alexander finally got to make his sacrifice in the temple of Herakles, the original cause of the siege. A naval review was held, along with athletic games. One of the catapults used to batter Tyre's walls was dedicated to the temple, as was one of the Tyrian triremes that were captured in the assault.[11] According to Diodorus, Alexander appointed a new king for Tyre, a man named Ballonymus.[12]

And, ever mindful of the gods, Alexander gave orders to remove the golden chains and ropes that had been used to secure the statue of Apollo to its base. His orders were that in the future, the name of the god would be known as Ἀπολλῶ Φιλαλέξανδρον.[13]

Apollō Philalexandron.

Apollo who loves Alexander.

THE UNCHAINED GOD

NINETEEN

LAMENTATION

Following the capture of Tyre, Alexander and his army marched south to Egypt, which surrendered to him without a fight. On the way he paused to capture the city of Gaza, a brutal siege in which Alexander was wounded. In Egypt he was able to have priests and an oracle confirm what he had always suspected—he was, in fact, a god.[1]

While Alexander was in Egypt, his Aegean naval commander arrived, a man named Hegelokhos. He brought with him captives, the leaders of cities that had switched sides and gone over to the Persians. The Persian fleet had been eliminated as a threat, and the Persian admirals were on the run, reduced to hiring pirate ships. Alexander's plan to defeat the Persian navy by land had proven wildly successful. Macedonia was now the strongest naval power in the eastern Mediterranean. Alexander sent the captives back to their cities, where they were executed by their fellow citizens.[2]

From Egypt Alexander retraced his path north, past Tyre, and then east into Syria and Mesopotamia, where he met Darius and his army for the second time. In a fierce battle on a dusty plain at a place called Gaugamela he

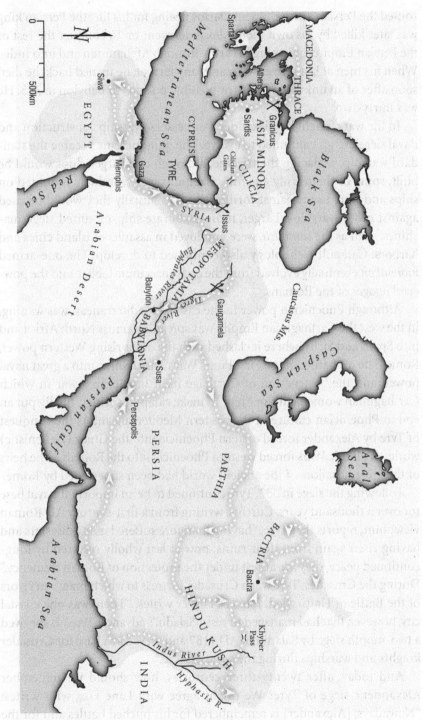

MAP 5. Alexander's route through Egypt and Asia.

routed the Persian army and sent Darius fleeing for his life; the Persian king was later killed by his own men. Alexander went on to conquer the rest of the Persian Empire, marching his army through Afghanistan and into India. When his men at last refused to march any farther, he turned back; he died soon after of an unknown fever (or possibly poison) in Babylon in 323. He was thirty-two.

In the wars fought by Alexander's successors, warship construction and naval siege tactics continued to evolve. The quinquereme became the standard warship, replacing the trireme, although ever larger ships would be built, some of them truly gigantic. Catapults were routinely mounted on ships and were used against fortifications; eventually they would be used against other warships. Larger, more-elaborate ship-mounted siege machines, such as the *sambuca*, were employed in assaults of island cities and harbors. Catapult technology also continued to develop. The one-armed *monankon* eventually evolved from the early inaccurate lobber into the powerful *onager* of the Romans.

Although Phoenician power in the eastern Mediterranean was waning, in the west the Carthaginian Empire was spreading across North Africa and into Spain and Sicily, where it clashed with the other rising Western power, Rome. The sea battles of the First Punic War turned Rome into a great naval power, and the destruction of Carthage itself in 146, in a war in which Carthaginian women cut their hair to make catapult springs, finally put an end to Phoenician culture in the western Mediterranean. As the conquest of Tyre by Alexander forced eastern Phoenicia into the Greek (Hellenistic) world, the Punic Wars forced western Phoenicia into the Roman.[3] The heirs of the greatest sailors of the ancient world had been superseded by Rome.

Following the siege in 332, Tyre continued to be an important naval base for over a thousand years. Curtius, writing from a first-century AD Roman viewpoint, reports that Tyre, "having therefore suffered many disasters and having risen again from their ruins, now at last wholly restored by long-continued peace, they are at rest under the protection of Roman clemency." During the Crusades, Tyre was a Crusader fortress to which many survivors of the Battle of Hattin fled. John D. Hosler writes, "There was one coastal city, however, that had managed to resist Saladin's advance: Tyre." It survived a two-month siege by Saladin in AD 1187 and served as a base for Crusader knights and warships during the siege of Acre.[4]

And today, after twenty-three centuries, how should we remember Alexander's siege of Tyre? We might agree with Lane Fox, who writes: "Nowadays, [Alexander] is remembered for his pitched battles and for the extreme length of his march, but on his contemporaries, perhaps, it was as a stormer of walled cities that he left his most vigorous impression. Both before him and after him, the art was never mastered with such success." This sentiment is echoed by Heckel, who says "it was the capture of Tyre that did the most to enhance Alexander's reputation for invincibility," and by Cartledge, who writes, "If Alexander deserves permanent commemoration as a general, then it is above all in his capacity as a besieger, and of all his sieges Tyre was his masterpiece."[5]

Or, like Ezekiel, we might simply say:

> In their wailing they raise a lamentation for you,
> and lament over you:
> "Who was ever destroyed like Tyre
> in the midst of the sea?"[6]

Appendix A

Historians of Alexander the Great

Arrian: Lucius Flavius Arrianus, a second-century AD Greek historian.
Curtius: Quintus Curtius Rufus, a first-century AD Roman historian.
Diodorus: Diodorus Siculus ("of Sicily"), a first-century BC Greek historian.
Justin: Marcus Junianus Justinus Frontinus, a second-century AD Roman historian.
Plutarch: Plutarchos, a first-century AD Greek biographer.

The accounts of Curtius, Diodorus, and Justin are considered by most scholars to be based largely on a common source, referred to as the "Alexander Vulgate," written by Cleitarchus of Alexandria at the end of the fourth century BC.[1] In the opinion of James Romm, editor of *The Landmark Arrian*, Cleitarchus is "the shadowy Greek who produced the narrative that underlies most of Diodorus, Quintus Curtius, and Justin, and a handful of even less responsible writers. This alternate tradition dramatized the Alexander story in highly diverting ways, but took far less trouble than Arrian did over accuracy. The gap between them is not as wide perhaps as between modern tabloid and broadsheet newspapers, but the analogy applies, I think."[2]

N. G. L. Hammond writes of Cleitarchus, "It is no accident that Cicero, Strabo (e.g., 505), Curtius (e.g., 9.5.21), Quintilian, Plutarch and Arrian distrusted him as a liar or, as we might say, regarded him as a writer of historical fiction."[3]

In the words of Lloyd Llewellyn-Jones, "we approach the life of Alexander only through the elaborately doctored later conceptions of his life and campaigns and love affairs, each with its own bias, and each encoding its own agenda. Innocent they are not. Historical reliability was never the point."[4]

Appendix B

Comparison of the End-of-Siege Accounts
of Three Historians

Event: First Breach in the Wall; Unsuccessful First Assault

Arrian

Alexander passed round to the wall projecting towards the south wind and towards Egypt, and tested the strength of the works everywhere. *Here first a large piece of the wall was thoroughly shaken, and a part of it was even broken and thrown down.* Then indeed for a short time he tried to make an assault to the extent of throwing a bridge upon the part of the wall where a breach had been made. But the Tyrians without much difficulty beat the Macedonians back.

Diodorus

Alexander lashed triremes together, mounted his various siege engines upon them, and *overthrew the wall for the space of a plethron.* Through this breach the Macedonians burst into the city, but the Tyrians rained on them a shower of missiles and managed to turn them back, and when night came, they rebuilt the fallen part of the wall.

Curtius

Alexander, bringing his fleet up to the city's defenses, *shattered the walls on every side with artillery, and in particular by the battering of rams.* The Tyrians hastily repaired the breaches by blocking them with rocks, and began also to build an inner wall, in order to protect themselves with this, if the first wall failed them.

Event: Ram Ships Attempt to Create Second Breach

Arrian

The third day after this, having waited for a calm sea, after encouraging the leaders of the regiments for the action, *he led the ships containing the military engines up to the city.*

Diodorus

He saw that the wall on the side of the naval base was weaker than elsewhere, and *brought up to that point his triremes lashed together and supporting his best siege engines.*

Curtius

Then two days were given to the soldiers for rest, and they were *ordered to bring up both the fleet and at the same time the machines,* in order that Alexander might terrify the enemy by an attack on all sides.

EVENT: Alexander Personally Attacks the Wall from a Tower

Diodorus

Now he *performed a feat of daring which was hardly believable* even to those who saw it. He flung a bridge across from a wooden tower to the city walls and crossing by it alone gained a footing on the wall.

Curtius

. . . he himself mounted a very lofty tower, with *great courage and still greater danger*; for being conspicuous for his royal garb and gleaming arms, he more than any other was a special target for missiles.

EVENT: Alexander Fights on Top of the Wall

Diodorus

Having as witness of his prowess the great army which had defeated the Persians, he ordered the Macedonians to follow him, and leading the way *he slew some of those who came within reach with his spear, and others by a blow of his saber.* He knocked down still others with the rim of his shield, and put an end to the high confidence of the enemy.

Curtius

And his exploits were well worth beholding; many defenders on the ramparts *he ran through with his spear, some he attacked hand to hand with sword and shield,* and hurled them headlong from the parapets. For the tower from which he was fighting was almost joined to the enemies' walls.

EVENT: Second Breach Is Created; Assault Is Successful (led by Alexander in Arrian)

Arrian

In the first place *he shook down a large piece of the wall; and when the breach appeared to be sufficiently wide,* he ordered the vessels conveying the military engines to retire, and brought up two others, which carried his bridges, which he intended to throw upon the breach in the wall. The shield-bearing guards occupied one of these vessels, which he had put under the command of Admetos; and the other was occupied by the regiment of Koinos, called the Foot Companions. Alexander himself, with the shield-bearing guards, intended to scale the wall where it might be practicable.

Diodorus

Simultaneously in another part of the city the *battering ram, put to its work, brought down a considerable stretch of wall;* and when the Macedonians entered through this breach ...

Curtius

And now, *after the blows of many rams had loosened the structure of the stones, the fortifications had begun to give way,* and the fleet had entered the port, and some of the Macedonians had made their way into the towers deserted by the enemy.

EVENT: Alexander Leads His Men into the City

Arrian

When Alexander's ships drew close to the city and the bridges were thrown from them upon the wall, the shield-bearing guards mounted valiantly along these upon the wall; for their captain, Admetos, proved himself brave on that occasion, and Alexander accompanied them, both as a courageous participant in the action itself, and as a witness of brilliant and dangerous feats of valor performed by others. The first part of the wall that was captured was where Alexander had posted himself; the Tyrians being easily beaten back from it, as soon as the Macedonians found firm footing, and at the same time a way of entrance not abrupt on every side. Admetos was the first to mount the wall; but while cheering on his men to mount, he was struck with a spear and died on the spot. After him, Alexander with the Companions got possession of the wall; and when some of the towers and the parts of the wall between them were in his hands, he advanced through the battlements to the royal palace, because the descent into the city that way seemed the easiest.

Diodorus

... and Alexander's party poured over the bridge on to the wall, the city was taken.

Sources

Arrian: https://www.gutenberg.org/files/46976/46976-h/46976-h.htm

Diodorus: https://penelope.uchicago.edu/Thayer/E/Roman/Texts/Diodorus_Siculus/17C*.html

Curtius: https://babel.hathitrust.org/cgi/pt?id=mdp.39015008158415&view=1up&seq=9

All emphasis added.

Notes

A NOTE ON SOURCES, NAMES, AND DATES

1. Brian Campbell and Lawrence A. Tritle, eds., *The Oxford Handbook of Warfare in the Classical World* (Oxford: Oxford University Press, 2013), xiii.
2. For a thorough discussion of the origin of *phoinix*, see Michael C. Astour, "The Origin of the Terms 'Canaan,' 'Phoenician,' and 'Purple,'" *Journal of Near Eastern Studies* 24, no. 4 (October 1965): 346-50.
3. Nina Jidejian, *Tyre through the Ages* (Beirut: Dar El-Mashreq, 1969), xvi.
4. James Romm, ed., *The Landmark Arrian: The Campaigns of Alexander*, trans. Pamela Mensch (New York: Anchor, 2012).

INTRODUCTION

1 Arrian, *Anabasis of Alexander*, trans. P. A. Brunt (Cambridge, MA: Harvard University Press, 1976), 1.18.5. (reference is to book 1, chapter 18, section 5)
2. Robin Lane Fox, *Alexander the Great* (London: Allen Lane, 1973), 134.

PROLOGUE: THE PROPHECY

1. Glenn E. Markoe, *Phoenicians* (Berkeley: University of California Press, 2000), 129.
2. Ibid., 117.
3. Jidejian, *Tyre*, 54.
4. An argument has been made that Ezekiel's prophecy is not about the Babylonian siege but rather about the much later siege by Alexander in 332. See Benjamin Garstad, "Nebuchadnezzar's Siege of Tyre in Jerome's Commentary on Ezekiel," *Vigiliae Christianae* 70 (2016): 175-92.

CHAPTER 1: THE SYRIAN GATES

1. J. F. C. Fuller, *The Generalship of Alexander the Great* (London: Eyre & Spottiswoode, 1958), 99.
2. Lloyd Llewellyn-Jones, *Persians: The Age of the Great Kings* (New York: Basic Books, 2022), 139; A. F. Rainey, "The Satrapy 'Beyond the River,'" *Australian Journal of Biblical Archaeology* 1, no. 2 (1969): 51-78.
3. Xenophon, *Anabasis*, trans. Carleton L. Brownson (Cambridge, MA: Harvard University Press, 1998), 1.4.

4. Tim Rood, "Xenophon's Parasangs," *Journal of Hellenic Studies* 130 (2010): 51-66; Christopher J. Tuplin, "Achaemenid Arithmetic: Numerical Problems in Persian History," *Topoi. Orient-Occident. Supplément 1* (1997): 365-421; Lane Fox, *Alexander*, 519; Donald W. Engels, *Alexander the Great and the Logistics of the Macedonian Army* (Berkeley: University of California Press, 1978), 47-52; Arrian, *Anabasis of Alexander*, appendix page 490.

5. Arrian, *Anabasis of Alexander*, 2.6.2.

6. Quintus Curtius, *History of Alexander*, trans. John C. Rolfe (Cambridge, MA: Harvard University Press, 1946), 3.8.15; Arrian, *Anabasis of Alexander*, 2.7.1, says only that Darius had the captured Macedonians tortured and killed.

7. Fuller, *Generalship of Alexander the Great*, 99.

8. Ibid.

9. Lane Fox, *Alexander*, 166.

10. Arrian, *Anabasis of Alexander*, 2.4.7.

11. For an excellent map depicting the mountains, seacoast, and two "gates" (Greek: Syriai Pylai and Amanikai Pylai) that are key to these movements, see map 67 in Richard J. A. Talbert, ed., *Barrington Atlas of the Greek and Roman World* (Princeton, NJ: Princeton University Press, 2000). The location in Syria from which Darius's army began its march is not known with certainty.

12. Fuller, *Generalship of Alexander the Great*, 98, says Alexander may not have been aware of the existence of the Amanic Gates.

13. Lane Fox, *Alexander*, 166.

14. Arrian, *Anabasis of Alexander*, 2.7.3.

CHAPTER 2: "MEN WHO DINE ON SHARPENED SWORDS"

1. Lane Fox, *Alexander*, 109; Arrian, *Anabasis of Alexander*, 1.11.6; Philip de Souza, "War at Sea," in *The Oxford Handbook of Warfare in the Classical World*, ed. Brian Campbell and Lawrence A. Tritle (Oxford: Oxford University Press, 2013), 375; J. S. Morrison and J. F. Coates, *Greek and Roman Oared Warships* (Oxford: Oxbow, 1996), 3; Diodorus of Sicily, *The Library of History*, trans. C. Bradford Welles (Cambridge, MA: Harvard University Press, 1963), 17.17.2; Morrison and Coates, *Greek and Roman Oared Warships*, 3-4.

2. Robin Lane Fox, *The Search for Alexander* (Boston: Little, Brown, 1980), 68. But Lane Fox adds, "No account of the battle, however, commands authority." Fuller, *Generalship of Alexander the Great*, 35, says, "Little has been recorded of the battle." Tradition holds that Alexander led a cavalry charge, but the use of cavalry in this battle has been questioned by some scholars. See Matthew A. Sears and Carolyn Willekes, "Alexander's Cavalry Charge at Chaeronea, 338 BCE," *Journal of Military History* 80 (October 2016): 1017-35; and Paul A. Rahe, "The Annihilation of the Sacred Band at Chaeronea," *American Journal of Archaeology* 85, no. 1 (January 1981): 84-87.

3. Fuller, *Generalship of Alexander the Great*, 36.

4. Ibid., 37.

5. Victor Davis Hanson, *The Wars of the Ancient Greeks* (London: Cassell, 1999), 153.

6. Llewellyn-Jones, *Persians*, 352.

7. Romm, *Landmark Arrian*, 4; Arrian, *Anabasis of Alexander*, 1.11.2.

8. Lane Fox, *Alexander*, 70-71, says "it suited Alexander to leave Sparta alone."

9. Lane Fox, *Search for Alexander*, 104.

10. Edward M. Anson, "Hellenistic Land Warfare," in *A Companion to Greek Warfare*, ed. Waldemar Heckel, F. S. Naiden, E. Edward Garvin, and John Vanderspoel (Chichester, UK: Wiley Blackwell, 2021), 42.

11. Hanson, *Wars*, 149.

12. Ibid., 151.

13. Duncan B. Campbell, "Ancient Catapults: Some Hypotheses Reexamined," *Hesperia: The Journal of the American School of Classical Studies at Athens* 80, no. 4 (September-December 2011): 681. The complete line in a slightly different translation is: "Don't you know you fight against men, / that dine on just-sharpened swords, / and who eat up flaming torches as an appetizer? / Straight after that, after dinner a slave / brings on a dessert of Cretan arrows / instead of chickpeas, and broken shards of arrows too." Eoghan Moloney, "The Macedonian Kings and Greek Theatre," in *Greek Theatre in the Fourth Century BC*, ed. Eric Csapo, Hans Rupprecht Goette, J. Richard Green, and Peter Wilson (Berlin/Boston: De Gruyter, 2014), 242.

14. Lane Fox, *Alexander*, 78. Lane Fox, *Search for Alexander*, 110. "Hoplite" is defined in the *Oxford English Dictionary* as "a heavy-armed foot-soldier of ancient Greece." From the Greek *hoplon* (ὅπλον) meaning a weapon, piece of armor, or heavy shield.

15. Minor M. Markle III, "Macedonian Arms and Tactics under Alexander the Great," *Studies in the History of Art: Symposium Series I: Macedonia and Greece in Late Classical and Early Hellenistic Times* 10 (1982): 94; Nick Sekunda, *The Army of Alexander the Great* (London: Osprey, 1984), 27.

16. Fuller, *Generalship of Alexander the Great*, 51; Lane Fox, *Search for Alexander*, 110; Lane Fox, *Alexander*, 77-78; Sekunda, *Army of Alexander the Great*, 27; Simon Anglim, Phyllis G. Justice, Rob S. Rice, Scott M. Rusch, and John Serrati, *Fighting Techniques of the Ancient World 3000 BC–AD 500: Equipment, Combat Skills, and Tactics* (New York: St. Martin's Press, 2002), 36.

17. "Sarissa seems to be a Macedonian word applied to the spear in general." Nicholas Sekunda, "Military Forces," in *The Cambridge History of Greek and Roman Warfare*, ed. Philip Sabin, Hans van Wees, Michael Whitby (Cambridge: Cambridge University Press, 2007), 329. "[E]ighteen feet long, with a foot-long iron blade," Lane Fox, *Alexander*, 76. However, Sekunda, *Army of Alexander the Great*, 27, says "the most distinctive feature of the sarissa was its small iron head, which made it more suitable for piercing armor than the large-headed Greek hoplite spear." Disagreement about the length of the sarissa may stem in part from the fact that it was used by many different armies over a long period of time. It became the standard infantry weapon of the armies of the Hellenistic kingdoms that emerged from Alexander's empire. The weapon fell out of favor after sarissa-armed phalanx formations were defeated by more-flexible sword-armed Roman legions. During the European Renaissance, the weapon was rediscovered and used by Swiss pikemen and German Landsknechts.

18. Fuller, *Generalship of Alexander the Great*, 50; Lane Fox, *Alexander*, 76; Lane Fox, *Search for Alexander*, 108; Anglim et al., *Fighting Techniques*, 33; Sekunda, *Army of Alexander the Great*, 27; Hanson, *Wars*, 149; Markle, "Macedonian Arms," 89; John Warry, *Warfare in the Classical World* (Norman: University of Oklahoma Press, 1995), 68.

19. There is some debate among scholars as to the exact date of Philip's introduction of these reforms. See for example Edward M. Anson, "The Introduction of the 'Sarissa' in Macedonian Warfare," *Ancient Society* 40 (2010): 51-68. For an in-depth analysis of the sarissa, see Minor M. Markle III, "The Macedonian Sarissa, Spear, and Related Armor," *American Journal of Archaeology* 81, no. 3 (Summer 1977): 323-339.

20. Hanson, *Wars*, 150; Lane Fox, *Alexander*, 77.

21. See for example R. D. Milns, "Philip II and the Hypaspists," *Historia: Zeitschrift fur Alte Geschichte* (September 1967): 509-12; J. R. Ellis, "Alexander's Hypaspists Again," *Historia: Zeitschrift fur Alte Geschichte* (4th Quarter 1975): 617-18; Edward M. Anson, "The Hypaspists: Macedonia's Professional Citizen-Soldiers," *Historia: Zeitschrift fur Alte Geschichte* (2nd Quarter 1985): 246-48; and R. D. Milns, "The Hypaspists of Alexander III: Some Problems," *Historia: Zeitschrift fur Alte Geschichte* (2nd Quarter 1971): 186-95.

22. Hanson, *Wars*, 150; Fuller, *Generalship of Alexander the Great*, 49; Sekunda, *Army of Alexander the Great*, 30; Anglim et al., *Fighting Techniques*, 36; Markle, "Macedonian Arms," 98.

23. Lane Fox, *Search for Alexander*, 110; Lane Fox, *Alexander*, 78.

24. James Romm, *Demetrius Sacker of Cities* (New Haven, CT: Yale University Press, 2022), 4-5. This argument is inconsistent with Alexander's frequent use of Greek mercenary soldiers, who were similarly armed.

25. Fuller, *Generalship of Alexander the Great*, 51.

26. Lane Fox, *Alexander*, 78.

27. Fuller, *Generalship of Alexander the Great*, 51.

28. Lane Fox, *Search for Alexander*, 110-111. Peltasts, from the word "pelta," which the *Oxford English Dictionary* defines as "a light shield, typically crescent-shaped but sometimes small and round." From the ancient Greek *peltē* (πέλτη).

29. Fuller, *Generalship of Alexander the Great*, 51; Lane Fox, *Search for Alexander*, 110-111.

30. Lane Fox, *Alexander*, 174.

31. Ibid., 74; Lane Fox, *Search for Alexander*, 108.

32. Markle, "Macedonian Sarissa," 324.

33. Lane Fox, *Alexander*, 75.

34. Sekunda, *Army of Alexander the Great*, 16. The same argument is given in Markle, "Macedonian Arms," 89.

35. Sekunda, *Army of Alexander the Great*, 16; Markle, "Macedonian Sarissa," 334.

36. Lane Fox, *Alexander*, 74; Hanson, *Wars*, 150.

37. Anglim et al., *Fighting Techniques*, 100; Lane Fox, *Alexander*, 74.

38. Michael J. Decker, *The Sasanian Empire at War: Persia, Rome, and the Rise of Islam, 224-651* (Yardley, PA: Westholme, 2022), xxix.

39. Sekunda, *Army of Alexander the Great*, 20.

40. Lane Fox, *Search for Alexander*, 109.

41. Markle, "Macedonian Arms," 104.

42. Fuller, *Generalship of Alexander the Great*, 51.

43. Ibid., 51.

44. Hanson, *Wars*, 175.

45. Ibid., 175-76; Lane Fox, *Alexander*, 72.

46. Lane Fox, *Search for Alexander*, 106.

47. Duncan B. Campbell, *Ancient Siege Warfare: Persians, Greeks, Carthaginians and Romans 546-146 BC* (Oxford: Osprey, 2005), 23.

48. E. W. Marsden, "Macedonian Military Machinery and Its Designers under Philip and Alexander," in *Ancient Macedonia II: Papers Read at the Second International Symposium Held in Thessaloniki, 19-24 August 1973* (Thessaloniki, Greece: Institute for Balkan Studies, 1977), 212.

49. Paul Bentley Kern, *Ancient Siege Warfare* (Bloomington: Indiana University Press, 1999), 198.

50. William M. Murray, "The Development of a Naval Siege Unit under Philip II and Alexander III," in *Macedonian Legacies: Studies in Ancient Macedonian History and Culture in Honor of Eugene N. Borza*, ed. Timothy Howe and Jeanne Reames (Claremont: Regina, 2008), 31-55.

CHAPTER 3: INVASION

1. Arrian, *Anabasis of Alexander*, 1.11.3; Diodorus, *Library of History*, 17.17.4; Lane Fox, *Alexander*, 116. Fuller, *Generalship of Alexander the Great*, 88, gives similar figures, arriving at a slightly smaller total of forty thousand.

2. Lane Fox, *Alexander*, 117; Arrian, *Anabasis of Alexander*, 1.12.7.
3. Arrian, *Anabasis of Alexander*, 1.14.4; Diodorus, *Library of History*, 17.19.5; Fuller, *Generalship of Alexander the Great*, 147.
4. Arrian, *Anabasis of Alexander*, 1.12.9-10.
5. E. Badian, "The Battle of the Granicus: A New Look," in *Ancient Macedonia II: Papers Read at the Second International Symposium Held in Thessaloniki, 19-24 August 1973* (Thessaloniki, Greece: Institute for Balkan Studies, 1977), 286.
6. Arrian, 1.14.5-7; Plutarch, *Lives: Alexander and Caesar* (Cambridge, MA: Harvard University Press, 1919), 16.
7. Diodorus, *Library of History*, 17.19.3.
8. Lane Fox, *Alexander*, 122.
9. Ibid., 121.
10. Lane Fox, *Search for Alexander*, 141.
11. Badian, "Battle of the Granicus," 271-272. The *Oxford English Dictionary* defines "paradoxography" as "a literary genre, originating in early Alexandrian Greece, in which natural or man-made phenomena considered remarkable or fantastic are described."
12. Peter Green, *Alexander of Macedon: A Historical Biography* (Berkeley: University of California Press, 1991), 489-512.
13. Arrian, *Anabasis of Alexander*, 1.15.3-4.
14. Ibid., 1.15.5; Plutarch, *Lives*, 16.
15. Fuller, *Generalship of Alexander the Great*, 152-53.
16. Plutarch, *Lives*, 16; Arrian, *Anabasis of Alexander*, 1.16.2.

CHAPTER 4: THE INFLUENCE OF SEA POWER

1. Lane Fox, *Search for Alexander*, 145; Llewellyn-Jones, *Persians*, 61.
2. Arrian, *Anabasis of Alexander*, 1.17.9.
3. Ibid., 1.18.4; Romm, *Landmark Arrian*, 36. The ancient city of Miletus was on the coast of Asia Minor. Over centuries, the Maeander River has silted up the bay on which the city was located, and today its ruins are inland.
4. Arrian, *Anabasis of Alexander*, 1.18.4-5, 1.19.3.
5. Ibid., 1.18.5; Diodorus, *Library of History*, 17.29.2.
6. Lane Fox, *Search for Alexander*, 145; Lane Fox, *Alexander*, 132.
7. Romm, *Landmark Arrian*, 36; Edward M. Anson, "The Persian Fleet in 334," *Classical Philology* 84, no. 1 (1989): 44.
8. Arrian, *Anabasis of Alexander*, 1.18.7-8.
9. Ibid., 1.18.9.
10. Lane Fox, *Alexander*, 133.
11. Cynthia M. Harrison, "Triremes at Rest: On the Beach or in the Water?," *Journal of Hellenic Studies* 119 (1999): 168.
12. Arrian, *Anabasis of Alexander*, 1.19.8, 1.19.11.
13. Diodorus, *Library of History*, 17.22.5.
14. Arrian, *Anabasis of Alexander*, 1.20.1.
15. Lane Fox, *Alexander*, 134.
16. Waldemar Heckel, *In the Path of Conquest* (Oxford: Oxford University Press, 2020), 64.
17. Lane Fox, *Search for Alexander*, 146.
18. Romm, *Landmark Arrian*, 4; Diodorus, *Library of History*, 17.23.1.
19. Pekka Hamalainen, *Indigenous Continent: The Epic Contest for North America* (New York: Liveright, 2022), 32; Si Sheppard, *Tenochtitlan 1519-21* (Oxford: Osprey, 2018), 11.

20. For an analysis of other parallels between Alexander and Cortés, see Brian Bosworth, "A Tale of Two Empires: Hernán Cortés and Alexander the Great," in *Alexander the Great in Fact and Fiction*, ed. A. B. Bosworth and E. J. Baynham (Oxford: Oxford University Press, 2000), 23.

21. Marsden, "Macedonian Military Machinery," 212.

22. David Whitehead and P. H. Blyth, *Athenaeus Mechanicus, On Machines* (Stuttgart: Franz Steiner Verlag, 2004), 181.

23. Herodotus, *The Persian Wars, Volume IV: Books 8-9*, trans. A. D. Godley (Cambridge, MA: Harvard University Press, 1925), 8.87.

24. Barry Strauss, *The Battle of Salamis: The Naval Encounter That Saved Greece—and Western Civilization* (New York: Simon & Schuster, 2004), 180-87.

25. Arrian, *Anabasis of Alexander*, 1.20.3.

26. Ibid., 1.23.5.

27. Lane Fox, *Search for Alexander*, 147-48.

28. Lane Fox, *Alexander*, 143.

29. Lane Fox, *Search for Alexander*, 159.

30. Arrian, *Anabasis of Alexander*, 2.3.8.

31. Lane Fox, *Search for Alexander*, 163.

32. Lane Fox, *Alexander*, 153.

33. Arrian, *Anabasis of Alexander*, 2.2.3.

34. Curtius, *History of Alexander*, 3.1.19-21.

35. N. G. L. Hammond, *Sources for Alexander the Great: An Analysis of Plutarch's "Life" and Arrian's "Anabasis Alexandrou"* (Cambridge: Cambridge University Press, 1993), 219.

36. Lane Fox, *Alexander*, 162.

37. Ibid., 157; A. B. Bosworth, *Conquest and Empire: The Reign of Alexander the Great* (Cambridge: Cambridge University Press, 1988), 53.

38. Lane Fox, *Alexander*, 162.

39. Arrian, *Anabasis of Alexander*, 2.6.1. The exact location of Sochi is not known.

40. Ibid., 2.6.2.

CHAPTER 5: THE KING'S BATH

1. Fuller, *Generalship of Alexander the Great*, 156; Lane Fox, *Alexander*, 168; Bosworth, *Conquest and Empire*, 60; W. W. Tarn, *Alexander the Great 1: Narrative* (Cambridge: Cambridge University Press, 1948), 24; Jonah 2:10 (RSV).

2. Arrian, *Anabasis of Alexander*, 2.8.2.

3. Curtius, *History of Alexander*, 3.8.18.

4. Ibid., 3.8.20-21.

5. Arrian, *Anabasis of Alexander*, 2.8.2.

6. Curtius, *History of Alexander*, 3.8.12.

7. Fuller, *Generalship of Alexander the Great*, 159-160.

8. Lane Fox, *Alexander*, 170; Fuller, *Generalship of Alexander the Great*, 154; Tarn, *Alexander the Great 1*, 24; Engels, *Alexander the Great*, 131-34; Bosworth, *Conquest and Empire*, 60.

9. Tarn, *Alexander the Great 1*, 26; Fuller, *Generalship of Alexander the Great*, 157; Lane Fox, *Alexander*, 170; Arrian, *Anabasis of Alexander*, 2.8.8.

10. Tarn, *Alexander the Great 1*, 26.

11. Curtius, *History of Alexander*, 3.8.24-25.

12. Diodorus, *Library of History*, 17.33.5.

13. Curtius, *History of Alexander*, 3.11.9.

14. Ibid., 3.11.10; Diodorus, *Library of History*, 17.34.

15. Bosworth, *Conquest and Empire*, 61.

16. Arrian, *Anabasis of Alexander*, 2.11.5-6.

17. Diodorus, *Library of History*, 17.35.1.

18. Llewellyn-Jones, *Persians*, 149.

19. Plutarch, *Lives*, 20.6.

20. Llewellyn-Jones, *Persians*, 152.

21. Diodorus, *Library of History*, 17.35.4; Curtius, *History of Alexander*, 3.11.20.

22. Curtius, *History of Alexander*, 3.11.21-22.

23. Diodorus, *Library of History*, 17.35.5-7.

24. Ibid., 17.36.2; Arrian, *Anabasis of Alexander*, 2.11.9.

25. Llewellyn-Jones, *Persians*, 82.

26. Curtius, *History of Alexander*, 3.11.23.

27. Diodorus, *Library of History*, 17.36.5.

28. Plutarch, *Lives*, 20.7-8.

CHAPTER 6: BABYLON . . . OR PHOENICIA?

1. Lane Fox, *Search for Alexander*, 182; Curtius, *History of Alexander*, 3.13.

2. Arrian, *Anabasis of Alexander*, 2.13.3.

3. Lane Fox, *Alexander*, 178.

4. Curtius, *History of Alexander*, 4.1.36.

5. Arrian, *Anabasis of Alexander*, 2.13.4-5; Romm, *Landmark Arrian*, 78.

6. Arrian, *Anabasis of Alexander*, 2.13.5.

7. Romm, *Landmark Arrian*, 79.

8. Lane Fox, *Alexander*, 180; Tarn, *Alexander the Great 1*, 36; Waldemar Heckel, *The Conquests of Alexander the Great* (Cambridge: Cambridge University Press, 2008), 65.

9. Theodore A. Dodge, *Alexander; A History of the Origin and Growth of the Art of War from the Earliest Times to the Battle of Ipsus, 301 BC, with a Detailed Account of the Campaigns of the Great Macedonian* (Boston, New York: Houghton, Mifflin, 1918), 328.

10. Edmund F. Bloedow, "The Siege of Tyre in 332 BC. Alexander at the Crossroads in His Career," *La parola del passato* 301 (1998): 279.

11. Llewellyn-Jones, *Persians*, 339-340.

12. Plutarch, *Lives*, 24.2.

13. Glanville Downey, *Ancient Antioch* (Princeton, NJ: Princeton University Press, 1963), 27.

14. Ibid., 28.

15. Romm, *Landmark Arrian*, 80; Lane Fox, *Alexander*, 180.

16. Arrian, *Anabasis of Alexander*, 2.14.1-3.

17. Romm, *Landmark Arrian*, 80.

18. Ibid., 81.

19. Arrian, *Anabasis of Alexander*, 2.14.8-9.

CHAPTER 7: THE PURPLE LAND

1. Jidejian, *Tyre*, 143; Strabo, *Geography*, trans. Horace Leonard Jones (Cambridge, MA: Harvard University Press, 1930), 16.2.23; Donald Harden, *The Phoenicians* (New York: Frederick A. Praeger, 1962), 146.

2. Jidejian, *Tyre*, 150.

3. Athenaeus, *The Learned Banqueters*, trans. S. Douglas Olson (Cambridge, MA: Harvard University Press, 2010), 12.526.

4. Philip Andrew Johnston and Brett Kaufman, "Metallurgy and Other Technologies," in *The Oxford Handbook of the Phoenician and Punic Mediterranean*, ed. Carolina Lopez-Ruiz and Brian R. Doak (Oxford: Oxford University Press, 2019), 403.

5. Ville Vuolanto, "lex Oppia," *Oxford Classical Dictionary*, February 25, 2019, https://oxfordre.com/classics.

6. 2 Chronicles 2:7 (RSV). Scholars have questioned the historicity of the biblical texts' accounts of a temple-building alliance between Solomon and the Phoenicians: "The general situation in tenth-century Israel would not have been propitious to large-scale projects." Guy Bunnens, "Phoenicia in the Later Iron Age," in *The Oxford Handbook of the Phoenician and Punic Mediterranean*, ed. Carolina Lopez-Ruiz and Brian R. Doak (Oxford: Oxford University Press, 2019), 65.

7. Markoe, *Phoenicians*, 163. This scene was depicted by Peter Paul Rubens in his painting *The Discovery of Purple by Hercules's Dog* at the Musée Bonnat in Bayonne, France.

8. Harden, *Phoenicians*, 22. Harden notes, "The name of the mythical bird—the Phoenix—is thought to be an independent derivation from the same adjective." The Romans applied the Latinized form of the Greek word, *Poeni*, to the Phoenician colonies in the western Mediterranean; hence the term "Punic" for the series of wars between Rome and the Phoenician colony of Carthage.

9. "Of all explanations of the Greek *Phoinix*, 'Phoenician,' (plur. *Phoinikes*) and *Phoinike*, 'Phoenicia,' the most convincing is certainly the derivation from *phoinix*, 'purple,' referring to the characteristic Phoenician trade." Astour, "Origin of the Terms," 348.

10. Harden, *Phoenicians*, 66.

11. The cor (or kor) was a Hebrew unit of both wet and dry volume. The size is uncertain. Josephus, *Jewish Antiquities*, trans. Ralph Marcus (Cambridge, MA: Harvard University Press, 1963) gives two different values for the cor. In 3.321, he writes that "seventy cors of flour" are equivalent to "forty-one Attic medimni," whereas in 15.314 he writes "the kor equals ten Attic medimnoi." According to the 2015 English edition of *The Brill Dictionary of Ancient Greek*, the Attic medimnos equals 52 liters. Rax Kletter writes that the "Kor could never be a vessel, because it was too big. We do not know the exact size, but it is assumed to be c. 150–220 liters." Rax Kletter, "Vessels and Measures: The Biblical Liquid Capacity System," *Israel Exploration Journal* 64, no. 1 (2014): 29.

12. Mark Woolmer and Glenn E. Markoe, *A Short History of the Phoenicians* (London: I. B. Tauris, 2017), 153-154.

13. Strabo, *Geography*, 16.2.25; Pliny, *Natural History*, trans. D. E. Eichholz (Cambridge, MA: Harvard University Press, 1962), 36.65.

14. Harden, *Phoenicians*, 20; Madadh Richey, "The Alphabet and its Legacy," in *The Oxford Handbook of the Phoenician and Punic Mediterranean*, ed. Carolina Lopez-Ruiz and Brian R. Doak (Oxford: Oxford University Press, 2019), 245.

15. Markoe, *Phoenicians*, 68, 197.

16. Harden, *Phoenicians*, 141.

17. Corinne Bonnet, "The Hellenistic Period and Hellenization in Phoenicia," in *The Oxford Handbook of the Phoenician and Punic Mediterranean*, ed. Carolina Lopez-Ruiz and Brian R. Doak (Oxford: Oxford University Press, 2019), 101.

18. Harden, *Phoenicians*, 82-83.

19. Ibid., 85-86.

20. Ibid., 103.

21. Markoe, *Phoenicians*, 120, 131; Woolmer and Markoe, *Short History*, 71.

22. Herodotus, *Persian Wars*, 1.199.

23. Stephanie Lynn Budin, *The Myth of Sacred Prostitution in Antiquity* (Cambridge: Cambridge University Press, 2008), 1, 87.

24. Paolo Xella, "Religion," in *The Oxford Handbook of the Phoenician and Punic Mediterranean*, ed. Carolina Lopez-Ruiz and Brian R. Doak (Oxford: Oxford University Press, 2019), 287-288. Burial sites containing urns with burned bones of children "have been dubbed 'tophets,' after a biblical site where worshipers 'burned sons and daughters in a fire' (Jeremiah 7:31-32)." Matthew M. McCarty, "The Tophet and Infant Sacrifice," in *The Oxford Handbook of the Phoenician and Punic Mediterranean*, ed. Carolina Lopez-Ruiz and Brian R. Doak (Oxford: Oxford University Press, 2019), 311.

25. Harden, *Phoenicians*, 95, 104.

26. Markoe, *Phoenicians*, 132.

27. Xella, "Religion," 288.

CHAPTER 8: THE SHIPS OF PERSIA

1. Thomas Collelo, ed., *Lebanon: A Country Study* (Washington, DC: Federal Research Division, Library of Congress, 1989), 43-44.

2. Harden, *Phoenicians*, 25, 141.

3. Ibid., 20.

4. Duane W. Roller, "Phoenician Exploration," in *The Oxford Handbook of the Phoenician and Punic Mediterranean*, ed. Carolina Lopez-Ruiz and Brian R. Doak (Oxford: Oxford University Press, 2019), 645-646; Keith DeVries and Michael L. Katzev, "Greek, Etruscan and Phoenician Ships and Shipping," in *A History of Seafaring Based on Underwater Archaeology*, ed. George Bass (New York: Walker, 1972), 39.

5. Timothy Champion, "The Appropriation of the Phoenicians in British Imperial Ideology," *Nations and Nationalism* 7, no. 4 (2001): 451-65.

6. Herodotus, *Persian Wars*, 4.42; Roller, "Phoenician Exploration," 649.

7. There is some confusion about this canal in the ancient sources. Some scholars argue that the canal was not completed by Necos but by King Darius I of Persia. Others think the canal Darius completed was a different one. See Carol A. Redmount, "The Wadi Tumilat and the 'Canal of the Pharaohs,'" *Journal of Near Eastern Studies* 54, no. 2 (April 1995): 127-135, and Llewellyn-Jones, *Persians*, 116.

8. Harden, *Phoenicians*, 170.

9. Roller, "Phoenician Exploration," 646-647.

10. John W. Betlyon, "Coins," in *The Oxford Handbook of the Phoenician and Punic Mediterranean*, ed. Carolina Lopez-Ruiz and Brian R. Doak (Oxford: Oxford University Press, 2019), 387.

11. The exact date when the Phoenician cities were incorporated into the Persian Empire is unclear. It may have been during the reign of Cyrus the Great. See Markoe, *Phoenicians*, 49.

12. Llewellyn-Jones, *Persians*, 90; W. W. Tarn, "The Fleet of Xerxes," *Journal of Hellenic Studies* 28 (1908): 206.

13. Jidejian, *Tyre*, 60-61.

14. Herodotus, *Persian Wars*, 7.89-90.

15. For an exhaustive mathematical analysis that attempts to derive the origin of 1,207 for the number of triremes in the fleet, see Tarn, "Fleet of Xerxes," 202-33.

16. Llewellyn-Jones, *Persians*, 251.

17. Herodotus, *Persian Wars*, 7.44, 7.128.

18. Strauss, *Battle of Salamis*, xvii, xviii.

CHAPTER 9: SURRENDER

1. In the Revised Standard Version of the Bible, Arados is called Arvad, and the city was known for supplying "rowers for Tyre" (Ezekiel 27:8). In AD 1302, Pope Clement V awarded the city and island to the Knights Templar for use as a base by the order.

2. Fuller, *Generalship of Alexander the Great*, 207.

3. Tarek Galal Abdelhamid, "Notes on the Architecture and History of the Fortifications of the Island of Arwad in Syria," *Levant* 54, no. 1 (2022): 97-123.

4. Arrian, *Anabasis of Alexander*, 2.13.8.

5. Lane Fox, *Alexander*, 178; Romm, *Landmark Arrian*, 79.

6. Xella, "Religion," 276.

7. H. Machler, "Books, Greek and Roman," *Oxford Classical Dictionary*, March 7, 2016.

8. Llewellyn-Jones, *Persians*, 340.

9. Markoe, *Phoenicians*, 60.

10. Diodorus, *Library of History*, 16.45.4.

11. Bosworth, *Conquest and Empire*, 65. This is not the same Straton who surrendered Arados to Alexander.

12. Arrian, *Anabasis of Alexander*, 2.15.6.

13. Curtius, *History of Alexander*, 4.1.

14. Justin, *Epitome of the Philippic History of Pompeius Trogus, Books 11-12: Alexander the Great*, trans. J. C. Yardley, commentary by Waldemar Heckel (Oxford: Clarendon, 1997), 11.10.8-9; Diodorus, *Library of History*, 17.47.1-6.

15. Lane Fox, *Alexander*, 181, says the siege began in "early January."

16. Arrian, *Anabasis of Alexander*, 2.15.6-7.

17. Xella, "Religion," 276.

18. Burr C. Brundage, "Herakles the Levantine: A Comprehensive View," *Journal of Near Eastern Studies* 17, no. 4 (October, 1958): 230.

19. Arrian, *Anabasis of Alexander*, 2.16.1.

20. Curtius, *History of Alexander*, 4.2.3.

21. N. G. L. Hammond, *Three Historians of Alexander the Great: The So-Called Vulgate Authors, Diodorus, Justin and Curtius* (Cambridge: Cambridge University Press, 1983), 125.

22. Arrian, *Anabasis of Alexander*, 2.16.1; Martin Hammond, trans., *Arrian: Alexander the Great, the "Anabasis" and the "Indica"* (Oxford: Oxford University Press, 2013), 288; Romm, *Landmark Arrian*, 82.

23. Bosworth, *Conquest and Empire*, 65. The exact month (January or February 332) is uncertain. J. E. Atkinson writes, "The awakening of Herakles was celebrated 'probably in January' . . . and the siege of Tyre began in January." J. E. Atkinson, *Commentary on Q. Curtius Rufus' "Historiae Alexandri Magni" Books 3 and 4* (Amsterdam: J. C. Gieben, 1980), 296.

24. Romm, *Landmark Arrian*, 82.

25. Xella, "Religion," 278-279.

26. Arrian, *Anabasis of Alexander*, 2.17.7.

27. Old Tyre (Greek: *Palaetyrus*) was called *Ushu* in cuneiform texts. Jidejian, *Tyre*, 1.

28. Lane Fox, *Alexander*, 181; Diodorus, *Library of History*, 17.40.3.

29. Curtius, *History of Alexander*, 4.2.15.

30. Adriaan Lanni, "The Laws of War in Ancient Greece," *Law and History Review* 26, no. 3 (Fall, 2008): 478.

31. Homer, *Iliad*, trans. A. T. Murray, rev. William F. Wyatt (Cambridge, MA: Harvard University Press, 2003), 1.394.

32. Lanni, "Laws of War," 475.

33. Curtius, *History of Alexander*, 4.2.15.

34. Atkinson, *Commentary*, 298; Arrian, *Anabasis of Alexander*, 2.24.3. Mensch in Romm, *Landmark Arrian*, 94, and Hammond in *Arrian: Alexander the Great*, 65, both translate this phrase as "cut their throats."

35. Curtius uses the Latin word for herald (*caduceator*) in 4.2.15. Arrian uses the Greek word for herald, *kērux* (κῆρυξ), in other sections of the *Anabasis of Alexander* that do not deal with Tyre (4.22.6 for example).

36. Bosworth, *Conquest and Empire*, 65; Justin, *Epitome*, 145.

37. Fuller, *Generalship of Alexander the Great*, 208; Lane Fox, *Alexander*, 181.

38. Harden, *Phoenicians*, 66.

39. Marcus Junianus Justinus, *Epitome of the Philippic History of Pompeius Trogus*, trans. Rev. John Selby Watson (London: Henry G. Bohn, 1853), 18.4-6, https://www.forumromanum.org/literature/justin/english/index.html.

40. Elissa appears again (as Dido) in the *Aeneid*, where Virgil has her fall in love with Aeneas. When Aeneas leaves her to continue his journey, Dido is heartbroken and commits suicide. In the seventeenth century AD, the story of Dido and Aeneas was made into an opera by the English composer Henry Purcell.

41. Homer, *The Odyssey*, trans. Emily Wilson (New York: W. W. Norton, 2018), 14, 288-290; Susan Sheratt, "Greeks and Phoenicians: Perceptions of Trade and Traders in the Early First Millennium BC," in *Social Archaeologies of Trade and Exchange: Exploring Relationships among People, Places, and Things*, ed. Alexander A. Bauer and Anna S. Agbe-Davies (London: Taylor and Francis, 2016), 122.

42. Pamina Fernández Camacho, "Skilled at Grasping: The Phoenician Migrant and Exile as a Cautionary Stereotype from Classical Antiquity to Early Modern Europe," *Arethusa* 52, no. 2 (Spring 2019): 116.

43. Irene J. Winter, "Homer's Phoenicians: History, Ethnography, or Literary Trope?" in *The Ages of Homer: A Tribute to Emily Townsend Vermeule*, ed. Jane B. Carter and Sarah P. Morris (Austin: University of Texas Press, 1995), 256; Mark Peacock, "Rehabilitating Homer's Phoenicians: On Some Ancient and Modern Prejudices against Trade," *Ancient Society* 41 (2011): 18.

44. Curtius, *History of Alexander*, 4.4.18.

45. Justin, *Epitome*, 11.10.13-14.

46. Herodotus, *Persian Wars*, 3.19.

47. Diodorus, *Library of History*, 17.41.1.

48. Isocrates, *Evagoras. Helen. Busiris. Plataicus. Concerning the Team of Horses. Trapeziticus. Against Callimachus. Aegineticus. Against Lochites. Against Euthynus. Letters,* trans. Larue Van Hook (Cambridge, MA: Harvard University Press, 1945), 62.

49. Curtius, *History of Alexander*, 4.2.15.

50. Edmund F. Bloedow and Edmund J. Bloedow, "Alexander's Speech on the Eve of the Siege of Tyre," *L'Antiquité Classique* 63 (1994): 69.

51. Arrian, *Anabasis of Alexander*, 2.17.3-4.

52. Bloedow and Bloedow, "Alexander's Speech," 70; Curtius, *History of Alexander*, 4.5.14; Arrian, *Anabasis of Alexander*, app. 2, 456.

53. W. W. Tarn, *Alexander the Great 2: Sources and Studies* (Cambridge: Cambridge University Press, 1948), 286-287.

54. A. B. Bosworth, *A Historical Commentary on Arrian's History of Alexander* (Oxford: Clarendon, 1980): 238-239.

55. Curtius, *History of Alexander*, 4.2.17-18; Arrian, *Anabasis of Alexander*, 2.18.1.

56. Curtius, *History of Alexander*, 4.2.17.
57. Arrian, *Anabasis of Alexander*, 2.18.1.
58. Ibid., 2.18.2.

CHAPTER 10: THE MOLE

1. *Oxford English Dictionary* online, www.oed.com; Henry George Liddell and Robert Scott, *A Greek-English Lexicon, 9th ed.* (Oxford: Clarendon, 1996); Charlton T. Lewis and Charles Short, *Harpers' Latin Dictionary. A New Latin Dictionary Founded on the Translation of Freund's Latin-German Lexicon* (New York: American Book Company, 1907), 1157.
2. Lane Fox, *Alexander*, 184.
3. Campbell, *Ancient Siege Warfare*, 26.
4. Diodorus, *Library of History*, 14.48.2-3.
5. Campbell, *Ancient Siege Warfare*, 24; John W. I. Lee, "The Fight for Ancient Sicily," *Archaeology* 64, no. 1 (January/February 2011): 38-41.
6. Diodorus, *Library of History*, 17.40.5; David Whitehead, *Philo Mechanicus: On Sieges* (Stuttgart: Franz Steiner Verlag, 2016), 13; Ian Worthington, *Alexander the Great: Man and God* (London: Routledge, 2004), 107.
7. Curtius, *History of Alexander*, 4.2.7; Bosworth, *Conquest and Empire*, 65; Lane Fox, *Alexander*, 181; Whitehead, *Philo Mechanicus*, 13.
8. Lane Fox, *Alexander*, 181; Paul Cartledge, *Alexander the Great: The Hunt for a New Past* (Woodstock, NY: Overlook Press, 2004), 147.
9. SEG (Society of Exploration Geophysicists), "Levantine Basin," https://wiki.seg.org/wiki/Levantine_Basin.
10. LCBI Lebanon News, "Ancient Greek Ruins Discovered Underwater South of Tyre," April 16, 2019, https://www.lbcgroup.tv/news/d/lebanon-news/438989/ancient-greek-ruins-discovered-underwater-south-of/en; Coral Diving Crete, "Ancient Wrecks Found in Lebanon and Croatia," June 5, 2019, https://www.coraldivingcrete.com/news/news-1018-ancient-wrecks-found-in-lebanon-and-croatia/.
11. Arrian, *Anabasis of Alexander*, 2.18.3.
12. Whitehead, *Philo Mechanicus*, 13.
13. Green writes that "the channel between Tyre and the mainland was over twenty feet deep" but gives no reference for the source of this figure. Green, *Alexander of Macedon*, 248.
14. This computation, 200 x (1/2 x 2,400 x 18) = 4,320,000, assumes that the change in depth occurs evenly over the 2,400 feet of length. The assumption is that the side view of the mole would be a triangle with a base of 2,400 feet and a height of 18 feet.
15. Lane Fox, *Alexander*, 184. For a thorough analysis of the origins of the wheelbarrow, see M. J. T. Lewis, "The Origins of the Wheelbarrow," *Technology and Culture* 35, no. 3 (July 1994): 453-75.
16. *Oxford English Dictionary*; Nick Marriner, Christophe Morhange, and Samuel Meule, "Holocene Morphogenesis of Alexander the Great's Isthmus at Tyre in Lebanon," *Proceedings of the National Academy of Sciences* 104, no. 22 (May 29, 2007): 9218–23; N. Marriner, J. P. Goiran, and C. Morhange, "Alexander the Great's tombolos at Tyre and Alexandria, Eastern Mediterranean," *Geomorphology* 100 (2008): 377–400.
17. Marriner et al., "Holocene Morphogenesis," 9218, 9219.
18. Ibid., 9220.
19. Romm, *Landmark Arrian*, 86.
20. Arrian, *Anabasis of Alexander*, 2.18.5.
21. Ibid., 2.18.4.

22. Polyaenus, *Stratagems of War*, trans. R. Shepherd (Chicago: Ares, 1974), 4.3.3.

23. Curtius, *History of Alexander*, 4.2.16.

24. Diodorus, *Library of History*, 17.40.5; Fuller, *Generalship of Alexander the Great*, 209.

25. Curtius, *History of Alexander*, 4.2.8.

26. Ibid., 4.2.18; Arrian, *Anabasis of Alexander*, 2.18.3.

27. Stephen English, *The Sieges of Alexander the Great* (Barnsley, UK: Pen & Sword Military, 2009), 60-61.

28. Arrian, *Anabasis of Alexander*, 2.21.4.

29. Whitehead, *Philo Mechanicus*, 13.

30. Bosworth, *A Historical Commentary*, 247; Whitehead and Blyth, *Athenaeus Mechanicus*, 180; Whitehead, *Philo Mechanicus*, 154; Campbell, *Ancient Siege Warfare*, 61; Fik Meijer, *A History of Seafaring in the Classical World* (London: Croom Helm, 1986), 128; Hammond, *Arrian: Alexander the Great*, 289.

31. English, *Sieges of Alexander*, 12; Lane Fox, *Alexander*, 181.

32. Kern, *Ancient Siege Warfare*, 209; Fuller, *Generalship of Alexander the Great*, 208; Heckel, *Conquests of Alexander the Great*, 67; Woolmer and Markoe, *Short History*, 55; W. W. Tarn, *Hellenistic Military & Naval Developments* (New York: Biblo and Tannen, 1966), 110; Worthington, *Alexander the Great*, 107; Green, *Alexander of Macedon*, 247.

33. Whitehead, *Philo Mechanicus*, 154.

CHAPTER 11: TYRE STRIKES BACK

1. Diodorus, *Library of History*, 17.41.1; Curtius, *History of Alexander*, 4.2.20.

2. Diodorus, *Library of History*, 17.41.8; Plutarch, *Lives: Alexander and Caesar*, 24; Curtius, *History of Alexander*, 4.3.22.

3. Arrian, *Anabasis of Alexander*, 2.18.5.

4. Curtius, *History of Alexander*, 4.2.22.

5. Diodorus, *Library of History*, 17.42.2.

6. Strauss, *Battle of Salamis*, xviii.

7. Curtius, *History of Alexander*, 4.2.23.

8. Arrian, *Anabasis of Alexander*, 2.18.6; Curtius, *History of Alexander*, 4.2.23; Diodorus, *Library of History*, 17.42.1.

9. Diodorus, 17.42.4; Tarn, *Alexander the Great 2*, 121.

10. E. W. Marsden, *Greek and Roman Artillery: Historical Development* (Oxford: Clarendon, 1969), 118.

11. Curtius, *History of Alexander*, 4.2.23; English, *Sieges of Alexander*, 63; Curtius, *History of Alexander*, 4.2.24.

12. Arrian, *Anabasis of Alexander*, 2.18.5, 2.18.6.

13. Fuller, *Generalship of Alexander the Great*, 209-210; Tarn, *Alexander the Great 1*, 38; Bosworth, *Conquest and Empire*, 65.

14. Morrison and Coates, *Greek and Roman Oared Warships*, 345.

15. Campbell, *Ancient Siege Warfare*, 4.

16. Lane Fox, *Alexander*, 183.

17. Marsden, "Macedonian Military Machinery," 212.

18. Kern, *Ancient Siege Warfare*, 163, 181.

19. Lane Fox, *Alexander*, 191.

20. Marsden, "Macedonian Military Machinery," 220.

21. Whitehead and Blyth, *Athenaeus Mechanicus*, 86; Marsden, "Macedonian Military Machinery," 221.

22. English, *Sieges of Alexander*, 15. He argues that the Tyrians "may well have tried to secure ropes to [the towers] and drag them, using ships, into the sea." However, it seems implausible that a trireme could generate enough force to move what must have been a very heavy tower, even if it had been on wheels.

23. Ibid., 67.

24. For a thorough discussion of whether the mobile towers of Diades had wheels, see David Whitehead, "Alexander the Great and the *Mechanici*," in *East and West in the World Empire of Alexander: Essays in Honour of Brian Bosworth*, ed. Pat Wheatley (Oxford: Oxford University Press, 2015), 87-91.

25. Lane Fox, *Search for Alexander*, 185.

26. Whitehead and Blyth, *Athenaeus Mechanicus*, 90.

27. Romm, *Demetrius*, 56.

28. Whitehead and Blyth, *Athenaeus Mechanicus*, 182, 183.

29. Ibid., 183, 184; Bosworth, *Historical Commentary*, 240.

30. Arrian, *Anabasis of Alexander*, 2.19.1; Curtius, *History of Alexander*, 4.3.1; Arrian, *Anabasis of Alexander*, 2.19.1.

31. Romm, *Landmark Arrian*, 86; Hammond, *Arrian: Alexander the Great*, 59. The Cambridge Greek Lexicon gives a definition for the word *klēmatōn* (κλημάτων) of "cut vine-branch" and a definition for the word *klēmatis* (κλημάτις) of "vine-branch used as firewood."

32. English, *Sieges of Alexander*, 65.

33. Arrian, *Anabasis of Alexander*, 2.19.1; Curtius, *History of Alexander*, 4.3.2; Arrian, *Anabasis of Alexander*, 2.19.3.

34. Arrian, *Anabasis of Alexander*, 2.19.2; Fuller, *Generalship of Alexander the Great*, 210; Lane Fox, *Alexander*, 185; Bosworth, *Historical Commentary*, 241.

35. Arrian, *Anabasis of Alexander*, 2.19.2.

36. Curtius, *History of Alexander*, 4.3.2; Arrian, *Anabasis of Alexander*, 2.19.3.

37. Romm, *Landmark Arrian*, 86.

38. Bosworth, *Historical Commentary*, 241; Hammond, *Arrian: Alexander the Great*, 59.

39. Arrian, *Anabasis of Alexander*, 2.19.3-4.

40. Curtius, *History of Alexander*, 4.3.4-5.

41. Arrian, *Anabasis of Alexander*, 2.19.5.

42. Curtius, *History of Alexander*, 4.3.6-7.

43. Ibid., 4.3.11.

CHAPTER 12: "THE SHIPS IN ALL THEIR NUMBERS!"

1. Arrian, *Anabasis of Alexander*, 2.19.6.

2. Lane Fox, *Alexander*, 185; Arrian, *Anabasis of Alexander*, 2.19.6; Curtius, *History of Alexander*, 4.3.8.

3. Diodorus, *Library of History*, 17.42.6.

4. Curtius, *History of Alexander*, 4.3.9.

5. Ibid., 4.3.8.

6. Atkinson, *Commentary*, 302.

7. Arrian, *Anabasis of Alexander*, 2.19.6.

8. Ibid.

9. Ibid., 2.20.1-2.

10. Lane Fox, *Alexander*, 185.

11. Arrian, *Anabasis of Alexander*, 2.20.3.

12. Hammond, *Arrian: Alexander the Great*, 60.

13. Arrian, *Anabasis of Alexander*, 2.20.3.

14. William M. Murray, *The Age of Titans: The Rise and Fall of the Great Hellenistic Navies* (Oxford: Oxford University Press, 2012), 96.

15. Curtius, *History of Alexander*, 4.3.11; Arrian, *Anabasis of Alexander*, 2.20.5.

16. Matthew Trundle, "The Business of War: Mercenaries," in *The Oxford Handbook of Warfare in the Classical World*, ed. Brian Campbell and Lawrence A. Tritle (Oxford: Oxford University Press, 2013), 342.

17. Ibid., 336.

18. Engels, *Alexander the Great*, 55.

19. Michael Morrison, "Old Testament Laws: Harvest Seasons of Ancient Israel," Grace Communion International, https://archive.gci.org/articles/harvest-seasons-of-ancient-israel/.

20. Engels, *Alexander the Great*, 55.

21. Josephus, *Jewish Antiquities*, trans. Ralph Marcus (Cambridge, MA: Harvard University Press, 1937), 11.317.

22. Curtius, *History of Alexander*, 4.2.24 says the tribesmen attacked the Macedonians in the Lebanon mountains, on the west side of the Bekaa valley, rather than the Antilebanon mountains to the east.

23. Arrian, *Anabasis of Alexander*, 2.20.4-5.

24. Plutarch, *Lives: Alexander and Caesar*, 24.

25. In the *Iliad*, Phoenix taught the young Achilles "warfare and debate." As an old man, Phoenix accompanied the Greeks to Troy and attempted to heal the schism between Achilles and Agamemnon. C. J. Mackie, "Achilles' Teachers: Chiron and Phoenix in the *Iliad*," *Greece & Rome* 44, no. 1 (April 1997): 1-10.

26. Elizabeth Carney, "Artifice and Alexander History," in *Alexander the Great in Fact and Fiction*, ed. A. B. Bosworth and E. J. Baynham (Oxford: Oxford University Press, 2000), 275.

27. See for example Richard Stoneman, ed., *Alexander the Great: The Making of a Myth* (London: British Library, 2022).

28. Lane Fox, *Search for Alexander*, 40; Lane Fox, *Alexander*, 186.

29 Homer, *The Iliad*, trans. Robert Fagles (New York: Penguin, 1990), 115. Alexander was reputed to have kept the *Iliad* with him on campaign.

30. DeVries, "Greek, Etruscan and Phoenician Ships and Shipping," 41. According to Morrison and Coates, *Greek and Roman Oared Warships*, 255, the Greek term for "long ships" was *makrai nees* (μακραὶ νῆες) and for "round ships" was *strongyloi nees* (στρογγύλοι νῆες).

31. Morrison and Coates, *Greek and Roman Oared Warships*, 258.

32. De Souza, "War at Sea," 372.

33. J. S. Morrison, J. F. Coates, and N. B. Rankov, *The Athenian Trireme: The History and Reconstruction of an Ancient Greek Warship* (Cambridge: Cambridge University Press, 2000), 290.

34. Strauss, *Battle of Salamis*, xvii.

35. Ibid., xvii-xix.

36. Morrison and Coates, *Greek and Roman Oared Warships*, 326.

37. DeVries and Katzev, "Greek, Etruscan and Phoenician," 45; Strauss, *Battle of Salamis*, 148.

38. Strauss, *Battle of Salamis*, 147.

39. De Souza, "War at Sea," 377.

40. Ibid., 374.

41. Strauss, *Battle of Salamis*, xviii.

42. DeVries and Katzev, "Greek, Etruscan and Phoenician," 45; De Souza, "War at Sea," 374.

43. Meijer, *History of Seafaring*, 118; DeVries and Katzev, "Greek, Etruscan and Phoenician," 46.

44. Meijer, *History of Seafaring*, 117.

45. Ibid., 118.

46. Ibid., 121; Morrison and Coates, *Greek and Roman Oared Warships*, xiii.

47. Morrison and Coates, *Greek and Roman Oared Warships*, 260.

48. Meijer, *History of Seafaring*, 117.

49. Lionel Casson argues that these ships could not have been much wider than triremes because they were housed in the same ship sheds, which had a limited width. Lionel Casson, *Ships and Seamanship in the Ancient World* (Baltimore: Johns Hopkins University Press, 1995), 102.

50. Morrison and Coates, *Greek and Roman Oared Warships*, 257, 285.

51. Ibid., 269.

52. Another possibility advocated by some scholars is that the quinquereme had a single level of oars, with five rowers manning each oar. Adrian Goldsworthy, *The Fall of Carthage: The Punic Wars 265–146 BC* (London: Cassell, 2000), 99; Tarn, *Hellenistic Military*, 125-126.

53. W. W. Tarn, "The Fleets of the First Punic War," *Journal of Hellenic Studies* 27 (1907): 60.

54. Curtius, *History of Alexander*, 4.3.11.

55. Pnytagoras was the king of the Cypriot city of Salamis. Romm, *Landmark Arrian*, 88; Curtius, *History of Alexander*, 4.3.11. The Cypriot city has the same name as the Greek island of Salamis, site of the famous sea battle between Greeks and Persians in 480.

56. Arrian, *Anabasis of Alexander*, 2.20.6.

57. Diodorus, *Library of History*, 17.41.1.

58. Herodotus, *Persian Wars*, 7.89.

59. Arrian, *Anabasis of Alexander*, 2.20.8; Diodorus, *Library of History*, 17.42.3-5.

60. Curtius, *History of Alexander*, 4.3.12; Arrian, *Anabasis of Alexander*, 2.20.9.

61. Arrian, *Anabasis of Alexander*, 2.20.8.

CHAPTER 13: BY LAND AND SEA

1. According to Tarn, the Greek word for catapult—καταπέλτης (*katapeltēs*)—"means something which, unlike the hand-bow, would pierce a πέλτη [*peltē*] or shield." Tarn, *Hellenistic Military*, 104.

2. Diodorus, *Library of History*, 17.41.3-4.

3. Hanson, *Wars*, 155; Marsden, *Greek and Roman Artillery*, 48; Campbell, *Ancient Siege Warfare*, 26. Although most scholars think catapults originated in Sicily, Leigh Alexander argues that catapults originated with the Assyrians. Leigh Alexander, "The Origin of Greek and Roman Artillery," *Classical Journal* 41, no. 5 (February 1946): 208-212.

4. Marsden, *Greek and Roman Artillery*, 86.

5. Ibid., 15.

6. *The Oxford English Dictionary* defines "torsion" as "the action of twisting, or turning a body spirally by the operation of contrary forces acting at right angles to its axis." Archaeologists have unearthed catapult bolt heads made of bronze with the name Philip (ΦΙΛΙΠΠΟ) clearly inscribed on them. Marsden, "Macedonian Military Machinery," 215, 216. T. E. Rihll, *The Catapult: A History* (Yardley, PA: Westholme, 2007), 89.

7. Fuller, *Generalship of Alexander the Great*, 45; Tarn, *Hellenistic Military*, 106.

8. Marsden, *Greek and Roman Artillery*, 87.

9. Tarn, *Hellenistic Military*, 114. In Tarn's view, the well-known story by Appian of Carthaginian women cutting their hair for use on catapults during the Roman siege was worth recording not because women cut their hair for this purpose but because these women were from wealthy families and would never have sold their hair but were willing to donate

it in defense of their city. Ibid., 115; Appian, *Roman History Volume 2*, ed. and trans. Brian McGing (Cambridge, MA: Harvard University Press, 2019), 8.1.441.

10. Hanson, *Wars*, 158; Marsden, *Greek and Roman Artillery*, 118.

11. Marsden, *Greek and Roman Artillery*, 24, 103; Rihll, *Catapult*, 86.

12. Arrian, *Anabasis of Alexander*, 2.21.3.

13. Campbell, *Ancient Siege Warfare*, 44; Marsden, *Greek and Roman Artillery*, 61, 97; Tarn, *Hellenistic Military*, 115.

14. English, *Sieges of Alexander*, 5.

15. From the Greek *monas* (μονάς) meaning "one" and *ankōn* (ἀγκών) meaning "arm." The Greek word μονάγκων (*monankōn*) is often transliterated as "*monagkōn*" (e.g., Rihll, *Catapult*, 77; English, *Sieges of Alexander*, 4; Whitehead, *Philo Mechanicus*, 281), although the Greek letter gamma (γ) has the sound of the English "n" rather than "g" when followed by a kappa (κ). James Morwood, *Oxford Grammar of Classical Greek* (Oxford: Oxford University Press, 2001), 1.

16. English, *Sieges of Alexander*, 4.

17. Marsden, *Greek and Roman Artillery*, 80.

18. Ibid., 53; G. Rawlinson, *Five Great Monarchies of the Ancient Eastern World* (London: John Murray, 1871), 472.

19. Whitehead, *Philo Mechanicus*, 281. Philon was writing half a century after Alexander. He is thought to have written his treatise in the city of Alexandria, which had not yet been founded at the time of the siege of Tyre. The 1996 edition of the Liddell and Scott *Greek-English Lexicon* defines πετροβόλοις as "an engine for throwing stones."

20. Rihll, *Catapult*, 76-77.

21. D. B. Campbell, "Review of T. Rihll, The Catapult: A History," in *American Journal of Archaeology* 112, no. 1 (January 2008), www.ajaonline.org/book-review/536. The quote from Rihll's book is on p. 61.

22. E. P. Barker, "Palintonon and Euthutonon," *Classical Quarterly* 14, no. 2 (1920): 85. This argument apparently does not apply to wheelbarrows, which scholars believe were developed from two-wheeled carts. Lewis, "Origins of the Wheelbarrow," 453.

23. Barker, "Palintonon and Euthutonon," 85.

24. Ibid.

25. English, *Sieges of Alexander*, 4-5; Barker, "Palintonon and Euthutonon," 85.

26. Rihll, *Catapult*, 87, 88; Tarn, *Hellenistic Military*, 117.

27. Diodorus, *Library of History*, 17.43.3.

28. Ibid., 17.43.2; Curtius, *History of Alexander*, 4.3.13.

29. Arrian, *Anabasis of Alexander*, 2.21.1.

30. Bosworth, *Historical Commentary*, 246.

31. Tarn, *Hellenistic Military*, 120.

32. Murray, "Development," 32.

33. Whitehead, "Alexander the Great and the *Mechanici*," 78; Diodorus, *Library of History*, 17.43.4; Arrian, *Anabasis of Alexander*, 2.21.1; Curtius, *History of Alexander*, 4.3.14-15.

34. Atkinson, *Commentary*, 304.

35. Curtius, *History of Alexander*, 4.3.15.

36. Atkinson, *Commentary*, 304.

37. Marsden, *Greek and Roman Artillery*, 117.

38. Curtius, *History of Alexander*, 4.3.13-14; Diodorus, *Library of History*, 17.43.5.

39. Arrian, *Anabasis of Alexander*, 2.21.5.

40. Fuller, *Generalship of Alexander the Great*, 213.

41. Arrian, *Anabasis of Alexander*, 2.21.5-6.

42. Ibid., 2.21.6, 2.21.7; Lane Fox, *Alexander*, 188; Hammond, *Arrian: Alexander the Great*, 62.
43. Bosworth, *Historical Commentary*, 248; Romm, *Demetrius*, 56; Murray, *Age of Titans*, 149; Tarn, *Hellenistic Military*, 115.
44. Curtius, *History of Alexander*, 4.3.16-18.
45. As discussed in chapter 6, the details of the timing and content of the letters from Darius to Alexander, as recorded by the ancient historians, are inconsistent and difficult to reconcile. This book presents the timing and details as recorded by Arrian. Bosworth suggests that this letter may have been received during Alexander's second visit to Tyre in 331, as he was returning from Egypt. Bosworth, *Historical Commentary*, 256.
46. Arrian, *Anabasis of Alexander*, 2.25.1.
47. Ibid., 2.25.2; Plutarch, *Lives*, 29.4; Bosworth, *Historical Commentary*, 257.
48. Arrian, *Anabasis of Alexander*, 2.25.3.

CHAPTER 14: SHIPS AND LADDERS

1. Diodorus, *Library of History*, 17.44.2-3; Quintus Curtius, *History of Alexander*, 4.3.24.
2. Tarn, *Alexander the Great 2*, 121.
3. English, *Sieges of Alexander*, 75. While it is unclear how hot this sand would have been when it hit the attackers, materials become visibly red hot at between 500 and 1,000 degrees Celsius (932 and 1,832 degrees Fahrenheit). Peter M. B. Walker, ed., *Larousse Dictionary of Science and Technology* (New York: Larousse, 1995), 920.
4. Whitehead, *Philo Mechanicus*, 154.
5. Bosworth, *Historical Commentary*, 247.
6. H. G. Liddell and R. Scott, *Greek-English Lexicon with a Revised Supplement* (Oxford: Clarendon, 1996); *The Brill Dictionary of Ancient Greek* (Leiden, Netherlands: Brill, 2015); J. Diggle, editor in chief, *The Cambridge Greek Lexicon* (Cambridge: Cambridge University Press, 2021).
7. Arrian, *Anabasis of Alexander* (Brunt trans.); Hammond, trans., *Arrian: Alexander the Great*; Romm, ed., *Landmark Arrian* (Mensch trans.); Diodorus, *Library of History* (Welles trans.); Chinnock, trans., *Arrian, Anabasis of Alexander*.
8. Like all nouns in ancient Greek, *epibathra* takes on different endings depending on number (singular or plural) and case—how the word is used in the sentence: as the subject (nominative), the object (accusative), or showing possession (genitive). For singular, the endings are -*a* (nominative) and -*an* (accusative); for plural the endings are *ai* (nominative), -*as* (accusative), and -*ōn* (genitive).
9. Vitruvius, *On Arcitecture*, trans. Frank Granger (Cambridge, MA: Harvard University Press, 1934), 10.13.8, 372.
10. Whitehead, "Athenaeus (2) Mechanicus," *Oxford Classical Dictionary*, January, 30, 2020, https://doi.org/10.1093/acrefore/9780199381135.013.914; Jan Stronk, *Semiramis' Legacy: The History of Persia According to Diodorus of Sicily* (Edinburgh: Edinburgh University Press, 2017), 308; Plutarch, *Life of Demetrius*, trans. Bernadotte Perrin (Cambridge, MA: Harvard University Press, 1920), 8.2; Christos Makrypoulias, "Siege Warfare: The Art of Re-capture," in *Brill's Companions to the Byzantine World Volume 3: A Companion to the Byzantine Culture of War, ca. 300-1204*, ed. Yannis Stouraitis (Leiden, Netherlands: Brill, 2018), 366; Frederick Winter, *Studies in Hellenistic Architecture* (Toronto: University of Toronto Press, 2006), 184; David Whitehead, "Siege Warfare," in *A Companion to Greek Warfare*, ed. Waldemar Heckel, F. S. Naiden, E. Edward Garvin, and John Vanderspoel (Hoboken, NJ: John Wiley & Sons, 2021), 117; David Whitehead, "Fact and Fantasy in Greek Military Writers," *Acta antiqua Academiae Scientiarum Hungaricae* 48 no. 1 (2008), 150; Duncan B. Campbell, *Besieged: Siege Warfare in the Ancient World* (Oxford: Osprey, 2006), 62.

11. In both of these cases (Syracuse and Rhodes), the use of the *sambuca* was apparently not successful.

12. Bosworth, *Historical Commentary*, 247.

13. Whitehead and Blyth, *Athenaeus Mechanicus,* 89; Heckel, *Conquests of Alexander the Great,* 68; Tarn, *Hellenistic Military,* 111-112.

14. English, *Sieges of Alexander,* 74.

15. Polybius, *The Histories,* trans. W. R. Paton, revised by Frank W. Walbank and Christian Habicht (Cambridge, MA: Harvard University Press, 2011), 8.4-6.

16. Tarn, *Alexander the Great 2,* 120.

17. Bosworth, *Historical Commentary,* 251.

18. Murray, *Age of Titans,* 89.

19. Murray, "Development," 39.

20. Ibid., 35.

21. Murray, *Age of Titans,* 98.

22. Arrian, *Anabasis of Alexander,* 1.19.5.

23. Murray, *Age of Titans,* 305.

24. For a thorough discussion of this issue, see David A. Guenther, "Diodorus Siculus and the *Purgos* at Tyre: Did Alexander Put Towers on Ships?," *Classical Philology* 119, no. 3 (July 2024): 421-25.

25. Adrian Goldsworthy, *Philip and Alexander: Kings and Conquerors* (New York: Basic Books, 2020), 304.

26. Arrian, *Anabasis of Alexander,* 2.27.5-6. Worthington avoids the distinction between scaling ladders and boarding bridges, stating that Alexander's ships "were equipped with stone-throwing catapults and scaling bridges." Worthington, *Alexander the Great,* 109.

CHAPTER 15: DESPERATE MEASURES

1. Diodorus, *Library of History,* 17.43.7; Curtius, *History of Alexander,* 4.3.24; Tarn, *Alexander the Great 2,* 120, 122.

2. Diodorus, *Library of History,* 17.44.4; Curtius, *History of Alexander,* 4.3.24.

3. Diodorus, *Library of History,* 17.43.1,17.45.4; Whitehead, *Philo Mechanicus: On Sieges,* 276.

4. Diodorus, *Library of History,* 17.43.7.

5. Ibid., 17.43.10; Campbell, *Besieged,* 62.

6. Tarn, *Alexander the Great 2,* 120; Hammond, *Three Historians,* 175.

7. Diodorus, *Library of History,* 17.45.3.

8. Ibid., 17.43.1.

9. English, *Sieges of Alexander,* 74-75; Patrick Romane, "Alexander's Siege on Tyre," *Ancient World* 16, no. 3 (Winter 1987): 87.

10. Bosworth, *Conquest and Empire,* 66; Lane Fox, *Alexander,* 188; Fuller, *Generalship of Alexander the Great,* 210; Tarn, *Alexander the Great 2,* 120-121.

11. Curtius, *History of Alexander,* 4.3.19-20.

12. Atkinson, *Commentary,* 305; Curtius, *History of Alexander,* 4.3.20.

13. Atkinson, *Commentary,* 305.

14. Manuel Alvarez Marti-Aguilar, "The Gadir-Tyre Axis," in *The Oxford Handbook of the Phoenician and Punic Mediterranean,* ed. Carolina Lopez-Ruiz and Brian R. Doak (Oxford: Oxford University Press, 2019), 622.

15. Curtius, *History of Alexander,* 4.3.23; Atkinson, *Commentary,* 306; Xella, "Religion," 289.

16. Atkinson, *Commentary,* 308; Curtius, *History of Alexander,* 4.4.3-5.

17. Curtius, *History of Alexander,* 4.4.5.

18. Harrison, "Triremes," 170-71.

19. Arrian, *Anabasis of Alexander*, 2.21.8, 2.21.9; Bosworth, *Historical Commentary*, 249.

20. Arrian, *Anabasis of Alexander*, 2.21.9-22.1-2.

21. Ibid., 2.22.3.

22. Ibid., 2.22.4-5.

23. Curtius, *History of Alexander*, 4.4.9.

CHAPTER 16: THE BREACH

1. Stanley Gevirtz, "On Canaanite Rhetoric: The Evidence of the Amarna Letters from Tyre," *Orientalia* 42 (1973): 165.

2. Curtius, *History of Alexander*, 4.4.1.

3. Diodorus, *Library of History*, 17.45.7.

4. Lloyd Llewellyn-Jones, "Wives, Other Women and Boyfriends," in *Alexander the Great: The Making of a Myth*, ed. Richard Stoneman (London: British Library, 2022), 159; Fuller, *Generalship of Alexander the Great*, 214-215; Lane Fox, *Alexander*, 190; Bosworth, *Historical Commentary*, 253.

5. Arrian, *Anabasis of Alexander*, 2.22.6-7.

6. Ibid., 2.22.7; Romm, *Landmark Arrian*, 91; Hammond, *Arrian: Alexander the Great*, 64.

7. Vitruvius, *On Architecture*, 10.13.2; Josephus, *The Jewish War*, trans. H. St. J. Thackeray (Cambridge, MA: Harvard University Press, 1927), 3.7.19; Procopius, *History of the Wars* (*Gothic War*), trans. H. B. Dewing (Cambridge, MA: Harvard University Press, 1916), 1.21.8.

8. Josephus, *Jewish War*, 3.7.19; Procopius, *History*, 1.21.11.

9. Arrian, *Anabasis of Alexander*, 2.22.7. In Romm, *Landmark Arrian*, 91, Pamela Mensch also translates *gephuras* as "gangways." Hammond, *Arrian: Alexander the Great*, 64, translates the word as "ramps."

10. Arrian, *Anabasis of Alexander*, 2.23.1.

11. Ibid., 2.23.2; Romm, *Landmark Arrian*, 91; Hammond, *Arrian: Alexander the Great*, 64; Polybius, *Histories*, 8.4-6.

12. Bosworth, *Historical Commentary*, 251. ἐπιβάθραι (*epibathrai*) are what Bosworth considers to be siege ladders. In Bosworth's view, the siege ladders are also described by Arrian's term *gephuras*. See chapter 14. Compare this with English's statement (also discussed in chapter 14) that the red-hot sand was poured onto Macedonian soldiers as they climbed up ladders. Here Bosworth is arguing that by using what he considers to be siege ladders and climbing to the top of the wall, the Macedonians would *avoid* red-hot sand being poured on them.

13. English presents an argument related to this point, writing, "Diodorus tells us that triremes were lashed together and siege towers built on them, thus allowing the rams to attack higher up the walls where they would be weaker." Stephen English, "The Campaigns of Alexander the Great" (PhD diss., Durham University, 2009), 124. Given the effect that a heavy ram swinging high in a tower would have on a ship's center of gravity, this explanation seems unlikely.

14. Bosworth, *Historical Commentary*, 253; Romm, *Landmark Arrian*, 92.

15. Arrian, *Anabasis of Alexander*, 2.23.4.

16. Bosworth, *Historical Commentary*, 250-251; Diodorus, *Library of History*, 17.46.2; Bosworth, *Historical Commentary*, 251.

17. Murray, *Age of Titans*, 99; Arrian, *Anabasis of Alexander*, 2.22.7.

18. Fuller, *Generalship of Alexander the Great*, 214-215; Lane Fox, *Alexander*, 190.

19. Arrian, *Anabasis of Alexander*, 2.23.2.

20. Romm, *Landmark Arrian*, 91.

21. Arrian, *Anabasis of Alexander*, 2.23.3. It isn't clear what "run ashore" means in this context, since there were no beaches on Tyre. The *Landmark Arrian* translation by Pamela Mensch reads "make landings wherever this could be managed."

22. Arrian, *Anabasis of Alexander*, 2.23.5. Tarn writes that the full name of the Shield Bearers (*hypaspists*) was "the hypaspists of the Companions." Tarn, *Alexander the Great 2*, 148.

23. Romm, *Landmark Arrian*, 92; Bosworth, *Historical Commentary*, 253.

24. Arrian, *Anabasis of Alexander*, 2.23.4-6.

25. Ibid., *Anabasis of Alexander*, 2.24.1, 2.24.2.

CHAPTER 17: THE LAND SIEGE

1. Diodorus, *Library of History*, 17.42.5-7, 17.43.1-3.

2. Ibid., 17.43.4; Arrian, *Anabasis of Alexander*, 2.22.7

3. Diodorus, *Library of History*, 17.43.3.

4. Tarn, *Alexander the Great 2*, 120.

5. Ibid., 68.

6. Bosworth, *Historical Commentary*, 250-251.

7. Ibid., 247.

8. Hammond, *Three Historians*, 175.

9. Diodorus, *Library of History*, 17.43.6-17.44.5, 17.45.3-4.

10. Ibid., 17.45.5-6.

11. Ibid., 17.45.6.

12. Bosworth, *Historical Commentary*, 253; Hammond, *Three Historians*, 42.

13. Goldsworthy, *Philip and Alexander*, 304.

14. Campbell, *Besieged*, 65.

15. Goldsworthy, *Philip and Alexander*, 304; Green, *Alexander of Macedon*, 261.

16. Diodorus, *Library of History*, 17.45.7-17.46.1, 17.46.2; Bosworth, *Historical Commentary*, 249, 251.

17. Diodorus, *Library of History*, 17.46.3.

18. Hammond, *Three Historians*, 176.

19. Romane, "Alexander's Siege," 88.

20. Curtius, *History of Alexander*, 4.3.25-4.4.2.

21. Ibid., 4.3.13, 4.4.6-9.

22. Ibid., 4.4.10.

23. Ibid., 4.4.10; Tarn, *Alexander the Great 2*, 121.

24. Curtius, *History of Alexander*, 4.4.10-11.

25. Ibid., 4.4.12.

26. Ibid., 4.4.12-13.

CHAPTER 18: THE UNCHAINED GOD

1. Arrian, *Anabasis of Alexander*, 2.24.3, 2.24.4; Diodorus, *Library of History*, 17.46.3; Curtius, *History of Alexander*, 4.4.16.

2. Arrian, Anabasis of Alexander, 2.24.5.

3. Curtius, *History of Alexander*, 4.4.14, 4.4.15-16.

4. Ibid., 4.4.17; Diodorus, *Library of History*, 17.46.4.

5. Markoe, *Phoenicians*, 196.

6. See Elizabeth D. Carney, "Women and War in the Greek World," in *A Companion to Greek Warfare*, ed. Waldemar Heckel, F. S. Naiden, E. Edward Garvin, and John Vanderspoel (Chichester, UK: Wiley Blackwell, 2021), 339-348.

7. Kathy L. Gaca, "Reinterpreting the Homeric Simile of 'Iliad' 16.7-11: The Girl and Her Mother in Ancient Greek Warfare," *American Journal of Philology* 129, no. 2 (Summer 2008): 146.

8. Jennifer Martinez Morales, "Women on the Walls? The Role and Impact of Women in Classical Greek Sieges," in *Brill's Companion to Sieges in the Ancient Mediterranean*, ed. Jeremy Armstrong and Matthew Trundle (Boston: Brill, 2019), 163.

9. Jonathan Gottschall, *The Rape of Troy: Evolution, Violence, and the World of Homer* (Cambridge: Cambridge University Press, 2008), 68; Homer, *Iliad*, 2.355, 9.325.

10. Diodorus, *Library of History*, 17.46.6.

11. Arrian, *Anabasis of Alexander*, 2.24.5-6.

12. Diodorus, *Library of History*, 17.46.6.

13. Ibid.

CHAPTER 19: LAMENTATION

1. Arrian, *Anabasis of Alexander*, 3.25.4-3.27.7, 3.4.5.

2. Ibid., 3.2.3-7.

3. Harden, *Phoenicians*, 22.

4. Curtius, *History of Alexander*, 4.4.21; John D. Hosler, *The Siege of Acre, 1189-1191: Saladin, Richard the Lionheart, and the Battle That Decided the Third Crusade* (New Haven, CT: Yale University Press, 2018), 8.

5. Lane Fox, *Alexander*, 137; Heckel, *In the Path of Conquest*, 108; Cartledge, *Alexander the Great*, 175.

6. Ezekiel 27:32 (RSV).

APPENDIX A

1. Bosworth and Baynham, *Alexander the Great*, 6-7.

2. Adam Wallitt, "Two Great Historians Talk Alexander the Great Part 3," *Forbes*, December 20, 2010, https://www.forbes.com/sites/booked/2010/12/20/two-historians-talk-alexander-the-great-part-3/?sh=15aec7611c78.

3. Hammond, *Three Historians*, 82-83.

4. Llewellyn-Jones, "Wives," 159.

Bibliography

ANCIENT WRITERS IN TRANSLATION: HISTORIANS OF ALEXANDER

Arrian. *Anabasis of Alexander*. Translated by P. A. Brunt. Cambridge, MA: Harvard University Press, 1976. (Book 2 describes the siege of Tyre.)

Diodorus of Sicily. *The Library of History*. Translated by C. Bradford Welles. Cambridge, MA: Harvard University Press, 1963. (Book 17 describes the siege of Tyre.)

Justin. *Epitome of the Philippic History of Pompeius Trogus, Books 11-12: Alexander the Great*. Translated by J. C. Yardley, commentary by Waldemar Heckel. Oxford: Clarendon, 1997. (Book 11 contains a brief description of the siege of Tyre. There is extensive commentary by Heckel.)

Plutarch. *Lives: Alexander and Caesar*. Translated by Bernadotte Perrin. Cambridge, MA: Harvard University Press, 1919. (Part 24 contains a brief description of the siege of Tyre.)

Quintus Curtius. *History of Alexander*. Translated by John C. Rolfe. Cambridge, MA: Harvard University Press, 1946. (Book 4 describes the siege of Tyre.)

OTHER ANCIENT WRITERS IN TRANSLATION

Appian. *Roman History Volume 2*. Edited and translated by Brian McGing. Cambridge, MA: Harvard University Press, 2019.

Athenaeus. *The Learned Banqueters*. Translated by S. Douglas Olson. Cambridge, MA: Harvard University Press, 2010.

Herodotus. *The Persian Wars, Volume IV: Books 8-9*. Translated by A. D. Godley. Cambridge, MA: Harvard University Press, 1925.

Homer. *Iliad*. Translated by A. T. Murray, revised by William F. Wyatt. Cambridge, MA: Harvard University Press, 2003.

———. *The Iliad*. Translated by Robert Fagles. New York: Penguin, 1990.

———. *The Odyssey*. Translated by Emily Wilson. New York: W. W. Norton, 2018.

Isocrates. *Evagoras. Helen. Busiris. Plataicus. Concerning the Team of Horses. Trapeziticus. Against Callimachus. Aegineticus. Against Lochites. Against Euthynus. Letters.* Translated by Larue Van Hook. Cambridge, MA: Harvard University Press, 1945.

Josephus. *Jewish Antiquities.* Translated by Ralph Marcus. Cambridge, MA: Harvard University Press, 1963.

———. *The Jewish War.* Translated by H. St. J. Thackeray. Cambridge, MA: Harvard University Press, 1927.

Justinus, Marcus Junianus. *Epitome of the Philippic History of Pompeius Trogus.* Translated by Rev. John Selby Watson. London: Henry G. Bohn, 1853. https://www.forumromanum.org/literature/justin/english/index.html.

Pindar. *Nemean Odes. Isthmian Odes. Fragments.* Edited and translated by William H. Race. Cambridge, MA: Harvard University Press, 1997.

Pliny. *Natural History.* Translated by D. E. Eichholz. Cambridge, MA: Harvard University Press, 1962.

Plutarch. *Life of Demetrius.* Translated by Bernadotte Perrin. Cambridge, MA: Harvard University Press, 1920.

Polyaenus. *Stratagems of War.* Translated by R. Shepherd. Chicago: Ares, 1974.

Polybius. *The Histories.* Translated by W. R. Paton, revised by Frank W. Walbank and Christian Habicht. Cambridge, MA: Harvard University Press, 2011.

Pomponius Mela. *Description of the World.* Translated by F. E. Romer. Ann Arbor: University of Michigan Press, 1998.

Procopius. *History of the Wars (Gothic War).* Translated by H. B. Dewing. Cambridge, MA: Harvard University Press, 1916.

Strabo. *Geography.* Translated by Horace Leonard Jones. Cambridge, MA: Harvard University Press, 1930.

Vitruvius. *On Architecture.* Translated by Frank Granger. Cambridge, MA: Harvard University Press, 1934.

Xenophon. *Anabasis.* Translated by Carleton L. Brownson. Cambridge, MA: Harvard University Press, 1998.

OTHER SOURCES

Abdelhamid, Tarek Galal. "Notes on the Architecture and History of the Fortifications of the Island of Arwad in Syria." *Levant* 54, no. 1 (2022): 97-123.

Alexander, Leigh. "The Origin of Greek and Roman Artillery." *Classical Journal* 41, no. 5 (February 1946): 208-212.

Anglim, Simon, Phyllis G. Justice, Rob S. Rice, Scott M. Rusch, and John Serrati. *Fighting Techniques of the Ancient World 3000 BC—AD 500: Equipment, Combat Skills, and Tactics.* New York: St. Martin's Press, 2002.

Anson, Edward M. "Hellenistic Land Warfare." In *A Companion to Greek Warfare,* edited by Waldemar Heckel, F. S. Naiden, E. Edward Garvin, and John Vanderspoel, 42-57. Chichester UK: Wiley Blackwell, 2021.

————. "The Hypaspists: Macedonia's Professional Citizen-Soldiers." *Historia: Zeitschrift fur Alte Geschichte* (2nd Quarter 1985): 246-48.

————. "The Introduction of the 'Sarisa' in Macedonian Warfare." *Ancient Society* 40 (2010): 51-68.

————. "The Persian Fleet in 334." *Classical Philology* 84, no. 1 (1989): 44-49.

Astour, Michael C. "The Origin of the Terms 'Canaan,' 'Phoenician,' and 'Purple.'" *Journal of Near Eastern Studies* 24, no. 4 (October 1965): 346-50.

Atkinson, J. E. *A Commentary on Q. Curtius Rufus' "Historiae Alexandri Magni" Books 3 and 4*. Amsterdam: J. C. Gieben, 1980.

Badian, E. "The Battle of the Granicus: A New Look." In *Ancient Macedonia II: Papers Read at the Second International Symposium Held in Thessaloniki, 19-24 August 1973*. Thessaloniki, Greece: Institute for Balkan Studies (1977), 271-93.

Barker, E. P. "Palintonon and Euthutonon." *Classical Quarterly* 14, no. 2 (1920): 82-86.

Betlyon, John W. "Coins." In *The Oxford Handbook of the Phoenician and Punic Mediterranean*, edited by Carolina Lopez-Ruiz and Brian R. Doak, 385-400. Oxford: Oxford University Press, 2019.

Bloedow, Edmund F. "The Siege of Tyre in 332 BC. Alexander at the Crossroads in His Career." *La parola del passato* 301 (1998): 255-293.

Bloedow, Edmund F., and Edmund J. Bloedow. "Alexander's Speech on the Eve of the Siege of Tyre." *L'Antiquité Classique* 63 (1994): 65-76.

Bonnet, Corinne. "The Hellenistic Period and Hellenization in Phoenicia." In *The Oxford Handbook of the Phoenician and Punic Mediterranean*, edited by Carolina Lopez-Ruiz and Brian R. Doak, 99-110. Oxford: Oxford University Press, 2019.

Bosworth, A. B. *Conquest and Empire: The Reign of Alexander the Great*. Cambridge: Cambridge University Press, 1988.

————. *A Historical Commentary on Arrian's History of Alexander*. Oxford: Clarendon, 1980.

Bosworth, A. B., and E. J. Baynham, eds. *Alexander the Great in Fact and Fiction*. Oxford: Oxford University Press, 2000.

Bosworth, Brian. "A Tale of Two Empires: Hernán Cortés and Alexander the Great." In *Alexander the Great in Fact and Fiction*, edited by A. B. Bosworth and E. J. Baynham, 23-49. Oxford: Oxford University Press, 2000.

Brundage, Burr C. "Herakles the Levantine: A Comprehensive View." *Journal of Near Eastern Studies* 17, no. 4 (October, 1958): 225-36.

Budin, Stephanie Lynn. *The Myth of Sacred Prostitution in Antiquity*. Cambridge: Cambridge University Press, 2008.

Bunnens, Guy. "Phoenicia in the Later Iron Age." In *The Oxford Handbook of the Phoenician and Punic Mediterranean*, edited by Carolina Lopez-Ruiz and Brian R. Doak, 57-74. Oxford: Oxford University Press, 2019.

Camacho, Pamina Fernández. "Skilled at Grasping: The Phoenician Migrant and Exile as a Cautionary Stereotype from Classical Antiquity to Early Modern Europe." *Arethusa* 52, no. 2 (Spring 2019): 107-128.

Campbell, Brian, and Lawrence A. Tritle, eds. *The Oxford Handbook of Warfare in the Classical World*. Oxford: Oxford University Press, 2013.

Campbell, D. B. "Review of T. Rihll, The Catapult: A History." *American Journal of Archaeology* 112, no. 1 (January, 2008): www.ajaonline.org/book-review/536.

Campbell, Duncan B. "Ancient Catapults: Some Hypotheses Reexamined." *Hesperia: The Journal of the American School of Classical Studies at Athens* 80, no. 4 (September-December 2011): 677-700.

———. *Ancient Siege Warfare: Persians, Greeks, Carthaginians and Romans 546-146 BC*. Oxford: Osprey, 2005.

———. *Besieged: Siege Warfare in the Ancient World*. Oxford: Osprey, 2006.

Carney, Elizabeth D. "Artifice and Alexander History." In *Alexander the Great in Fact and Fiction*, edited by A. B. Bosworth and E. J. Baynham, 263-285. Oxford: Oxford University Press, 2000.

———. "Women and War in the Greek World." In *A Companion to Greek Warfare*, edited by Waldemar Heckel, F. S. Naiden, E. Edward Garvin, and John Vanderspoel, 339-348. Chichester UK: Wiley Blackwell, 2021.

Cartledge, Paul. *Alexander the Great: The Hunt for a New Past*. Woodstock, NY: Overlook Press, 2004.

Casson, Lionel. *Ships and Seamanship in the Ancient World*. Baltimore: Johns Hopkins University Press, 1995.

Champion, Timothy. "The Appropriation of the Phoenicians in British Imperial Ideology." *Nations and Nationalism* 7, no. 4 (2001): 451-65.

Chinnock, E. J., trans. *The Anabasis of Alexander, or, The History of the Wars and Conquests of Alexander the Great, Literally Translated with a Commentary, from the Greek of Arrian the Nicomedian*. London: Hodder and Stoughton, 1884.

Collelo, Thomas, ed. *Lebanon: A Country Study*. Washington, DC: Federal Research Division, Library of Congress, 1989.

Coral Diving Crete. "Ancient Wrecks Found in Lebanon and Croatia." June 5, 2019. https://www.coraldivingcrete.com/news/news-1018-ancient-wrecks-found-in-lebanon-and-croatia/.

Decker, Michael J. *The Sasanian Empire at War: Persia, Rome, and the Rise of Islam, 224-651*. Yardley PA: Westholme, 2022.

De Souza, Philip. "War at Sea." In *The Oxford Handbook of Warfare in the Classical World*, edited by Brian Campbell and Lawrence A. Tritle, 369-94. Oxford: Oxford University Press, 2013.

DeVries, Keith, and Michael L. Katzev. "Greek, Etruscan and Phoenician Ships and Shipping." In *A History of Seafaring Based on Underwater Archaeology*, edited by George Bass, 37-64. New York: Walker, 1972.

Dodge, Theodore A. *Alexander; A History of the Origin and Growth of the Art of War from the Earliest Times to the Battle of Ipsus, 301 BC, with a Detailed Account of the Campaigns of the Great Macedonian*. Boston, New York: Houghton, Mifflin, 1918.

Downey, Glanville. *Ancient Antioch.* Princeton, NJ: Princeton University Press, 1963.

Ellis, J. R. "Alexander's Hypaspists Again." *Historia: Zeitschrift fur Alte Geschichte* (4th Quarter 1975): 617-18.

Engels, Donald W. *Alexander the Great and the Logistics of the Macedonian Army.* Berkeley: University of California Press, 1978.

English, Stephen. "The Campaigns of Alexander the Great." PhD diss., Durham University, 2009.

—. *The Sieges of Alexander the Great.* Barnsley, UK: Pen & Sword Military, 2009.

Fuller, J. F. C. *The Generalship of Alexander the Great.* London: Eyre & Spottiswoode, 1958.

Gaca, Kathy L. "Reinterpreting the Homeric Simile of 'Iliad' 16.7-11: The Girl and Her Mother in Ancient Greek Warfare." *American Journal of Philology* 129, no. 2 (Summer, 2008): 145-171.

Garstad, Benjamin. "Nebuchadnezzar's Siege of Tyre in Jerome's Commentary on Ezekiel." *Vigiliae Christianae* 70 (2016): 175-92.

Gevirtz, Stanley. "On Canaanite Rhetoric: The Evidence of the Amarna Letters from Tyre." *Orientalia* 42 (1973): 162-177.

Goldsworthy, Adrian. *The Fall of Carthage: The Punic Wars 265–146 BC.* London: Cassell, 2000.

—. *Philip and Alexander: Kings and Conquerors.* New York: Basic Books, 2020.

Gottschall, Jonathan. *The Rape of Troy: Evolution, Violence, and the World of Homer.* Cambridge: Cambridge University Press, 2008.

Green, Peter. *Alexander of Macedon: A Historical Biography.* Berkeley: University of California Press, 1991.

Guenther, David A. "Diodorus Siculus and the *Purgos* at Tyre: Did Alexander Put Towers on Ships?" *Classical Philology* 119, no. 3 (July 2024): 421-25.

Hamalainen, Pekka. *Indigenous Continent: The Epic Contest for North America.* New York: Liveright, 2022.

Hammond, Martin, trans. *Arrian: Alexander the Great, the "Anabasis" and the "Indica."* Oxford: Oxford University Press, 2013.

Hammond, N. G. L. *Sources for Alexander the Great: An Analysis of Plutarch's "Life" and Arrian's "Anabasis Alexandrou."* Cambridge: Cambridge University Press, 1993.

—. *Three Historians of Alexander the Great: The So-Called Vulgate Authors, Diodorus, Justin and Curtius.* Cambridge: Cambridge University Press, 1983.

Hanson, Victor Davis. *The Wars of the Ancient Greeks.* London: Cassell, 1999.

Harden, Donald. *The Phoenicians.* New York: Frederick A. Praeger, 1962.

Harrison, Cynthia M. "Triremes at Rest: On the Beach or in the Water?" *Journal of Hellenic Studies* 119 (1999): 168-71.

Heckel, Waldemar. *The Conquests of Alexander the Great.* Cambridge: Cambridge University Press, 2008.

———. *In the Path of Conquest*. Oxford: Oxford University Press, 2020.

Heckel, Waldemar, F. S. Naiden, E. Edward Garvin, and John Vanderspoel, eds. *A Companion to Greek Warfare*. Chichester, UK: Wiley Blackwell, 2021.

Hosler, John D. *The Siege of Acre, 1189-1191: Saladin, Richard the Lionheart, and the Battle That Decided the Third Crusade*. New Haven, CT: Yale University Press, 2018.

Institute for Balkan Studies. *Ancient Macedonia II: Papers Read at the Second International Symposium Held in Thessaloniki, 19-24 August 1973*. Thessaloniki, Greece: Institute for Balkan Studies, 1977.

Jidejian, Nina. *Tyre through the Ages*. Beirut: Dar El-Mashreq, 1969.

Johnston, Philip Andrew, and Brett Kaufman. "Metallurgy and Other Technologies." In *The Oxford Handbook of the Phoenician and Punic Mediterranean*, edited by Carolina Lopez-Ruiz and Brian R. Doak, 401-22. Oxford: Oxford University Press, 2019.

Kern, Paul Bentley. *Ancient Siege Warfare*. Bloomington: Indiana University Press, 1999.

Kletter, Rax. "Vessels and Measures: The Biblical Liquid Capacity System." *Israel Exploration Journal* 64, no. 1 (2014): 22-37.

Lane Fox, Robin. *Alexander the Great*. London: Allen Lane, 1973.

———. *The Search for Alexander*. Boston: Little, Brown, 1980.

Lanni, Adriaan. "The Laws of War in Ancient Greece." *Law and History Review* 26, no. 3 (Fall 2008): 469-89.

LCBI Lebanon News. "Ancient Greek Ruins Discovered Underwater South of Tyre." April 16, 2019. https://www.lbcgroup.tv/news/d/lebanon-news/438989/ancient-greek-ruins-discovered-underwater-south-of/en.

Lee, John W. I. "The Fight for Ancient Sicily." *Archaeology* 64, no. 1 (January/February 2011): 38-41.

Lewis, M. J. T. "The Origins of the Wheelbarrow." *Technology and Culture* 35, no. 3 (July, 1994): 453-475.

Llewellyn-Jones, Lloyd. *Persians: The Age of the Great Kings*. New York: Basic Books, 2022.

———. "Wives, Other Women and Boyfriends." In *Alexander the Great: The Making of a Myth*, edited by Richard Stoneman, 159-167. London: British Library, 2022.

Lopez-Ruiz, Carolina, and Brian R. Doak, eds. *The Oxford Handbook of the Phoenician and Punic Mediterranean*. Oxford: Oxford University Press, 2019.

Mackie, C. J. "Achilles' Teachers: Chiron and Phoenix in the *Iliad*." *Greece & Rome* 44, no. 1 (April 1997): 1-10.

Makrypoulias, Christos. "Siege Warfare: The Art of Re-capture." In *Brill's Companions to the Byzantine World Volume 3: A Companion to the Byzantine Culture of War, ca. 300-1204*, edited by Yannis Stouraitis, 356-393. Leiden, Netherlands: Brill, 2018.

Markle, Minor M., III. "Macedonian Arms and Tactics under Alexander the Great." *Studies in the History of Art: Symposium Series I: Macedonia and Greece in Late Classical and Early Hellenistic Times* 10 (1982): 86-111.

———. "The Macedonian Sarissa, Spear, and Related Armor." *American Journal of Archaeology* 81, no. 3 (Summer 1977): 323-39.

Markoe, Glenn E. *Phoenicians.* Berkeley: University of California Press, 2000.

Marriner, Nick, Christophe Morhange, and Samuel Meule. "Holocene Morphogenesis of Alexander the Great's Isthmus at Tyre in Lebanon." *Proceedings of the National Academy of Sciences* 104, no. 22 (May 29, 2007): 9218–23.

Marriner, N., J. P. Goiran, and C. Morhange. "Alexander the Great's Tombolos at Tyre and Alexandria, Eastern Mediterranean." *Geomorphology* 100 (2008): 377–400.

Marsden, E. W. *Greek and Roman Artillery: Historical Development.* Oxford: Clarendon, 1969.

———. "Macedonian Military Machinery and Its Designers under Philip and Alexander." In *Ancient Macedonia II: Papers Read at the Second International Symposium Held in Thessaloniki, 19-24 August 1973,* 211-23. Thessaloniki, Greece: Institute for Balkan Studies, 1977.

Marti-Aguilar, Manuel Alvarez. "The Gadir-Tyre Axis." In *The Oxford Handbook of the Phoenician and Punic Mediterranean,* edited by Carolina Lopez-Ruiz and Brian R. Doak, 617-26. Oxford: Oxford University Press, 2019.

McCarty, Matthew M. "The Tophet and Infant Sacrifice." In *The Oxford Handbook of the Phoenician and Punic Mediterranean,* edited by Carolina Lopez-Ruiz and Brian R. Doak, 311-24. Oxford: Oxford University Press, 2019.

Meijer, Fik. *A History of Seafaring in the Classical World.* London: Croom Helm, 1986.

Milns, R. D. "The Hypaspists of Alexander III: Some Problems." *Historia: Zeitschrift fur Alte Geschichte* (2nd Quarter 1971): 186-95.

———. "Philip II and the Hypaspists." *Historia: Zeitschrift fur Alte Geschichte* (September 1967): 509-12.

Moloney, Eoghan. "The Macedonian Kings and Greek Theatre." In *Greek Theatre in the Fourth Century BC,* edited by Eric Csapo, Hans Rupprecht Goette, J. Richard Green, and Peter Wilson, 231-248. Berlin/Boston: De Gruyter, 2014.

Morales, Jennifer Martinez. "Women on the Walls? The Role and Impact of Women in Classical Greek Sieges." In *Brill's Companion to Sieges in the Ancient Mediterranean,* edited by Jeremy Armstrong and Matthew Trundle, 150-168. Boston: Brill, 2019.

Morrison, J. S., and J. F. Coates. *Greek and Roman Oared Warships.* Oxford: Oxbow, 1996.

Morrison, J. S., J. F. Coates, and N. B. Rankov. *The Athenian Trireme: The History and Reconstruction of an Ancient Greek Warship.* Cambridge: Cambridge University Press, 2000.

Morrison, Michael. "Old Testament Laws: Harvest Seasons of Ancient Israel." Grace Communion International. https://archive.gci.org/articles/harvest-seasons-of-ancient-israel/.

Morwood, James. *Oxford Grammar of Classical Greek*. Oxford: Oxford University Press, 2001.

Murray, William M. *The Age of Titans: The Rise and Fall of the Great Hellenistic Navies*. Oxford: Oxford University Press, 2012.

———. "The Development of a Naval Siege Unit under Philip II and Alexander III." In *Macedonian Legacies: Studies in Ancient Macedonian History and Culture in Honor of Eugene N. Borza*, edited by Timothy Howe and Jeanne Reames, 31-55. Claremont: Regina, 2008.

Oxford Classical Dictionary. https://oxfordre.com/classics.

Peacock, Mark. "Rehabilitating Homer's Phoenicians: On Some Ancient and Modern Prejudices against Trade." *Ancient Society* 41 (2011): 1-29.

Rahe, Paul A. "The Annihilation of the Sacred Band at Chaeronea." *American Journal of Archaeology* 85, no. 1 (January, 1981): 84-87.

Rainey, A. F. "The Satrapy 'Beyond the River.'" *Australian Journal of Biblical Archaeology* 1, no. 2 (1969): 51-78.

Rawlinson, G. *Five Great Monarchies of the Ancient Eastern World*. London: John Murray, 1871.

Redmount, Carol A. "The Wadi Tumilat and the 'Canal of the Pharaohs.'" *Journal of Near Eastern Studies* 54, no. 2 (April 1995): 127-135.

Richey, Madadh. "The Alphabet and Its Legacy." In *The Oxford Handbook of the Phoenician and Punic Mediterranean*, edited by Carolina Lopez-Ruiz and Brian R. Doak, 241-56. Oxford: Oxford University Press, 2019.

Rihll, T. E. *The Catapult: A History*. Yardley, PA: Westholme, 2007.

Roller, Duane W. "Phoenician Exploration." In *The Oxford Handbook of the Phoenician and Punic Mediterranean*, edited by Carolina Lopez-Ruiz and Brian R. Doak, 645-53. Oxford: Oxford University Press, 2019.

Romane, Patrick. "Alexander's Siege on Tyre." *Ancient World* 16, no. 3 (Winter 1987): 79-90.

Romm, James. *Demetrius: Sacker of Cities*. New Haven, CT: Yale University Press, 2022.

———, ed. *The Landmark Arrian: The Campaigns of Alexander*. Translated by Pamela Mensch. New York: Anchor, 2012.

Rood, Tim. "Xenophon's Parasangs." *Journal of Hellenic Studies* 130 (2010): 51-66.

Sears, Matthew A., and Carolyn Willekes. "Alexander's Cavalry Charge at Chaeronea, 338 BCE." *Journal of Military History* 80 (October 2016): 1017-35.

SEG (Society of Exploration Geophysicists). "Levantine Basin." https://wiki.seg.org/wiki/Levantine_Basin.

Sekunda, Nicholas. "Military Forces." In *The Cambridge History of Greek and Roman Warfare*, edited by Philip Sabin, Hans van Wees, Michael Whitby, 325-357. Cambridge: Cambridge University Press, 2007.

Sekunda, Nick. *The Army of Alexander the Great*. London: Osprey, 1984.

Sheppard, Si. *Tenochtitlan 1519-21*. Oxford: Osprey, 2018.

Sheratt, Susan. "Greeks and Phoenicians: Perceptions of Trade and Traders in the Early First Millennium BC." In *Social Archaeologies of Trade and Exchange: Exploring Relationships among People, Places, and Things*, edited by Alexander A. Bauer and Anna S. Agbe-Davies, 119-142. London: Taylor and Francis, 2016.

Stoneman, Richard, ed. *Alexander the Great: The Making of a Myth*. London: British Library, 2022.

Strauss, Barry. *The Battle of Salamis: The Naval Encounter That Saved Greece—and Western Civilization*. New York: Simon & Schuster, 2004.

Stronk, Jan. *Semiramis' Legacy: The History of Persia According to Diodorus of Sicily*. Edinburgh: Edinburgh University Press, 2017.

Talbert, Richard J. A., ed. *Barrington Atlas of the Greek and Roman World*. Princeton, NJ: Princeton University Press, 2000.

Tarn, W. W. *Alexander the Great 1: Narrative*. Cambridge: Cambridge University Press, 1948.

———. *Alexander the Great 2: Sources and Studies*. Cambridge: Cambridge University Press, 1948.

———. "The Fleet of Xerxes." *Journal of Hellenic Studies* 28 (1908): 202-33.

———. "The Fleets of the First Punic War." *Journal of Hellenic Studies* 27 (1907): 48-60.

———. *Hellenistic Military & Naval Developments*. New York: Biblo and Tannen, 1966.

Trundle, Matthew. "The Business of War: Mercenaries." In *The Oxford Handbook of Warfare in the Classical World*, edited by Brian Campbell and Lawrence A. Tritle, 330-50. Oxford: Oxford University Press, 2013.

Tuplin, Christopher J. "Achaemenid Arithmetic: Numerical Problems in Persian History." *Topoi. Orient-Occident. Supplément 1* (1997): 365-421.

Wallitt, Adam. "Two Great Historians Talk Alexander the Great Part 3." *Forbes*, December 20, 2010. https://www.forbes.com/sites/booked/2010/12/20/two-historians-talk-alexander-the-great-part-3/?sh=15aec7611c78.

Warry, John. *Warfare in the Classical World*. Norman: University of Oklahoma Press, 1995.

Whitehead, David. "Alexander the Great and the *Mechanici*." In *East and West in the World Empire of Alexander: Essays in Honour of Brian Bosworth*, edited by Pat Wheatley, 75-91. Oxford: Oxford University Press, 2015.

———. "Fact and Fantasy in Greek Military Writers." *Acta antiqua Academiae Scientiarum Hungaricae* 48, no. 1 (2008): 139-155.

———. *Philo Mechanicus: On Sieges*. Stuttgart: Franz Steiner Verlag, 2016.

———. "Siege Warfare." In *A Companion to Greek Warfare*. edited by Waldemar Heckel, F. S. Naiden, E. Edward Garvin, and John Vanderspoel, 109-125. Hoboken NJ: John Wiley & Sons, 2021.

Whitehead, David, and P. H. Blyth. *Athenaeus Mechanicus, On Machines*. Stuttgart: Franz Steiner Verlag, 2004.

Winter, Frederick. *Studies in Hellenistic Architecture*. Toronto: University of Toronto Press, 2006.

Winter, Irene J. "Homer's Phoenicians: History, Ethnography, or Literary Trope?" In *The Ages of Homer: A Tribute to Emily Townsend Vermeule*, edited by Jane B. Carter and Sarah P. Morris, 247-272. Austin: University of Texas Press, 1995.

Woolmer, Mark, and Glenn E. Markoe. *A Short History of the Phoenicians*. London: I. B. Tauris, 2017.

Worthington, Ian. *Alexander the Great: Man and God*. London: Routledge, 2004.

Xella, Paolo. "Religion." In *The Oxford Handbook of the Phoenician and Punic Mediterranean*, edited by Carolina Lopez-Ruiz and Brian R. Doak, 273-92. Oxford: Oxford University Press, 2019.

Acknowledgments

The hows and whys of Alexander's siege of Tyre have always fascinated me, and that lifetime of interest eventually led to this book. The difficulty of writing about Alexander is that there are so few ancient sources, and those few are often drawn from the same original accounts, which are lost to us. These ancient sources cover the siege quite briefly, raise many questions, and, as the book points out, often contradict one another. To augment these ancient sources, I've drawn on the work of a small army of classics scholars (as well as a few geologists), and I am extremely grateful for their careful study and analysis.

I want to thank the staff of the Knight Library at the University of Oregon for help in acquiring the books and journal articles I needed to complete this book. I also thank Professor Malcolm Wilson of the University of Oregon Classics Department for help with translations of ancient Greek.

The people at Westholme Publishing have been extremely supportive, and I owe them a great deal of thanks, especially the publisher, Bruce Franklin. I want to particularly thank Ron Silverman for his careful editing of the manuscript, Paul Rossmann for transforming my crude maps into very nice ones, and Trudi Gershenov for creating the beautiful cover design for the book.

Most importantly, I am thankful for the support of my wife, Dawn, without whose constant encouragement this book would never have been written.

Index